Funny Girls

Guffaws, Guts, and Gender in Classic American Comics

MICHELLE ANN ABATE

UNIVERSITY PRESS OF MISSISSIPPI / JACKSON

The University Press of Mississippi is the scholarly publishing agency of the Mississippi Institutions of Higher Learning: Alcorn State University, Delta State University, Jackson State University, Mississippi State University, Mississippi University for Women, Mississippi Valley State University, University of Mississippi, and University of Southern Mississippi.

www.upress.state.ms.us

Designed by Peter D. Halverson

The University Press of Mississippi is a member of the Association of University Presses.

Copyright © 2019 by Michelle Ann Abate
All rights reserved

First printing 2019
∞

Library of Congress Cataloging-in-Publication Data

Names: Abate, Michelle Ann, 1975– author.
Title: Funny girls : guffaws, guts, and gender in classic American comics / Michelle Ann Abate.
Description: Jackson : University Press of Mississippi, [2019] | Includes bibliographical references and index. |
Identifiers: LCCN 2018032191 (print) | LCCN 2018038969 (ebook) | ISBN 9781496820754 (epub single) | ISBN 9781496820761 (epub institutional) | ISBN 9781496820778 (pdf single) | ISBN 9781496820785 (pdf institutional) | ISBN 9781496820730 (hardcover : alk. paper) | ISBN 9781496820747 (pbk. : alk. paper)
Subjects: LCSH: Girls—Comic books, strips, etc. | Comic strip characters—Women. | Comic books, strips, etc.—United States—History and criticism. | LCGFT: Literary criticism.
Classification: LCC PN6714 (ebook) | LCC PN6714 .A28 2019 (print) | DDC 741.5/3522—dc23
LC record available at https://lccn.loc.gov/2018032191

British Library Cataloging-in-Publication Data available

Contents

Acknowledgments vii

Introduction
"It's a Bird! It's a Plane! It's an Elementary-Aged Girl!"
Remembering a Time in American Comics
When Young Female Protagonists Ruled 3

1. "Then I Could Have a Real Papa and Mama like Other Kids"
Little Orphan Annie, the Orphan Girl Formula, and the Nanny State 15

2. "I Slant My Gags to the Lawrence Welk Gum Chewers"
Nancy and the Vaudeville Aesthetic 41

3. From Battling Adult Authority to Battling the Opposite Sex
Little Lulu as Gag Panel and Comic Book 63

4. In Your Dreams
Little Audrey, Freudian Psychoanalysis, and Postwar Child Psychology 90

5. "From the Top, Stupid!"
The *Li'l Tomboy* Comic Book Series, Female Juvenile Delinquency, and the Comics Code 114

Epilogue
From Li'l to Big
The Legacy of Classic American Comics Starring Girls 152

Notes 171

Works Cited 178

Index 191

Acknowledgments

Don Markstein once observed, "Little girl stars litter the history of the cartoon medium" (*Little Mary Mixup*, para. 1). In examples ranging from Harold Gray's Little Orphan Annie and Lucy in Charles Schulz's *Peanuts* to Ernie Bushmiller's Nancy and Alice Otterloop in Richard Thompson's *Cul de Sac*, young female characters permeate commercial comics in the United States.

This project recognizes the long, rich, and important history of girl characters in American comics, transforming them from isolated figures who—in the words of Markstein—"litter the history of the cartoon medium" to a recurring demographic who constitute an influential character tradition. Accordingly, it seems only appropriate that I begin by thanking the many people whose support, input, and insights are scattered throughout these pages.

First and foremost, I want to express my deep gratitude to Katie Keene, my editor at the University Press of Mississippi, for her guidance and encouragement. I am also indebted to the anonymous outside readers of my manuscript. Their thoughtful, detailed, and helpful suggestions made my project stronger and more insightful.

At The Ohio State University, I am extremely fortunate to be immersed in an incredible environment for the study of comics. To that end, I am very grateful to Jenny Robb, Caitlin McGurk, and Susan Liberator at the Billy Ireland Cartoon Library and Museum for their expertise, assistance, and camaraderie. I also want to express my thanks to Jared Gardner, whose work has served as a model to me over the years and whose leadership—with ICAF, CXC, and *Inks*—has advanced the field in innumerable ways. I am likewise grateful to Karly Marie Grice for her keen editorial eye on early versions of several chapters.

I am equally indebted to many colleagues, organizations, and individuals outside OSU. First, I owe a big thanks to Joe Sutliff Sanders. His wisdom, his generosity, and his humor have guided me through many tricky situations, both inside and outside of these pages. Joe, you are both a scholar and a gentleman, and I am so very fortunate to know you. I want to express my gratitude to Regina Marchi and Laura M. Jiménez for their excellent feedback and insightful suggestions about a completely different version of chapter 1. I am also appreciative of the vibrant community of comics scholars at the International Comic Arts Forum (ICAF), as well as the Cartoon Crossroads Columbus (CXC). I have learned much over the years from your formal presentations and informal conversation. Finally, I want to thank my comics buddies in children's literature: Annette Wannamaker and Gwen Athene Tarbox. From trading new books and attending events to talking about our favorite cartoonists and titles, I relish being able to share my love of sequential art with you.

This project was supported by the Institute for Advanced Study, a research center of the Office of the Vice Provost for Research at Indiana University Bloomington. I would like to extend a special thanks to Heather Elizabeth Blair, Suzanne Godby Ingalsbe, the staff at the IAS, and the archivists at the Lilly Library for making my time at IU not simply so productive but so pleasurable. The Robert Klein Comic Book Collection at the Lilly Library was invaluable to this project in general and to the epilogue in particular.

Chapter 3 appeared in a slightly modified form in the *Journal of Graphic Novels and Comics* 7, no. 4 (2016): 381–402. A version of chapter 5 also appeared in the same journal, vol. 6, no. 1 (2015): 59–90. I am grateful to Taylor and Francis for permission to reprint.

Finally, I'd like to dedicate this book to my grandfathers, George Charles Schwelle (1909–78) and Morris "Mo" Abate (1919–60), neither of whom I ever had the pleasure—or the honor—of knowing. Both men were avid readers of daily newspapers, including the comics section. While working on this project, I have often thought about how these fun, feisty, and formidable female characters who so delight me must have delighted my grandfathers as well. Scott McCloud famously titled the third chapter of *Understanding Comics* "Blood in the Gutter." For me, there were also bloodlines.

Funny Girls

Introduction

"It's a Bird! It's a Plane! It's an Elementary-Aged Girl!"

Remembering a Time in American Comics
When Young Female Protagonists Ruled

• •

Open up any article about comics in twenty-first-century American culture, and you'll likely see one topic being discussed: the rise of female fans. As the popular website Autostraddle discussed in 2015, "Monthly titles like *Lumberjanes*, *Ms. Marvel*, *Batgirl*, and *The Unbeatable Squirrel* have been showing that girls and young women . . . represent a huge number of comic fans and buyers" (Mey, para. 2). Both in mainstream media coverage and in scholarly circles, commentators have noted the massive growth of girls and women in the field: as readers, as characters, and as creators. While market researchers disagree on the precise breakdown of female comics fans in millennial American society, they place the figure somewhere "between 41 and 47 percent" (Berlatsky, para. 10). The implications, even for the more modest estimate of this phenomenon, are significant. As Scott McCloud flatly stated: "Girls are taking the comic book world by storm." He went on to assert that this trend has "set off an atom bomb, and it's completely changing the face of comics" (para. 7). Female cartoonists like Raina Telgemeier, Cece Bell, and Mariko Tamaki and Jillian Tamaki have enjoyed incredible success, releasing narratives that are both best-selling and award winning. Likewise, titles featuring strong female protagonists, such as *Persepolis* (2000), *Fun Home* (2006), and *Hereville* (2010), have found a wide and enthusiastic fan base. For this reason, comics in millennial American culture have emerged, in the apt words of Jane Danziger-Russell, as a "mode of art and literature that has the potential to reach female readers and allow them to connect with strong and complex female characters" (1).

The increased presence of women and girls in comics in the United States is regarded as being so newsworthy because it represents such a massive shift in the gender dynamics historically associated with the industry. Echoing a sentiment that has been expressed by numerous past and present commentators, Erin Maxwell remarked: "Since Clark Kent got his first desk job, comic books have been a male-dominated field" (para. 1). As she elaborates, "Be it the audience, the creators or the titles themselves, the numbers were downright anemic when it came to female involvement" (para. 1). As a consequence, for generations in the United States, comics have been regarded as a literal boys' club: they were created by men, featured male characters, and catered to male audiences. Given this situation, the medium "has long been associated with the adolescent male in America" (Danziger-Russell, 1).

Although comics have been a masculinist form for many decades, this observation does not hold true for the genre's entire history. Throughout the first half of the twentieth century, the medium was enjoyed equally by both sexes. As Berlatsky has discussed, "Comics then were more like film or television—a mass entertainment option, rather than a niche one" (para. 4). Accordingly, both newspaper comic strips and stand-alone comic books were read not just by boys but by girls as well. "A Market Research Company of America report from 1944 found that 95 percent of all boys and 91 percent of all girls between six and 11 read comics" (Berlatsky, para. 4). Meanwhile, the figure for readers aged twelve to seventeen was comparable: "87 percent of boys and 81 percent of girls" (para. 4). Finally, the number of adult men and women who enjoyed comics in the mid-1940s was lower, but far from negligible. As Berlatsky reports, "41 percent of men and 28 percent of women between 18 and 30" were comics fans (para. 4).

In the same way that girls represented a large and important audience for comics in the first half of the twentieth century, they also represented a large and important cadre of popular characters. Many of the earliest, most successful, and most influential comics in the United States during this era featured young female protagonists. Marjorie Henderson Buell's Little Lulu, for example, was an immediate hit with audiences when she debuted in the *Saturday Evening Post* in 1935. The mischievous moppet was a regular feature in the magazine until 1944, when she left the *Post* to branch out into other media venues. Over the following decades, Little Lulu enjoyed successful runs in comic books, animated cartoons, television commercials, and movie shorts.

Ernie Bushmiller's Nancy matched Lulu's popularity. The eight-year-old girl first appeared as a secondary character in the newspaper comic *Fritzi*

Ritz in 1933. Just five years later, Nancy had become so beloved by fans that Bushmiller made her the strip's new eponymous star. The popularity of *Nancy* grew with every passing decade. As A. S. Hamrah has documented, by the 1950s, "*Nancy* appeared in about 500 US papers and appeared in translation in many others worldwide" (para. 4).

Finally, and perhaps most vividly of all, we have Harold Gray's Little Orphan Annie. From the time of her first appearance in the *New York Daily News* in 1924, the frizzy-haired ten-year-old held the nation in the palm of her little cartoon hand. For decades, Gray's strip "would be in the top five favorite comic strips in every poll conducted among newspaper readers" (Mullaney and Canwell, 5). Furthermore, echoing the experiences of her predecessor Little Lulu, Annie morphed into other facets of American popular culture: she was featured in a series of live-action films during the Great Depression, she was the star of a nationally syndicated radio broadcast during the 1930s and 1940s, and she was the inspiration for a wildly popular Broadway musical and feature-length Hollywood film during the 1970s and 1980s.

Far from embodying now-forgotten facets of twentieth-century culture, all three of these characters remain popular icons. *Little Lulu* comic books, toys, and collectibles are commonly sold at antique stores, flea markets, and auction sites like eBay. Meanwhile, Nancy's place in American culture is equally secure. Her highly recognizable visage has been the featured in a variety of well-known works of art, from Andy Warhol's painting *Nancy* (1961) to Joe Brainard's cult collection *The Nancy Book* (2008). Moreover, Bushmiller's character has never retired from the realm of American comics. New strips featuring Nancy and her pal Sluggo continue to be created by the cartoonist Guy Gilchrist. Finally, the celebrity enjoyed by Little Orphan Annie is difficult to overestimate. As Dean Mullaney and Bruce Canwell have observed, with her signature features of orange hair, red dress, and black shoes, Annie is well known even by individuals who have never read Gray's strips (5).

In spite of the strong commercial success, powerful historical impact, and enduring cultural legacy of girl protagonists in American comics during the first half of the twentieth century, little scholarly work has been done on them. No full-length study exploring the commercial, aesthetic, or sociopolitical significance of these female figures—and the many others like them—has been released. In addition, only a handful of critical essays have been published about most of these titles. Moreover, the bulk of these discussions, such as Mark Newgarden and Paul Karasik's classic essay "How to Read Nancy" (1988), examine these characters from a formalist perspective, discussing the comics' aesthetic features, rather than their social, political, and cultural significance. Even analyses that take a more historical approach—such as Stella Ress's "Bridging the Generation Gap: Little Orphan Annie in the Great Depression" or Maria Mazzenga's "The Home Front's Cartoony Face: World War Two through Orphan Annie's Eyes"—do not connect them with other popular girl characters in comics and thus do not treat them as part of a larger cultural phenomenon.

These figures have likewise been overlooked in recent books that examine the largely forgotten role that female characters have played in past and present American comics. Titles such as Maurice Horn's *Women in the Comics* (1977, 1981, 2001), Trina Robbins's *The Great Women Superheroes* (1996), and Mike Madrid's *Divas, Dames, and Daredevils: Lost Heroines of Golden Age Comics* (2013) and *Vixens, Vamps, and Vipers: Lost Villainesses of Golden Age Comics* (2014) challenge long-standing perceptions that comics in the United States have been populated almost exclusively by male figures. However, as the titles of these works imply, they focus on characters who are adult women, not preadolescent girls.

Ironically, the same observation also applies to Robbins's *From Girls to Grrrlz: A History of Women's Comics from Teens to Zines* (1999) and Madrid's *The Supergirls: Fashion, Feminism, Fantasy, and the History of Comic Book Heroines* (2009). Although Robbins titles her book *From Girls to Grrrlz* and dedicates her first chapter to the subject of girls' comics, she does not focus on young female characters. Using the 1941 debut of *Archie* as the starting point for her study, Robbins skips over strips like *Little Orphan Annie* and also largely equates the term "girls" with teenagers. In the same vein, Mike Madrid's *The Supergirls* also does not focus on any actual girls. Its title notwithstanding, his book explores a variety of female characters—Sheena, Wonder Woman, Lois Lane, and so on—who are adults.[1] Indeed, in an observation that applies to nearly all the other female comics characters who possess a similar moniker, Madrid remarks: "Although her name may not have implied it, the first Super-Girl was an adult woman" (*Supergirls*, 81). Consequently, while early comics characters who are adult women have enjoyed renewed interest, their preadolescent counterparts remain critically neglected.

This book offers a corrective to this problem. *Funny Girls* examines the important but long-overlooked cadre of young female protagonists in US comics during the first half of the twentieth century. Ranging from Little Orphan Annie, Nancy, and Little Lulu to Little Audrey of the Harvey Girls and Li'l Tomboy, the star of a fascinating but now forgotten comic book series by Charlton Publications, these characters are rich and compelling subjects in their own right while also collectively forming what I call a tradition of Funny Girls in American comics. For generations, figures like Little Orphan Annie, Nancy, and Little Audrey offered the nation's comics fans a consistent combination of feistiness, feminism, and, of course, fun. They made their readers laugh, but they also made them think. Much of the humor in comics like *Little Lulu, Nancy*, and *Little Audrey* arose from the title character's questioning traditional gender roles, defying expected codes of polite middle-class conduct, and challenging long-established social manners and mores. In so doing, they encouraged their readers—child and adult, male and female—to question the status quo. Decades before the emergence of second-wave feminism and more than a half century before the advent of the Girl Power movement, these figures gave readers exemplars of female independence, agency, and autonomy. They were outspoken, daring, and mischievous. In so doing, characters like Little Lulu and Li'l Tomboy reveal the tremendous power that young girls personally possessed—and could wield politically. Furthermore, given their shared identity as white, preadolescent girls, they embodied powerful points of collection about how race, gender, class, and age were constructed during these eras—along with the ways that these categories intersected and interacted. The period from the 1920s to the 1960s saw massive transformations in the societal status of women, cultural conceptions of childhood, and national attitudes about race and ethnicity. Such concerns are routinely reflected in *Little Lulu, Nancy*, and *Little Orphan Annie*. When such issues are viewed collectively, these comics did far more than simply provide leisure-time amusement; they also offered a mirror that invited their adult and child audiences to look at themselves and their society in a new way. For this reason, Little Lulu, Nancy, and Li'l Tomboy may have been Funny Girls, but they were also serious agents for cultural commentary and, in many respects, sociopolitical change.

When critics, scholars, and fans think about major developments in American comics from the first half of the twentieth century, they commonly think of events like the advent of the Sunday newspaper supplement, the rise of the comic book, and the backlash against the industry by individuals like Fredric Wertham. My project seeks to add another phenomenon to this history: the popularity of young female protagonists. Examining figures like Little Lulu, Nancy, and Little Orphan Annie—both individually and as part of a larger tradition—yields compelling new insights about the industry during the first half of the twentieth century. The characters and comics that I spotlight in these pages reveal important information about an influential, but neglected, aspect of the history of sequential art in the United States. Recognizing the cadre of Funny Girls who played such a significant role in the popular appeal and commercial success of American comics during the first half of the twentieth century challenges long-standing perceptions about the gender dynamics operating during this era. While the Golden Age of US comics is routinely remembered as the time when adult male characters like Happy Hooligan, Superman, and Walt Wallet dominated, it was also a time when elementary-aged girls like Little Lulu, Nancy, and Little Audrey were hugely popular. These strips offer compelling and heretofore overlooked insights about major sociopolitical issues such as the societal perceptions of children, popular representations of girlhood, and changing national attitudes regarding youth and youth culture. Finally, but just as importantly, strips like *Little Lulu*, *Little Orphan Annie*, and *Nancy* also shed light on another important phenomenon in comics: branding, licensing, and merchandising. Most of these characters existed across a wide spectrum of media platforms: they starred in newspaper strips, comic books, movie shorts, and television cartoons. In addition, these protagonists were heavily commercialized, with their likenesses appearing on toys, games, dolls, clothes, and collectibles. In this way, characters like Little Lulu, Little Audrey, and Little Orphan Annie embody instructive case studies in the relationship between sequential art and consumer capitalism.

ORGANIZATION AND METHODOLOGY

Given both the tremendous sociocultural significance of these figures and their understudied critical status, each chapter of *Funny Girls* serves a dual purpose. First, my discussion provides information about the origins, history, and evolution of each comic and character. I discuss every title's debut, its popular and critical reception, and its commercial as well as creative significance, past and present. That said, the chapters are not merely encyclopedia entries; they are also argument-driven analyses that offer original critical readings of the comics under consideration. In so doing, my discussions simultaneously demonstrate the massive popularity that these titles and characters enjoyed, and also reveal how they possess unexplored narrative complexity, aesthetic richness, and historical resonance.

In the field of comics studies today, it has become commonplace for critics to assert that sequential art is worthy of serious critical analysis. Indeed, such sentiments have become so routine that they have attained the status of cliché. Dylan Meconis, for example, includes statements of this nature in his list "How Not to Write Comics Criticism," which he first posted in September 2012.[2] That said, given that once hugely popular characters like Little Audrey and Little Lulu continue to be neglected, such assertions are still germane to young female protagonists in classic American comics. *Funny Girls* simultaneously recognizes and responds to those calls.

Chapter 1 spotlights the young female comics character who arguably started it all: Harold Gray's Little Orphan Annie. To that end, I explore a fundamental, but underexamined, aspect of the newspaper strip: Little Orphan Annie as an orphan girl story. When Gray's eleven-year-old moppet debuted in 1924, many of the most popular novels, poems, and films in the United States featured orphan girls as their protagonists. Given this situation, the comic's original audience would have immediately recognized Annie as participating in this phenomenon. My discussion demonstrates that, far from an incidental detail of the original historical context for *Little Orphan Annie*, the formula for orphan girl stories serves as both a creative starting point for the comic and its critical end point. So many of the plots, characters, and themes in the strip arise from this tradition and, ultimately, return to it. Placing *Little Orphan Annie* in the context of the orphan girl story—and tracing the way in which the genre operates in Gray's strip—yields new insights about the strip's connection with popular culture, the factors fueling its success, and its primary artistic kinships.

Chapter 2 explores Ernie Bushmiller's *Nancy*. In what embodies an overlooked facet of the strip, many of its signature traits, central characters, and core qualities can be traced back to one of the most popular modes of entertainment in the United States during the early twentieth century: vaudeville. From the gag humor employed throughout the comic and Nancy's penchant for linguistic misunderstandings to Sluggo's use of working-class dialect and the comedic exchanges that take place between him and Nancy, the strip is an amalgamation of vaudevillian elements. Understanding the way in which vaudeville permeates *Nancy* helps to account for the strip's tremendous appeal along with its long-standing low cultural esteem. Vaudeville was a wildly successful entertainment mode for generations in the United States, but it was never regarded as a sophisticated, serious, or highbrow form—a condition that mirrors that of Bushmiller's strip. At the same time, the elements of vaudeville in *Nancy* add a new facet to discussions of class, ethnicity, and race in the comic.

Chapter 3 examines Marjorie Henderson Buell's *Little Lulu*. When the now iconic figure moved from the *Saturday Evening Post*, where she had resided since the 1930s, to comic books during the 1950s, her character underwent numerous transformations. One compelling but formerly overlooked change is the nature of Lulu's rebellion. In the single-panel gag comics, the young girl was overwhelmingly targeting adults with her antics. In the comic books, however, her sworn enemy is the gang of neighborhood boys. The change from intergenerational conflicts during the prewar era to intragenerational ones postwar reveals a compelling and previously unexplored dimension to the literary, artistic, and cultural alterations to this character across different print formats. These details shed new light on Lulu's place in American mass culture, as well as the role that she played in its popular imagination. At the same time, the shift from plots that pitted children against adults in the 1930s to ones that pitted girls against boys in the 1950s reflects larger shifts in American culture regarding the gendering of children and the sexual segregation of childhood. When this beloved comics character shifted print formats in the 1950s, she also shifted social targets. I argue that this alteration did far more than merely permit the comic book version of Little Lulu to tell artistically new, socially different, and materially longer stories; it radically altered the aim and intent of Buell's original character, along with the commentary on gender, childhood, and American culture that it offered.

Chapter 4 features the cartoon-character-turned-comic-book-star Little Audrey. Appearing in her first issue in 1948, the spunky little character would become one of the most beloved and most widely recognized personalities in comics over the next quarter century. While the *Little Audrey* comic books were a wholly separate commercial and creative endeavor from the cartoon movie shorts, they retained one powerful link to the version on the big screen: the title character's penchant for dreaming. In numerous issues of the comic book, Little Audrey falls asleep and embarks on an imaginative adventure that constitutes the bulk of the story line. This chapter places the *Little Audrey* comic books in general and the dream sequences that occur within them in particular back within their original Freudian-infused postwar context. It is difficult to imagine that the comic's adult creators could have crafted these story lines—and child readers could have encountered them—and not been aware of the era's fascination with the somnolent workings of an individual's unconscious mind. From the opening panel to the final thought balloon, Little Audrey's dream sequences invite young people to join the growing legions of armchair psychoanalysts during the postwar period. However, these features do far more than simply expand the postwar reach of pop psychology. In an arguably even more important implication, they also challenge the era's prevailing views about child psychology. Freud believed that boys and girls experience only highly simplistic dreams that are mere wish fulfillments. However, the sequences in *Little Audrey* paint a far more complicated portrait of the unconscious mind of its juvenile character. Freudian analysis of her dream sequences uncovers profound anxieties about an array of pressing sociopolitical issues, such as the threat of nuclear war and the fears over communist infiltration—concerns that not only would have been readily recognizable to the comic book's young readers but also were likely shared by many of them. In this way, the *Little Audrey* comic books did more than merely participate in the widespread interest in psychoanalysis during the postwar period. By demonstrating the way in which children's dreams were often adult-style nightmares, they offered a rare critique of it. Accordingly, I explore what Freudian theory can reveal about the dream sequences in *Little Audrey* and, in turn, what the series' traffic in postwar psychoanalysis can tell us about the role that comics storytelling for young people played in efforts to question, resist, and challenge this climate.

Chapter 5 explores the rich and interesting but critically neglected *Li'l Tomboy* comic book series. Published by Charlton Comics from 1956 through 1960, the series did far more than simply challenge traditional gender roles for white, middle-class girls in the 1950s; it also challenged the newly established Comics Code. Although the title character's appearance may be conventionally feminine—shoulder-length hair, starched dresses, and even frilly underskirts—her behavior is not. From her debut in the October 1956 issue of *Li'l Genius*, she upends notions about appropriate female comportment: breaking rules, defying authority, and generally being mischievous. But this feisty female figure engaged in behavior that went far beyond simply defying postwar notions about appropriate feminine conduct for white, middle-class figures; it could often be seen as delinquent. In numerous issues, she commits petty theft, intentionally destroys private property, and sasses adult authority figures, including police officers. Moreover, Li'l Tomboy engages in these activities not simply under the watchful eye of the Comics Code Authority but, astoundingly, with its official seal of approval. During a time when the censors employed by the Authority office were at their most powerful and restrictive, Li'l Tomboy engaged in antics that far exceeded those that had been forbidden in other publications. Accordingly, this chapter tells the story of how, with the creation of Li'l Tomboy, Charlton Publications demonstrated that postwar gender conformity could be resisted and, even more significantly, so too could the Comics Code.

Finally, the epilogue makes a case that the tradition of Funny Girls calls for a reconsideration of the history of American comics both during the mid-twentieth century and during the opening decades of the new millennium.

Remembering and recouping characters like Little Lulu, Nancy, Li'l Tomboy, Little Orphan Annie, and Little Audrey restores the important place and powerful status that young female protagonists had in early American comics. The Golden Age was far from a literal or figurative "boys' club"; on the contrary, it was a period when comics featuring girls had a noteworthy presence and when they also exerted a substantial creative and cultural influence. At the same time, an awareness of this cadre of female characters changes our perspective on the growing presence of girls in comics during the twenty-first century. The bulk of discussions about the tremendous success of graphic novels featuring young female protagonists like Raina Telgemeier's *Smile* (2010), Vera Brosgol's *Anya's Ghost* (2011), or Mariko Tamaki and Jillian Tamaki's *This One Summer* (2014) cast them as a wholly new development in the field. However, these figures have strong literary antecedents. Events taking place in American comics in the early twenty-first century can be connected to those from the early twentieth century. Far from embodying a radical shift in US comics, the rise of fun, feisty, and formidable female protagonists represents the continuation of a tradition. Accordingly, the epilogue reveals that while the names of many of the characters profiled in these chapters include the diminutive "li'l" or "little," their cultural legacy has been big.

As this brief overview demonstrates, *Funny Girls* is interested in the unexamined role that young female protagonists have played in classic American comics. As such, I make no distinction between comics that appeared as newspaper strips, as comic books, and—in the epilogue—as graphic novels. My focus is on the artistic medium of comics, not the specific material format in which these titles and characters appeared. While one can certainly make a case that the creative possibilities, as well as the readerly experience, of a newspaper strip differ from those of a comic book (as well as those of a comic book or newspaper strip from a graphic novel), all these different formats are, first and foremost, sequential art. That said, *Funny Girls* does attempt to strike a balance between the two dominant physical formats for the medium in the era under consideration: newspapers and comic books. Accordingly, the first two chapters spotlight comics that appeared as daily strips; the final two chapters explore characters who were stars of comic books; and the third chapter, which appears between these discussions, examines the transformations that took place to a character when she moved from a magazine to a comic book. In so doing, I devote equitable amounts of space to the two main material venues for sequential art in the United States from the 1920s through the 1960s.

Furthermore, on the subject of methodology, while *Funny Girls* profiles female protagonists from the first half of the twentieth century, it is far from comprehensive. My goal is to spotlight some of the most commercially successful and historically influential figures, not to provide a comprehensive survey of them. A variety of other titles from this era feature girls as central characters and enjoyed mass popularity. Examples range from *Little Mary Mixup* (1918–57) and *Little Annie Rooney* (1927–66) to *The Adventures of Patsy* (1935–55) and *Little Iodine* (1943–83), to name just a few newspaper strips.[3] Meanwhile, in the realm of comic books, *Li'l Jinx* from the *Archie* series (debut, 1947; solo comic book series, 1956–57, 1971–73), along with *Little Audrey*'s two sidekicks, *Little Dot* (1953–76) and *Little Lotta* (1953–73), merits attention. I discuss all these figures in more detail in the epilogue. However, I hope that *Funny Girls* will inspire additional scholarly work on the full cast of feisty female characters who populated this period.

One final note about the pages that follow: while the feisty female protagonists featured in the subsequent chapters challenge the gender norms commonly associated with American comics during the first half of the twentieth century, they perpetuate another equally powerful feature: its racial dynamics. All the Funny Girls who permeated this era are white. As a result, female protagonists like Little Lulu, Little Audrey, and Li'l Tomboy worked to challenge the gender line, but not the racial one. In so doing, they reveal—to borrow a phrase from Nancy Larrick—the all-white world of American comics during this era while they also illustrate the limits of progressive politics that do not remain cognizant of intersectionality. Figures like Li'l Tomboy and Little Lulu—though historically important—cannot be unequivocally lauded as feminist champions for American girlhood, given that their conception of this category excludes, overlooks, or ignores nonwhite girls. Furthermore, as my discussions of *Li'l Tomboy* and *Nancy* in particular reveal, these comics frequently drew on negative stereotypes concerning nonwhite people, and they also routinely co-opted elements from nonwhite cultures. To be sure, all of these titles contained some degree of denigrating caricatures of racial and ethnic minority groups. As Robin Bernstein reminds us, these elements cannot simply be dismissed, minimized, or explained away as a "product of their era." Instead they reveal the highly racialized way that childhood, girlhood, and especially innocence were constructed, disseminated, and reinforced in the United States during these eras. As a result, recognizing these Funny Girls and the role that they played in classic American comics is important, but equally important is recognizing their sociocultural limitations and even political problems.

• • •

Jacqueline Danziger-Russell, in *Girls and Their Comics: Finding a Female Voice in Comic Book Narrative* (2013), makes the following observation about millennial American print culture: "Comics are gaining an esteemed place upon the bookshelves of girls and young women, and this is an adventure that certainly deserves to be chronicled" (33). My own project makes a similar point about a related phenomenon from nearly a century earlier. Whereas Danziger-Russell examines girls *and* their comics, the chapters that follow spotlight girls *in* the comics. The first half of the twentieth century contained a bevy of funny young female protagonists. To borrow Danziger-Russell's phrasing once again, their adventures certainly deserve to be chronicled. Moreover, telling this history is long overdue.

Chapter 1

"Then I Could Have a Real Papa and Mama like Other Kids"

Little Orphan Annie, the Orphan Girl Formula, and the Nanny State

• •

In the apt words of Worth Gatewood, Little Orphan Annie "has long since ceased to be simply a comic-strip figure. . . . She has become part of the American myth" (viii). For almost a century, the spunky eleven-year-old was one of the nation's most beloved, recognizable, and enduring characters. Created by Harold Gray and debuting in the *New York Daily News* on August 5, 1924, the *Little Orphan Annie* comic "reached the zenith of its popularity during the Thirties, when more than 500 newspapers in North America subscribed to it" (Smith, 23). For decades, Gray's creation "would be in the top five favorite comic strips in every poll conducted among newspaper readers" (Mullaney and Canwell, 5). As Maria Mazzenga has noted, the strip ranks among the most commercially successful comics of the twentieth century (431–34).

The popularity of *Little Orphan Annie* in US print culture precipitated her appearance in other mediums. From 1930 to 1940, Annie's exploits formed the basis for a wildly successful syndicated radio program. "*Adventure Time with Orphan Annie* held an audience of children estimated at six million . . . five evenings a week, from 5:45 to 6PM, EST" (Smith, 39). In addition, in 1976, the comic obtained a whole new cultural life, along with a cadre of fans, when it was adapted as a Broadway musical. Over the past ninety years, Harold Gray's moppet has also appeared in a variety of feature-length Hollywood films: first in 1932; then again in 1938; next, and by far most famously, in 1982; and finally, most recently, in 2014. Throughout this span, Annie has enjoyed a strong presence in American material culture. Her likeness has appeared on a wide array of consumer items, ranging from toys, clothes, books, and dolls to bedding, school supplies, jewelry, and dishes. Given both the diversity of these objects and their ubiquity, Dean Mullaney and Bruce Canwell called *Little Orphan Annie* nothing less than "an icon of American culture. Even those who've never read the comic strip are keenly aware of the spunky orphan, her loveable mutt Sandy, and her adoptive benefactor, Oliver 'Daddy' Warbucks" (5).

In what has become an oft-repeated anecdote about the origins of *Little Orphan Annie*, when Harold Gray first conceived of his new comic strip character, she was a he. As Bruce Smith has recounted, "Gray titled the strip 'Little Orphan Otto,' worked up a dozen sketches of a boy in various poses, and showed them to [Joseph Medill] Patterson," Gray's editor at the *Chicago Tribune* (9). Having pitched ideas for numerous other strips over the years, Gray "was braced for the familiar step of rejection" (9). Much to Gray's surprise, however, Patterson liked the idea, "but with one important alteration. 'The kid looks like a pansy to me,' the Captain said with a scowl. 'Put a skirt on him and we'll call him 'Little Orphan Annie'" (9).[1]

With this change, Gray's character joined a long tradition of orphan girls in American popular culture. As Claudia Nelson, Joe Sutliff Sanders, and Carol Singley have all written, young girls who were "invalids, orphans, or waifs" (Sanders, 145) constituted some of the most beloved protagonists in novels, poems, and films from the middle of the nineteenth century through the opening decades of the twentieth. Given this context, when Joseph Medill Patterson instructed Harold Gray to "put a skirt on" Little Orphan Otto and thereby create Little Orphan Annie, he was not encouraging his cartoonist to engage in an iconoclastic act. Instead he was having Harold Gray's creation participate in an established cultural phenomenon.

In this chapter, I explore this fundamental but underexamined aspect of Harold Gray's newspaper strip: Little Orphan Annie as an orphan girl story. Far from an incidental detail about its original historical context, the tradition serves as both a creative starting point for the comic and its critical end point. So many of the stories, characters, and themes in *Little Orphan Annie* arise from the orphan girl story and, ultimately, return to it. Placing *Little Orphan Annie* back in the context of the orphan girl story—and tracing the way in which this phenomenon operates in Gray's strip—yields new insights about the strip's connection with popular culture, the factors fueling its success, and its primary artistic kinships.

That said, *Little Orphan Annie*'s engagement with the orphan girl story is not one of simple participation. The newspaper strip replicates key facets of the formula while it revises others. In so doing, *Little Orphan Annie* offers a powerful commentary on this well-known genre, along with the larger sociocultural issues that it engages. Orphan girl stories have long been seen as possessing conservative messages that serve to maintain the status quo. The modifications that *Little Orphan Annie* makes to this tradition, however, serve a far different function. Throughout the comic, these changes challenge hegemonic notions about girlhood and family.

In the same way that Gray's newspaper strip modifies the orphan girl story to destabilize many of the sociocultural institutions that the formula had long been used to support, the comic also ultimately puts these progressive elements to far different sociopolitical ends. *Little Orphan Annie* uses orphanhood as a vehicle to critique not simply family ties or legal guardianship in the United States during the 1920s but also another issue that concerned the cartoonist: the nanny state. Annie repeatedly demonstrates that she doesn't need to be protected, coddled, or taken care of by Daddy Warbucks—and she likewise doesn't need such treatment by another wealthy, paternalistic benefactor: Uncle Sam.

At this point in criticism about *Little Orphan Annie*, Harold Gray's political beliefs are no secret. As the cartoonist famously said, he was a "Republican down to his toenails" (quoted in Smith, 58). Previous discussions about *Little Orphan Annie* suggest that Gray's politics surfaced in the comic strip during the 1930s, amid the Great Depression, the election of Franklin Delano Roosevelt, and the passage of the New Deal. The discussion that follows both challenges and extends this critical perspective, demonstrating that such elements are present in the comic from the beginning. Gray's famous character is not just an orphan; she is a case study about the effectiveness of laissez-faire capitalism.

"AND IF IT'S NOT TOO MUCH TROUBLE I'D LIKE A DOLLY TOO— AMEN": SENTIMENTALITY, SYMPATHY, AND SPIRITUAL UPLIFT

In the apt words of Claudia Mills, "As long as there have been novels about children, there have been novels about orphans" (227). This feature forms one of the most common tropes within both British and American literature. For example, in Great Britain, "The great novelists of the nineteenth century who explored the world of childhood created a gallery of memorable orphan children: Oliver Twist, David Copperfield, Jane Eyre, Silas Marner's Eppie" (Mills, 227). These figures have been just as pervasive in the United States. In examples such as Horatio Alger's *Ragged Dick* (1868), Mark Twain's *The Adventures of Huckleberry Finn* (1884), and Edgar Rice Burroughs's *Tarzan of the Apes* (1912), "American literature abounds with orphaned, homeless, destitute, or neglected children" (Singley, 3).

While orphaned children have long been a powerful archetype in the United States, stories featuring orphan girls rose to special prominence in the middle of the nineteenth century. The release of Susan Warner's *The Wide, Wide World* in 1850 inaugurated this trend. The book—which told the story of protagonist Ellen Montgomery, whose mother dies early in the novel and father passes away later in the text—was an "immediate success. *The Wide, Wide World* went into twenty-two editions in only three years" (Singley, 201).

The best-selling status of Warner's orphan girl story launched an entire subgenre of narratives along these lines. As Joe Sutliff Sanders has discussed, orphan girl stories constituted some of the most commercially successful and critically acclaimed books in the United States for the next seventy years (2–3). Bookended by Susanna Maria Cummins's *The Lamplighter* (1854) and L. M. Montgomery's *Emily of New Moon* (1923), titles included E. D. E. N. Southworth's *The Hidden Hand* (1859), Louisa May Alcott's *Eight Cousins* (1875), Kate Douglas Wiggin's *Rebecca of Sunnybrook Farm* (1903), Frances Hodgson Burnett's *A Little Princess* (1905), L. M. Montgomery's *Anne of Green Gables* (1908), Frances Hodgson Burnett's *The Secret Garden* (1911), Eleanor Porter's *Pollyanna* (1911), and Jean Webster's *Daddy-Long-Legs* (1912). These books were beloved by both adults and children during their era—and many remain classics today.[2]

When *Little Orphan Annie* debuted in the *New York Daily News* in 1924, the strip's original audience would have immediately recognized Annie as participating in this tradition. Even the specific name that Patterson suggested to Gray for his new comic strip announced its connection to the orphan girl tradition: "Little Orphan Annie" was an allusion to the much-loved poem "Little Orphant Annie," by James Whitcomb Riley (Smith, 3). First published in 1885, Riley's poem quickly became "an immensely popular piece of the nineteenth century" (Young, 310). In a telling index of the poem's national appeal, "Little Orphant Annie" was made into a silent film in 1918. Moreover, demonstrating the celebrity status that the poet had attained, the movie featured Riley in a cameo role (Negra, 34).

Harold Gray's newspaper strip does far more than simply allude to the orphan girl phenomenon via the name of its title character. The comic incorporates some of the genre's best-known features. From the portrayal of the protagonist as a pitiable figure worthy of sympathy to its presentation of the ways that children can emotionally soften and psychically rejuvenate even the most cantankerous adults, Gray's character possesses traits that made orphan girl stories so endearing. The success of *Little Orphan Annie* has often been attributed to the fact that she was a new type of character in American comics. During the 1910s and 1920s, the funny pages overwhelmingly featured male protagonists. As Gray himself once commented, "At the time, some 40 strips were using boys as the main characters; only three were using girls" (quoted in Harvey, "The Orphan's Epic," para. 5). Little Orphan Annie crossed the gender line and demonstrated that a girl could carry a strip. The redheaded eleven-year-old may have been a new type of character in US comics, but she was not one in the nation's print culture. On the contrary, Annie was the continuation of a long literary tradition—and this fact forms a significant and previously overlooked factor to her fame.

• • •

While the specific events of orphan girl stories varied, they all contained the same basic plot. As Diana Loercher Pazicky has written, these narratives featured a white, preadolescent girl who hailed from a respectable middle-class or upper-middle-class Protestant family (xiii–xvi). The narrative commenced with the death of one or both of her parents—or these events transpired just before the start of the action. Regardless of the exact timing of these occurrences, the end result was the same: they rendered the young girl destitute. As readers witness early in the novel, the formerly contented, cherished, and comfortable protagonist is now both penniless and alone. She has lost her family, and as a result, she has lost her financial stability.

This scenario lays the groundwork for a feature that was arguably the essential ingredient of orphan girl stories. In the words of Claudia Mills, the characters in these narratives were "much sentimentalized" (228). Both because the protagonists now found themselves in dire circumstances through no fault of their own and because they hailed from white, middle-class Protestant backgrounds, they were regarded with compassion and empathy rather than blame and condemnation (Pazicky, 149). As a result, from the time of their origins in the mid-nineteenth century through their presence in the early twentieth, orphan girls were intended to elicit readers' sympathy, not their scorn. Presented as physically alone, economically destitute, and emotionally vulnerable, these characters were "innately pitiable" ("Orphan Stories," para. 2).

Little Orphan Annie firmly locates itself within this tradition. The comic consistently presents the title character in highly sentimentalized ways that are designed to stir the reader's emotions—and win his or her sympathy. These features are firmly established in the debut strip (fig. 1.1). The first panel shows an older woman pointing her finger at the young girl and lecturing her: "Now, Annie, if these people who are coming to the 'home' tomorrow should adopt you I hope you'll always remember what a lot we've done for you here—you have been sheltered, clothed [and] fed since you were a baby entirely by charity—you should be very grateful" (Gray, 36). Although Annie responds politely—saying only "Yessum, Miss Asthma" (36)—Gray provides an abundance of visual clues to indicate that he does not want his readers to agree with these views. Instead, he wants them to see such comments as cruel and hurtful. Not only does the cartoonist give the caretaker of the orphanage the unflattering name of "Miss Asthma," but he also presents her in a severe way: she is tall and thin and has her hair pulled up in a tight bun. By contrast, Annie—with her baby doll dress and short ringlets—is a portrait of cherubic beauty and romantic innocence.

The second panel makes these features more explicit. Here Annie is presented in an even more pitiable manner: we see the adorable little girl on her hands and knees, scrubbing the floor with a brush. A wooden bucket of water sits to one side. Of course, this visual imagery alone would elicit strong sympathy. As Viviana Zelizer has documented, beginning in the 1880s and accelerating rapidly in the opening decades of the twentieth century, profound shifts took place in the United States with regard to popular attitudes regarding children's relationship to labor. In previous generations, young people were seen as possessing measurable economic value, with children working as farmhands, performing domestic chores, and even taking jobs outside the home to bring in wages (Zelizer, 100–101). For both urban and rural families, boys and girls contributed materially and monetarily. Consequently, having children was regarded as a financial asset; they helped to support households, both directly and indirectly (100–101).

In the opening decades of the twentieth century, however, this phenomenon began to change. American society increasingly felt that young people—especially those who were white, native born, and middle class—ought to spend their childhoods playing, not working. Progressive-era reforms steadily took children out of the labor market, while changes in child-rearing practices eliminated chores altogether, cut back on them drastically, or offered monetary compensation for their completion in the form of a weekly allowance. In this way, young people went from being economic assets within families to economic "burdens" on them (Zelizer, 198, 209). Children needed to be clothed, fed, and sheltered—all of which cost money—but they themselves did not contribute. These economically "useless" children, however, were worth this financial sacrifice because they

Figure 1.1. The very first *Little Orphan Annie* comic, August 5, 1924. By Harold Gray.

had value in another way: they were emotionally "priceless" (Zelizer, 3). As Zelizer notes, children brought joy, love, and happiness to parents—benefits that defied monetary valuation.

Although Gray's *Little Orphan Annie* takes it name from James Whitcomb Riley's 1885 poem "Little Orphant Annie," the relationship that the two characters possess with labor demonstrates the profound shifts that took place between the 1880s and the 1920s. As Claudia Nelson has summarized, Riley's narrative poem tells the story of a young girl who is "'bound out' to earn her own way in the world. In return for room and board, young Annie . . .

serves as maid-of-all-work for a large family" (1). By contrast, in Gray's comic strip, Annie's engagement in domestic drudge work—such as scrubbing the floor—is used to elicit sympathy. Rather than showing the white orphan girl rightfully "earning her keep" or usefully "contributing" to a household, the strip shows her being physically exploited and emotionally mistreated. Little girls exist to be loved and cherished by adults—not to be used as free sources of manual labor.

In case any doubts remain about Annie's opinion of Miss Asthma, a speech bubble makes them perfectly clear. "When she keeps reminding I'm an orphan and that I'm a charity girl it makes me *hate* her and *hate* the 'home' and *hate* myself for being so poor," the protagonist says aloud to herself while scrubbing the floor (Gray, 36). Far from regarding Miss Asthma's comments about her being grateful for the charity that she has received as blunt pragmatism or even brutal honesty, Annie finds them infuriating. The young girl understandably does not appreciate being reminded that she is a societal burden. Not surprisingly, she longs to find a loving family of her own and leave the orphanage. In comments that are clearly designed to pull the reader's heartstrings, Annie muses while she scrubs the floor: "Gee I wish some nice folks would adopt me—then I could have a real papa and mama like other kids" (36). Demonstrating the emotional power and cultural pervasiveness of such views by the early 1920s, the third panel repeats this exact scenario, only it shows Annie scrubbing dishes instead of floors.

The sentimentalism of the debut strip reaches its apex in the final panel. Annie's work-filled day at the orphanage has come to an end. We see the young white girl in her pajamas, kneeling beside her bed. The speech bubble above her head reveals her prayer to God: "And please make me a real good little girl so some nice people will adopt me—then I can have a papa and a mama to love," she asks (Gray, 36). Lest these sentiments are not already sufficiently touching, Annie adds one more request: "And if it's not too much trouble I'd like a dolly too—amen" (36). With these remarks, Gray's character arguably moves beyond the realm of pity and into pathos.

This scenario establishes the tone for numerous subsequent strips. Annie is routinely presented in highly sentimentalized ways. She is a sympathetic figure worthy of the reader's compassion. Miss Asthma is presented as a villain for not viewing Annie in this way, and so too are other adults who behave in a similar manner. In examples ranging from Mrs. Bottle, who only wants to adopt Annie as a source of free labor (Gray, 70–71), to Mrs. Warbucks, who brings the young girl home only to satisfy the sense of obligation that she feels to do more for charity (38), adults who treat the orphan girl in cold, pragmatic, or purely utilitarian ways are presented in a negative light. These individuals are not exhibiting the proper—and even *only*—affective response to the orphan girl.

Little Orphan Annie's adherence to the conventions of the orphan girl story extends beyond its use of sentimentality. Just as important as presenting the protagonist in sympathetic ways was presenting her as having a positive and even uplifting influence on the people whom she encounters. As Perry Nodelman has commented, in orphan girl novels, there is one outcome that the men and women who take in the destitute character do not know at the outset but quickly discover: "The child who is about to descend on them will transform their lives and make them happy" (146). Soon after she enters their lives, people in general and her new caretakers in particular undergo dramatic changes: "Bad ones become good ones; nasty people turn nice, uncharitable people give things away, [and] potential divorcees decide to stay married" (147). In many cases, rather than precipitating a radical reinvention of an individual's demeanor, orphan girls merely bring out areas of the personality that have been hurt, ignored, or neglected. In the words of Nodelman once again, "Most frequently, it turns out that the bad people were not really bad at all; while they have been soured by experience, they only need the presence of our remarkable heroine to rediscover their goodness" (147).

This feature likewise forms a central component to *Little Orphan Annie*. From the moment that Daddy Warbucks meets his adoptive daughter, the formerly cantankerous man is transformed into a playful, affectionate, and lighthearted caregiver. As Bruce Smith has observed about the comic, Daddy is "a man with deeply hurt feelings who believed nobody liked him because he'd made money from the war" (13). Indeed, as he reveals in the strip that appeared on October 3, 1924: "I thought money would make the Mrs. happy—I thought she'd be proud of me but I guess I was wrong" (Gray, 53). The image that accompanies these remarks demonstrates the depths of his sorrow. It shows the munitions mogul sitting dejectedly in a chair with his hands covering his face. "I've made nothing but mistakes all my life," he goes on to say mournfully (53). Akin to the orphan girls before her, Annie has—to borrow the language of Perry Nodelman—a "magic ability to awaken dormant joyousness" (147). Rather than taking days or even weeks to transpire, this phenomenon occurs immediately after Warbucks meets Annie. Encountering the orphan girl in the hallway of his home, he points his finger at her and barks: "Listen here, don't you ever dare to call me *Mr. Warbucks* again—" (Gray, 51; emphasis in original). His gruff tone, reprimanding words, and aggressive body language frighten the young girl. Emanata radiate from her head, and wiggly lines appear around her body, indicating that she is trembling. Even Annie's response, "Yes, Sir!" is created using shaky lines to convey her fear (51). The final panel, however, contains an unexpected twist: Daddy scoops Annie up in his arms and with a big smile tells her: "You can call me *Daddy*—see? (51; emphasis in original). Thus begins Daddy Warbucks's affectionate relationship with his adoptive daughter. In many ways, he becomes a different person when she is around. Her presence not only softens him; it rejuvenates him. The closing panel to the comic that appeared on October 6, 1924, for example, shows Daddy galloping gleefully through the house on his hands and knees like a horse. Annie sits atop his back, wearing a cowboy hat (Gray, 53). In this episode, and many other similar scenarios, Daddy Warbucks rediscovers not simply his youth but also his joie de vivre in Annie's presence.

• • •

For nearly a century, readers and critics have identified Charles Dickens, who was Harold Gray's favorite novelist, as exerting the greatest creative influence on *Little Orphan Annie*. Jeet Heer, for example, has written: "Gray was a voracious reader of Dickens and there is a great deal of the Victorian novelist in Annie" ("Dream Big," 24). In features ranging from the cartoonist's penchant for crafting character names like Doc Scalpel, Phil O. Buster, and Mrs. Bleeding Heart to his reliance on "coincidental meetings" for plot resolutions (24), *Little Orphan Annie* contains a variety of Dickensian elements.

Gray's decision to make his protagonist an orphan is often seen as another homage to his favorite Victorian writer (Doherty, para. 4). While *Little Orphan Annie* is undeniably influenced by Dickens, it is also powerfully indebted to the cadre of women novelists publishing on the other side of the Atlantic. From the basic premise of the comic's plot to the portrayal of its title character, *Little Orphan Annie* draws on the work of Susan Warner, L. M. Montgomery, Kate Douglas Wiggin, and Eleanor Porter. Remembering and recouping the tradition of the orphan girl story alters the comic strip's narrative kinships and cultural coordinates. *Little Orphan Annie* is at least as connected to the tradition of women's fiction as it is to the work of Charles Dickens, perhaps more so.

"AW, TRAIN YOUR OWN BRAT": GIVING THE ORPHAN GIRL SOME SASS—AND SCRAP

Little Orphan Annie's participation in the orphan girl tradition is not one of simple replication. The comic strip mirrors key aspects of this formula while modifying others. The changes that Gray's comic makes to the orphan girl story are as significant as its areas of conformity. These features allow the newspaper strip to challenge one of the most popular literary traditions of its era, along with an array of equally foundational aspects of American sociocultural life with which it engages. The modifications to the orphan girl story that appear in *Little Orphan Annie* offer a progressive and even radical critique of the construction of white, middle-class girlhood during the early twentieth century. These elements reveal how Gray's comic was not merely a product of the transformations that were taking place in American life during the 1920s; it was also a catalyst for them.

As Joe Sutliff Sanders has observed, all the protagonists featured in orphan girl narratives shared one personality trait: they were thoroughly schooled "in the art of being pleasant, of being *good* invalids, orphans, or waifs" (145; italics in original). Arising in part from the gender expectations associated with middle-class white Protestant girlhood and in part from the fact that these specific figures needed to ingratiate themselves to potential benefactors, orphan girls were rarely naughty. "Although these child protagonists have endured grief, loss, neglect, abuse, poverty, and friendlessness," Claudia Mills has commented, "they appear absolutely unscathed and unscarred by these experiences" (228). Orphan girls were known for their "model behavior" (Singley, 91). Such characters rarely misbehaved, and when they did, their "mistakes [were] honest ones" (Sanders, 67). The misstep was purely accidental, and they learned the appropriate lesson from the error immediately (67–69). Furthermore, orphan girls never engaged in this blunder again. In this way, as Carol Singley has observed, orphan girl stories served "as a disciplinary strategy aimed at ensuring a girl's piety, passivity, and obedience" (91).

Little Orphan Annie breaks from this convention. The title character differs from her orphan girl counterparts both in her attitude and in her actions. Annie frequently misbehaves, and she just as commonly does not regret her behavior. Instead she delights in, and even prides herself on, defying the manners and mores expected of "good" orphan girls. Harold Gray wastes no time revealing this aspect of his protagonist; he announces it, in fact, in the second strip (fig. 1.2). Appearing on August 6, 1924, the comic shows a wealthy couple visiting the orphanage with their young son. As the wife reveals when

Figure 1.2. *Little Orphan Annie*, August 6, 1924. By Harold Gray.

they enter Miss Asthma's office, they are thinking about adopting a girl "to be sort of a companion to our Lester" (Gray, 36). However, when the young boy meets Annie, his reaction is anything but friendly. Pointing his finger at her, Lester says mockingly: "Where did you find those clothes? In a grab bag?" (36). The young boy is not finished ridiculing Annie, however. He continues: "And that hair—wow! Orphans are always funny, but you're a riot!" (36).

Had this encounter occurred to one of Annie's orphan girl counterparts, she would likely have ignored the hurtful taunts or perhaps even tried to befriend Lester and thereby change his views about orphans. Gray's protagonist, however, responds in a far different way: she punches him in the face.

Figure 1.3. *Little Orphan Annie*, August 19, 1924. By Harold Gray.

"I'll teach you some manners!" Annie exclaims while charging at the boy full speed, her left fist smashing into his mouth. Both Miss Asthma and Lester's parents are shocked by the young girl's behavior, but—signaling an even greater difference from her orphan girl antecedents—Annie is unrepentant. Lester's father says haughtily, "If I had a rowdy like that I'd certainly train her" to Miss Asthma as he leaves her office, his son bawling. Without hesitating, Annie shoots back, "Aw, train your own brat" (Gray, 36).

Far from an isolated incident, this comic depicts a key facet of Annie's character. The young girl is both scrappy and sassy. Annie routinely talks back, and she also often physically fights back. Only two weeks after the incident with Lester, in the strip that appeared on August 19, 1924, Annie gets into another altercation with a peer. This time, she punches a boy whose dog is attacking the dog that she is walking. The kid and his friends are not only refusing to intervene but cheering on their pugnacious pooch (Gray, 40). The left hook that Annie delivers to the boy's face is even stronger than the punch that she planted on Lester. As Gray's drawing reveals, Annie's blow knocks the boy completely off his feet (fig. 1.3). The panel shows him falling backward, his legs sticking up in the air. In a further indication of the power

Figure 1.4. *Little Orphan Annie*, October 7, 1924. By Harold Gray.

of Annie's punch, the boy's arms are splayed open, his hat is shooting into the air, and stars are circling his head, suggesting that he has a concussion or, at the least, has been dazed (40).

Such behavior becomes a recurring feature of Annie's personality—and of the plot events in the strip. The spirited young girl frequently gets into physical skirmishes, usually with a naughty boy who is mistreating her, another person, or an animal. Annie's most common tactic is to wallop her adversaries with one of her powerful punches. As in the case of the boy who was cruelly allowing his large dog to attack Annie's small pup, she usually knocks them down with just one blow (fig. 1.4). However, she occasionally employs different methods. In the strip that appeared on October 8, 1924, for example, she chases away a group of boys who are ridiculing an elderly man on the street by pelting them with cobblestones (fig. 1.5). In the strip that appeared on January 9, 1925, a group of boys are hurting Sandy, and Annie wallops them with a wooden board (fig. 1.6).

Through these episodes, Gray's comic strip offers a powerful commentary on the type of protagonist commonly featured in orphan girl stories and, by extension, the type of behavior commonly expected of white, middle-class

Figure 1.5. *Little Orphan Annie*, October 8, 1924. By Harold Gray.

girls in American society as a whole. Instead of presenting Annie as weak, helpless, and passive, Gray shows her as tough, strong, and capable. In so doing, the comic strip calls into question prevailing societal views of girls as vulnerable and in need of protection. As Annie's sassiness and scrappiness demonstrate, not only are girls fully capable of standing up for themselves, but they need to do so. Being sweet, kind, and obedient in life is not an effective strategy. When an adult or another child is treating you cruelly and unfairly, docility does not work. Instead, girls need to speak up—and fight back. As the basic premise of the orphan girl narrative demonstrates, girls cannot always count on their families to take care of them, their guardians to protect them, and society to treat them kindly. Consequently, they must know how to protect themselves. As Harold Gray would often say about Annie, "She can take care of herself because she has to" (quoted in Gubar, para. 7). Given these circumstances, Gray went on to boast that Annie had a famous "fast left" and was "tougher than hell" (quoted in Gubar, para. 7).

Daddy Warbucks not only sanctions his adoptive daughter's unconventional actions; he praises them. After Annie punches a boy who is mistreating her in the comic from October 7, 1924, Daddy commends her: "Atta

Figure 1.6. *Little Orphan Annie*, January 9, 1925. By Harold Gray.

girl, Annie—a straight left turneth away wrath" (Gray, 54). In such passages, *Little Orphan Annie* demonstrates the importance of being more proactive and assertive. For generations, orphan girl stories idealized female passivity, presenting it as a laudable trait or model quality. *Little Orphan Annie* thoroughly rejects this feature of the formula and thus also the societal beliefs from which it arose.

Given the long-standing tradition of presenting orphan girls as obedient, polite, and well behaved—combined with the perceived desirability of these traits—one might expect that Annie's iconoclastic nature would be viewed in a negative light. Both her actions and attitudes deviated so far from the conventions of this tradition that they would understandably shock and perhaps even offend the comic's original audience. The portrayal of Annie as bold, sassy, and even pugnacious, however, did not impede her likability. On the contrary, these traits greatly enhanced it. As Ted Slampyak observed about the strip, "It always was good to open a newspaper and see a little girl who should be helpless but is out there, tough as nails, out to win the day. ... Everyone finds that inspiring" (quoted in Cohen, para. 15). In spite of getting into fights and talking back to adult authority figures, the young girl remained a character that Americans in the 1920s found not merely palatable but pleasing. In Slampyak's words once again, "The appeal of Annie is simply that she doesn't give up.... She doesn't have a lot of resources but she has a lot of spirit, a lot of pluck. She's got a lot of fight in her" (quoted in Cohen, para. 14).

The 1920s were a time of massive transformations to American society. From the challenges posed to traditional women's gender roles with the rise of the flapper and the upheavals caused by the massive influx of immigrants to the growing influence of African American culture amid the Harlem Renaissance and the shifts in daily life precipitated by new technological innovations like the radio, automobile, and motion picture, the United States underwent profound changes during this era. Exemplifying both the power and the pervasiveness of these shifts, figures such as Amos St. Germain and Frederick Lewis Allen have written that American society at the end of the 1920s was virtually unrecognizable from the form that it had taken at the beginning of the era. The decade marked the end of the Victorian way of life and the start of modernity.

While topics like Prohibition, women's suffrage, and the Great Migration are frequently mentioned in discussions about the upheavals of the 1920s, childhood in general and girlhood in particular are commonly omitted. Indeed, much attention has been paid to the massive transformations that were taking place to the gender roles of white, middle-class adult women with the rise of the flapper. With her short hair, even shorter shirts, and penchant for smoking, dancing, and drinking, the flapper challenged long-standing notions about women's manners and mores. As Frederick Lewis Allen observed, flappers "were making mincemeat" of Victorian codes of conduct that had been sacrosanct for generations (*Only Yesterday*, 74).

In spite of profound changes to the gender roles of adult middle-class white women in the 1920s, comparatively little is said about their preadolescent counterparts. There is an assumption that young girls from the same demographic were unaware of, or at least immune to, the decade's atmosphere of gender iconoclasm—in short, that while adult white women were thoroughly rejecting Victorian manners and mores, young girls continued to happily conform to them.

Little Orphan Annie offers an alternative perspective on this belief. Although the protagonist is not a flapper, she does engage in what Allen called "a first-class revolt against the accepted American order ... taking place during those early years of the Post-war Decade" (*Only Yesterday*, 73). In a previously overlooked facet to this phenomenon, young white girls were participants in the era's revolt against traditional gender roles. As *Little Orphan Annie* repeatedly demonstrates, long-standing conceptions about girlhood needed to be not simply fought but—echoing the protagonist's pugnaciousness—dealt a knockout blow.

In a recent essay, Pamela Robertson Wojcik asserted: "Annie needs to be situated within the complex and variable definitions of girlhood available in the 1930s" (13). While Gray's title character does offer a commentary on female gender roles during the Great Depression, she likewise does so for those that were in place during the Jazz Age when she made her debut. In the same way that Annie was in dialogue with the concept of "the new girl" during the 1930s—as Wojcik discusses—she was in close conversation with that of "the orphan girl" from the 1920s. Furthermore, the changes that Annie makes to this earlier female formula helped give rise to the phenomenon that followed. Examining the ways in which *Little Orphan Annie* both reflects and revises the orphan girl story reveals how these phases of the comic—as well as periods in US cultural history—are not unrelated; they are interconnected.

"JUST GIVE HER AN EVEN BREAK AND SHE'LL DO THE REST": THE ORPHAN CHARACTER AND/AS THE AMERICAN CHARACTER

The modifications that *Little Orphan Annie* makes to the orphan girl formula extend beyond the title character's personality. The strip also calls into question the basic plot of these narratives. "Although stories about boys and girls may begin with sentimental portrayals of departures from birth parents followed by trial adoptions," Carol Singley has written, "virtually all stories about girls end with the protagonist safely inscribed within the boundaries of family and home" (91). Novels featuring orphan girls document the protagonist's journey from abandonment to belonging, from losing a family to joining one, and from presenting a pitiable young girl who is all alone in the world to showcasing one who is now happily enveloped in a loving community. Furthermore, orphan girls do not simply want to be adopted; they are depicted as "needing the security of home" (91). A nuclear family provides these figures with a variety of essential elements—ranging from financial support and physical protection to material comfort and emotional well-being—that the girls are unable to obtain on their own. Consequently, as Joe Sutliff Sanders has observed, while various aspects of the orphan girl story changed over the decades, one feature remained constant: all these books featured the happy ending of the formerly orphaned girl being integrated into a loving new family (22).

Forming an even more radical departure from the orphan girl formula, *Little Orphan Annie* deviates from this feature. As her name implies, Gray's protagonist remains Little *Orphan* Annie. Although she is taken in by Daddy Warbucks and ostensibly becomes his adoptive daughter, she is frequently cast out of her new home. Either by her own choice or by circumstances beyond her control, Annie routinely leaves the safety and security of the Warbucks abode and fends for herself in the world. Indeed, this process by which Annie is reorphaned embodies one of the recurring features of the strip and forms a main vehicle for its story lines.

That said, this detail does far more than simply embody a useful plot device that allows Annie to experience a wide variety of exciting escapades, as numerous previous critics have contended. It also allows the comic strip to engage in sociopolitical commentary. Unlike Annie's orphan girl counterparts who suffer terribly on their own and need the physical protection, emotional comfort, and economic support of a family, Gray's protagonist has a far different experience. While Annie may find herself in conditions that are trying or even troublesome, she always perseveres. Contrary to prevailing beliefs that children in general and girls in particular need protection, Annie is emotionally resilient, physically capable, and economically resourceful. As her repeated abandonment and reorphaning demonstrate, Annie doesn't need anyone—not her biological family, not the orphanage, and not an adoptive mother or father. Far from being dependent, she consistently proves that she is self-sufficient.

Furthermore, Annie's repeated abandonment has implications that extend beyond challenging the importance of the patriarchal nuclear family and the necessity of adoption. It can also be seen as offering a powerful commentary on the American political landscape, especially its economic policies. In the same way that Annie does not need the protection, guardianship, or safety nets provided by parents, she also does not need ones provided by the state. The young girl does just fine without social welfare, civic charity, or government assistance. In this way, the progressive messages that Gray's comic strip contains about a young girl's physical strength, intellectual ability, and emotional resilience ultimately serve a conservative purpose. These liberal elements are paradoxically used to support neoliberal views about American society, politics, and especially the economy. Moreover, these features are present in Gray's comic years before the stock market crash, the start of the Great Depression, and the implementation of FDR's New Deal. *Little Orphan Annie* capitalizes on the popularity of the orphan girl story and uses this tradition to offer a pointed commentary on American capitalism. More specifically, Gray's portrayal of a young girl who has been liberated from restrictive gender roles becomes a means to promote his libertarian views about government and the economy.

• • •

The way in which Annie's repeated reorphaning demonstrates the benefits of being free, unencumbered, and unrestricted occurs from the first time that this event occurs. In the strip that appeared on October 25, 1924, Daddy announces that he is leaving on his first business trip. Almost immediately after his departure, Mrs. Warbucks returns Annie to the orphanage, telling Miss Asthma that the "trial" did not work out (Gray, 60). After being adopted by a couple who only want Annie as a free laborer in their dry goods store, she runs away. The young girl tramps through the countryside, sleeping under bridges, hitching rides with passing strangers, and keeping company with hoboes (85–86). She spends the night in a barn, where she startles the farmer, Byron Silo, when he arrives to tend to the animals in the morning (90). Byron and his wife welcome Annie into their home, where she becomes a cherished member of the family, as well as an asset to the farm. In a series of comics that appeared over the course of several weeks, Annie helps with the chores both inside and outside the house: she feeds the horses, milks the cows, chops firewood, helps haul grain to the mill, churns butter, and does laundry (91–95). Even more importantly, Annie repeatedly foils the machinations of a crooked banker, Mr. Willis, who is trying to swindle the Silos out of their farm. First, while running errands in town, Annie overhears Willis's plan to compel the couple to pay up on their mortgage note or forfeit their property, and she alerts them to it (105). Then she saves their entire crop season by recognizing that Mr. Willis has sold them bad seed (112). Finally, Annie and her dog Sandy repeatedly disrupt the efforts of the banker and his henchmen to sneak onto the property and sabotage the Silos' farming efforts.

When all of Annie's good deeds are viewed collectively, she is almost single-handedly responsible for the Silos having the best growing season in many years. As Mr. Silo says while they survey the fields one evening: "No, Annie, I don't remember ever seeing corn so far along or looking better this time o' year" (Gray, 127). Moreover, it is not simply this one crop that is prospering. "Yep, the oats are just starting to shoot up now," he adds, "we can't help but have a bumper crop this year" (127). Furthermore, Mr. Silo remarks in the third panel of the same strip: "This hay'll be ready to cut before very long—I'll bet it will make three tons to the acre" (127). Unfortunately, a fierce storm decimates the property. "Mary, we're ruined," Mr. Silo tells his wife after the weather clears. "The hail killed our crops and the wind wrecked the barn and as if that wasn't enough lightning burned our hay stacks—we've lost everything" (128). Once again, however, Annie's presence saves the day. Just when all seems lost, Daddy Warbucks pulls up in his car, looking for a place to get a drink of water (128). When he sees his long-lost adopted daughter, he immediately decides to assist the couple who have taken such good care of her. First, Daddy helps Mr. Silo make repairs around the farm (129). Additionally, he pays off the remaining balance on their mortgage (129). Finally, in an act that affirms the end of the Silos' troubles, Daddy punches Mr. Willis in the nose and growls at him to leave town and never come back: "There now, my fat friend—on yer way and don't stop—there'll be one of my men following you from now on and don't let him catch you, see?—My advice is to take that 7,000 bucks for railroad fare and when you're broke, *run—*" (131; emphasis in original).

Annie's residence with the Silos unfolds over the course of more than six months of daily comic strips, indicating that these experiences are not a momentary digression but a sustained and significant story line. Moreover, the episode embodies far more than merely an entertaining subplot designed to keep Gray's readers returning to the strip. Instead, Annie's time with the Silos also offers a poignant commentary on the role of government in people's lives. Neither Annie nor the Silos need federal assistance when they fall on tough times. Annie does not need child protective services or social welfare programs. While she certainly experiences hardship and difficulty when she is wandering on her own, she can handle it. She is hardworking, independent, and resourceful. The only thing that Annie needs to rely on is herself. While tramping through the countryside, she always manages to keep herself sheltered, fed, and safe. At several points, she even helps other people: Annie returns a lost pocketbook to a farmer, and she also rescues a boy who has fallen through thin ice (Gray, 87, 90). Not surprisingly, when the young girl first encounters Mr. Silo, she tells him: "Aw, I've always worked hard that's O.K. with me—I'm used to it" (91). These remarks encapsulate Annie's nature—as well as the key to her success. The protagonist doesn't need the local or federal government to step in and help her; she is fully capable of helping herself. The comic consistently condemns instances when Annie is exploited as a source of uncompensated labor. But it values and even celebrates hard work when the young girl engages in this practice voluntarily. Echoing one of primary tenets of laissez-faire capitalism, she is simply opposed to having her labor regulated, restricted, and exploited.

The Silos can likewise manage without government intervention. Although they face a myriad of difficult issues—a corrupt banker, a bad batch of seeds, and a natural disaster—they do not need federal assistance: not in the form of environmental protections, banking regulations, or government subsidies. On the contrary, the only things that the rural couple need to turn their difficult time around are hard work, perseverance, and a little bit of luck. Through this combination of their own efforts and the assistance of neighbors and friends like Annie and Daddy, they can overcome any obstacle.

This scenario recurs throughout the comic. At numerous points, Annie leaves the Warbucks home and fends for herself in the world. The young girl does not simply survive; she thrives. Annie is able to take care of herself as well as other people. In so doing, she demonstrates that she does not need guardianship on the familial, state, or federal level—and neither does anyone else. Gray's comic does not treat this aspect of Annie's personality as merely implied or tacit; Daddy Warbucks announces this quality soon after meeting her. In the comic published on September 29, 1924, he tells his wife: "Annie doesn't need charity—just give her an even break and she'll do the rest—charity!!—Bah!" (Gray, 51). By repeatedly demonstrating how the title character is capable, resilient, and self-sufficient, Gray's comic makes the case that so, too, are the American people. After all, if an eleven-year-old orphan girl can manage on her own, then surely the nation's adult citizens can as well. When tough times hit, Americans don't need the government to step in and save them; they need only themselves—and each other. Through their own hard work, combined with the assistance of their neighbors, friends, and community members, they can overcome any obstacle, persevere through any difficulty, and triumph over any crisis. Government assistance is not simply unnecessary; it is insulting.

For generations, orphan girl stories presented an adoptive family saving a young female protagonist from the cruelty of "the wide, wide, world"—to borrow the title of the 1850 novel by Susan Warner that inaugurated the trend. In *Little Orphan Annie*, this process is reversed. Gray's orphan girl saves various citizens from the clutches of what might be called "the wide, wide government." Harold Gray's comic strip contains elements that can be regarded as challenging conventional female gender roles by presenting Annie as tough, strong, and capable. Rather than making a statement about feminism, these traits are doing so about federalism. *Little Orphan Annie* is not so much pro-girl as it is antigovernment.

• • •

Discussions about the political nature of *Little Orphan Annie* are not new. Harold Gray was a highly partisan individual who subscribed to a specific sociocultural viewpoint. As Worth Gatewood said about Gray, he was "imbued with a Calvinist morality and a political conservatism slightly to the right of Ivan the Terrible" (ix). This statement is far from hyperbole. Jeet Heer has likewise said of the cartoonist: "He was famously reactionary" ("Limits," para. 1). Far from simply privately holding such sociopolitical beliefs, Gray incorporated them in *Little Orphan Annie*. More to the point, he unapologetically used the comic as a mouthpiece—or, perhaps more accurately, a bullhorn—for these views. During a time when comic strips staunchly avoided engaging with any culturally controversial subjects lest they alienate viewers and lose subscribers, "*Little Orphan Annie* became the first nationally syndicated comic strip to be unabashedly, unrelievedly, 'political'" (Harvey, para. 14). As R. C. Harvey has rightly observed, these elements were not occasionally "dropped into" or "externally imposed" on the comic. Instead, "the strip's politics were organic—integral to its story" (para. 16). From the worldview espoused by the title character to the business philosophy practiced by Daddy Warbucks, Republican conservatism formed as much of a signature facet to the comic strip as Annie's orange hair and her pet dog, Sandy. Over the years, *Little Orphan Annie* would take on a variety of politically charged issues, including the unions, social welfare programs, child labor laws, federal income tax, communism, and government regulation of business.

Gray's political commentary did not go unnoticed by the strip's readers or critics. On the contrary, it "stirred intense debate across the country. It made [Gray] many enemies, but he never backed down" (Smith, 2). By 1935, in fact, the Republican conservatism that permeated *Little Orphan Annie* prompted the *New Republic* to call Gray's comic "Hooverism in the Funnies." Meanwhile, another critic likened *Little Orphan Annie* to "John Birch Society propaganda" (Cohen, para. 34). Finally and most recently, Jay Maeder characterized the comic as "the Fox News Channel of the funny papers" (quoted in Cohen, para. 11).

That said, the intensely political nature of *Little Orphan Annie* is not regarded as being present in the comic from the beginning. As Jeet Heer has written, "Gray wasn't really a conservative in the 1920s: he was more of a general populist" ("CR Holiday," para. 1). The cartoonist's political views did not become more conservative until "the 1930s when the presidency of Franklin Roosevelt polarized American politics into those who saw the New Deal as the salvation for the working class and those who saw it as the end of American liberty" (para. 1). It was during this era that Gray and, by extension, Annie "became much more explicitly right-wing" (para. 1). Before the Great Depression, the comic is more often regarded as simply a sappy "soap opera" (Weales, 80). Instead of being driven by major national events, *Little Orphan Annie* was fueled by histrionic emotions, overblown characters, and "treacly adventures" (Gatewood, viii). It was during the 1930s when "*Little Orphan Annie* evolved from a crudely drawn melodrama" to a strip that possessed a more sophisticated artistic style, as well as a more pointed sociopolitical message (Heer, "CR Holiday," para. 1). These features were not present in the "*Annie* books till we hit the New Deal period" (para. 1). In sentiments that have been echoed by many subsequent critics, William H. Young asserted: "Until about 1931 . . . Gray kept his personal views pretty much to himself" (310).

Placing *Little Orphan Annie* back in the tradition of the orphan girl story challenges this viewpoint. Reading the comic strip in the context of this popular literary phenomenon reveals elements of sociopolitical commentary during a period that is commonly regarded as lacking this quality. Gray's strip may have been a "crudely drawn melodrama" when it appeared in the 1920s, but this feature did not mean it was devoid of serious social messages. On the contrary, the strip used the sentimentality of the orphan girl formula to offer a multifaceted cultural critique. Moreover, many of these messages—about the importance of personal freedom, the value of hard work, and the unnecessary nature of social safety nets—foreshadowed the ones that would appear later and more overtly in the strip. Reading *Little Orphan Annie* as an orphan girl story demonstrates that these elements are present both from the strip's origins and *because* of its origins. The orphan girl formula is not antithetical to the politics that would emerge in *Little Orphan Annie*. On the contrary, this literary phenomenon served as their starting point.

Unlike many of the other comics examined in this project, *Little Orphan Annie* has been the subject of sustained attention. Over the decades, the strip has been discussed in essays that have appeared in edited collections, articles that have been posted both on popular websites and in peer-reviewed academic journals, and full-length books released by mainstream presses. That said, the vast majority of these discussions focus on *Little Orphan Annie* during the 1930s and 1940s. Examples such as Maria Mazzenga's "The Home Front's Cartoony Face: World War Two through Orphan Annie's Eyes" and Stella Ress's "Bridging the Generation Gap: *Little Orphan Annie* in the Great Depression" identify these periods as the time when the comic was most interesting, complex, and influential.[3] As a result, such discussions either skip over strips from the 1920s entirely or give them short shrift. Bruce Smith's

The History of Little Orphan Annie, for example, devotes only one chapter to the comic's origins, evolution, and existence during the 1920s. Furthermore, the discussion itself spans a mere fifteen pages (6–21). Smith's book is not an anomaly. Rather, it reflects a long-standing phenomenon in both the popular and scholarly treatment of Gray's comic.

Reading *Little Orphan Annie* as an orphan girl story contests this practice. Placing the strip back within the context of this popular phenomenon demonstrates the literary and cultural richness of the comic during this era and, by extension, its capacity for sustained, serious analysis. *Little Orphan Annie* comics from the 1920s are ones not to merely skim but to thoughtfully study.

• • •

In examples that date back to Moses and Romulus and Remus, the theme of adoption has been a fixture in Western narratives for centuries. The concept has particular resonance in the United States. As Carol Singley has written, "Disrupted biological families and elective family units are a defining feature of American literature, in a way that is strikingly absent in other national literatures" (3). The origin of this phenomenon arises from the origin of the nation. "Adoption narratives are rooted in the American migratory experience: they reflect politically and culturally the severed ties to Great Britain and the construction of new forms of social and governmental organization" (4). Of course, in the decades following the Revolutionary War, millions of men and women would arrive on the nation's shores from locations around the globe. For these individuals, the United States became their adoptive country. Given this history, "Adoption, as a trope or narrative event, is notable in major American literary landmarks" (3).

Harold Gray's *Little Orphan Annie* revises the orphan girl story and, with it, the conception of adoption as an American literary trope. Whereas previous works positioned the *adopted* figure as an emblem of the national spirit and American experience, Gray's comic strip does so with a protagonist who remains an orphan in many ways. Annie possesses quintessential American qualities like self-reliance, hard work, and determination, not because she is adopted by Daddy Warbucks but because she is abandoned by him. It is through her repeated reorphaning that she both cultivates and exhibits traits that are commonly seen as embodying the national character.

The factors fueling Little Orphan Annie's long-standing attraction and multigenerational appeal have been widely discussed. As Lyle W. Shannon has commented, the character reflects "the symbols which have traditionally represented good in our society and she condemns some of the well known sins" (170). More specifically, Shannon goes on to explain, Annie embodies quintessential American traits: "Little Orphan Annie approves of honesty, brains, going straight, decency and fair dealing, curiosity, love of countrymen, Santa Claus, Providence, school, peace, prosperity and equal opportunity" (178). William H. Young echoed this observation, arguing that the character reflects core middle-class values, including hard work, faith, determination, and charity (312). Such assessments of Annie are anything but externally imposed. In a comic from 1939, Daddy Warbucks himself calls the young girl nothing less than "the symbol of America" (quoted in Weales, 80).

For nearly a century, the fact that *Little Orphan Annie* is an orphan girl story has largely been seen as unrelated to this quality. Given the way in which this literary tradition was inextricably tied to questions of familial and civic guardianship, the orphan girl origins of *Little Orphan Annie* are not extraneous; they are essential. At repeated points throughout the comic, Annie is reunited with Daddy Warbucks. Heeding the example of this plot element, we likewise need to reunite Gray's strip with this influential but overlooked literary heritage.

Chapter 2

"I Slant My Gags to the Lawrence Welk Gum Chewers"

Nancy and the Vaudeville Aesthetic

• •

Perhaps no newspaper strip in the history of American comics is simultaneously more revered and reviled than Ernie Bushmiller's *Nancy*. The comic's eight-year-old eponymous character made her debut in the long-standing *Fritzi Ritz* series on January 2, 1933, and was an immediate sensation. With her outspoken personality, mischievous nature, and quirky worldview, Nancy quickly became the star. As Brian Walker has written, when Bushmiller officially changed the strip's name to *Nancy* in 1938, the move "was a mere formality," for the young girl had already emerged as the comic's central character (46).

In the years that followed, *Nancy* did not simply maintain its appeal; the comic grew in popularity with each generation. In the 1930s, the strip "was being distributed to over 200 daily and 100 Sunday newspapers by United Feature Syndicate" (Walker, 19). Then, by the 1950s, "*Nancy* appeared in about 500 U.S. papers and appeared in translation in many others worldwide" (Hamrah, para. 4). Finally, at the peak of its circulation during the early 1970s, the comic ran in more than 880 dailies around the country (Walker, 228). As Brian Walker has noted, the strip "earned Bushmiller a handsome living" (135). By the time of the cartoonist's death in 1982, *Nancy* had become one of the most commercially successful comics in American history.

In spite of the tremendous public popularity of *Nancy*, the strip never enjoyed much critical, artistic, or cultural acclaim. As the cartoonist Shannon Wheeler said about Bushmiller and his creation: "He was no innovator.... He inspired no school or technique. His 'storytelling' consisted of rudimentary gags and the worst kind of puns" (quoted in Harvey, "The Lawrence Welk of Cartoonists," para. 2). Such viewpoints have been echoed by numerous other figures. Daniel Clowes, for example, has written how, early in his career as a cartoonist, he would buoy his ego by reminding himself "that I could draw better than 'that Nancy guy,' or at least with way more lines" (4). Similarly, R. C. Harvey, in an essay about the tremendous commercial success of *Nancy*, "professe[d] as much exasperation at the phenomenon as anyone" (para. 1). Finally, and perhaps most damningly of all, Brian Walker confessed: "As a little kid, I used to read *Nancy* regularly.... But as I got older, I learned to hate *Nancy*. I found it offensively dumb and an insult to my intelligence" (10). In sentiments that have been privately thought if not publicly uttered by many individuals, Walker went on to assert: "How could anybody, except children under the age of six and ancients (anyone over fifty), find this simple-minded, illiterate comic strip entertaining?" (10).

This chapter identifies a new source of possible influence on *Nancy* and offers an alternative explanation for the strip's paradoxical condition of being loved and hated in equal measure. In what embodies an overlooked facet of *Nancy*, many of the comic's signature traits, central characters, and core qualities can be traced back to one of the most popular modes of entertainment in the United States during the early twentieth century: vaudeville. From the gag humor employed in the strip and Nancy's penchant for linguistic misunderstandings to Sluggo's use of working-class dialect and the comedic exchanges that take place between him and Nancy, the strip is an amalgamation of vaudevillian elements.

Understanding the way in which vaudeville permeates *Nancy* helps to account for the strip's tremendous appeal, along with its long-standing low cultural esteem. Vaudeville was wildly successful for generations in the United States, but it was never regarded as a sophisticated, serious, or highbrow form—a condition that mirrors that of Bushmiller's strip. At the same time, the elements of vaudeville that can be traced through *Nancy* add a new facet to discussions of class, ethnicity, and race in the comic.

In an oft-repeated comment, in 1971, Ernie Bushmiller offered the following explanation about the success of *Nancy*: "I slant my gags to the Lawrence Welk gum chewers and it works" (quoted in Walker, 228). While critics commonly read Bushmiller's remark as a commentary on the cartoonist's commitment to offering wholesome fare during a time when comics were becoming increasingly edgy, it also offers an insight into his strip's aesthetic. *The Lawrence Welk Show* was a variety program modeled after vaudeville in many ways. In the pages that follow, I make a case that so, too, was Bushmiller's *Nancy*. Guy Gilchrist has commented that the strip's central character "can be, depending on the situation, a conceited prima donna or a fun-loving, cute and cheeky little girl" (para. 1). While Nancy's specific mood may change, one aspect of her personality remains the same: her status as vaudevillian.

"VAUDEVILLE MAD":
POPULAR ENTERTAINMENT IN FIN DE SIÈCLE AMERICA

In the apt words of Mark Hodin, "During the last decade of the 19th century, vaudeville became the nation's most popular entertainment form, drawing unprecedented numbers of spectators and appealing to members of diverse socioeconomic groups" (193). No single leisure-time activity even came close to rivaling the public popularity and commercial success of vaudeville. From the 1880s through the 1910s, the United States was, as Andrew Erdman has stated, "vaudeville mad" (163).

Although vaudeville dominated popular entertainment in the United States during the fin de siècle, it was not an inherently American art form. As the name implies, "vaudeville" was imported from France. "The word itself is traced back to the valley of the Vire River in Normandy, where *Val de Vire* was often pronounced *Vau de Vire*" (DiMeglio, 19). More specifically, "The area was one noted for its ballads and *vau-de-Vire* became a synonym for 'lively songs'" (19). The word "vaudeville" emerged from this tradition and quickly came to serve as an umbrella category. In the words of DiMeglio, "Vaudeville, as a term, was first used in the United States in 1840, when a Boston 'Vaudeville Saloon' advertised itself as an establishment where a variety program could be seen" (19). From there it spread quickly. "Vaudeville emerged from the concert saloon, burlesque hall, and dime museums of the 1880s, drawing on preexisting forms of variety entertainment" (Erdman, 163).

One of the reasons that vaudeville was able to become so popular was that, in the words of David Nasaw, it offered "something for everyone" (23). Any given show included a diverse array of acts, ranging from jugglers, dramatic sketches, acrobats, magicians, and actors to trained animals, Shakespearean monologists, comedy teams, dancers, and operatic soloists (Hodin, 193). As Gavin Jones has said about the performance ethos governing vaudeville, "The managers of vaudeville theaters saw their mission as the creation of stage shows that would appeal to the largest possible number of people" (162). As a consequence, vaudeville was able to cross the lines of gender, race, region, class, age, and aesthetic taste. Appearing during a time of massive immigration, rapid urbanization, and rampant industrialization, the diverse array of acts mirrored the diverse array of peoples and cultures within the nation.

In this way, although vaudeville was not an inherently American art form, it quickly came to be seen as an emblem of the nation. In 1899, the playwright and theater critic Edwin Royle argued that "vaudeville had taken such a hold in the United States because variety performance was itself somehow typically American, the various acts representing the great plurality and diversity of the nation" (Hodin, 193). As Mark Hodin has noted, "Most subsequent scholarly analyses of vaudeville have followed Royle's conception of theatrical nationhood" (193). All the acts featured in a vaudeville performance "did their separate, highly individual parts, yet all somehow integrating into the whole, serving as a symbol of Americanism" (DiMeglio, 199).

These elements made vaudeville "the most popular area of the entertainment media for approximately thirty years" (DiMeglio, 202). Indeed, it is difficult to overestimate the success of this performance mode. By the early twentieth century, "Some two thousand theaters, scattered throughout the United States and Canada, played nothing but vaudeville. Mae West observed that it would have taken her six years just to play each theater" (11). Far from saturating the market, vaudeville venues were in great demand. "According to Schenk, ten people attended a vaudeville show to every one who patronized other forms of entertainment" (11). Such popularity was not surprising, given that the performers who appeared on the vaudeville stage formed a veritable who's who of American celebrities from the early twentieth century. Ethel Barrymore, Will Rogers, Eddie Cantor, Al Jolson, Bert Williams, Ethel Waters, Sophie Tucker, W. C. Fields, Mae West, Fanny Brice, George Burns, Gracie Allen, Bob Hope, Fred Astaire, Milton Berle, Buster Keaton, Charlie Chaplin, Lionel Barrymore, and Gypsy Rose Lee all either got their start in vaudeville or appeared regularly on the circuit. Looking back on his experiences in vaudeville, Eddie Cantor "called this period the 'Golden Days of Comedy'" in the United States, "when 'unforgettable giants would warm our hearts and tickle our funny bones'" (quoted in DiMeglio, 43).

The meteoric rise of vaudeville in the United States was rivaled only by its equally dramatic fall. As Albert F. McLean Jr. has written, by 1915—a mere two decades after vaudeville had made its mainstream debut—it was already in decline (1). In the years that followed, the rise of motion pictures and then the advent of radio were "beginning to draw away from the entertainment to which it had once flocked" (Erdman, 164). Ultimately these new modes of entertainment proved too great a competition. By the opening years of the 1930s, vaudeville theaters had disappeared, with some closing their doors, others changing their format to traditional stage plays, and still others transforming themselves into movie theaters (Sobel, 99–100).

Even though vaudeville's life span in American popular culture was relatively short, its legacy has been long. Decades after vaudevillians ceased to appear on live stages, this performance mode continued to exert a tremendous influence on the nation's popular entertainment. As Howard Taubman has discussed, the stars of vaudeville "formed a pool of talent from which the new mediums, radio and television, drank thirstily" (128). Bob Hope echoed this observation. "If vaudeville had died, television was the box they put it in," he famously remarked (quoted in Gabler, 6). In examples ranging from NBC's *Texaco Star Theater*, hosted by Milton Berle, to *The Lawrence Welk Show*, which aired until 1982—the year of Ernie Bushmiller's death—vaudeville's approach, style, and content continued to permeate American entertainment throughout the twentieth century. For this reason, Albert McLean Jr. asserted that vaudeville occupies a "permanent place in the popular imagination" (211).

ALL THE WORLD'S A STAGE: ERNIE BUSHMILLER AND VAUDEVILLE

Ernie Bushmiller did not simply live and work during the heyday of vaudeville in the United States; he had a variety of personal, professional, and even familial connections to it. Bushmiller was born on August 23, 1905, in the South Bronx near 137th Street. Of course, New York City during this era was the geographic hub and artistic epicenter of vaudeville. In the words of John E. DiMeglio, "That great metropolis of New York City supplied vaudeville's pulse" (119). Many of the biggest, best, and most prestigious vaudeville theaters were located in the Big Apple. For example, DiMeglio continues, "The one and only Palace Theatre was its heart," located at Forty-seventh Street and Broadway in midtown Manhattan. "Descriptions of the Palace are a veritable vaudeville bill by themselves. It has been called the 'Taj Mahal of vaudeville' and the 'Mecca of every vaudevillian,' 'the Seventh Heaven of the vaudevillians' dream,' show business' 'nirvana,' and 'the temple of vaudeville'" (119).

The Palace was not the only prominent vaudeville theater located in Bushmiller's hometown. Just south of midtown Manhattan, "the Union Square area where Pastor's Music Hall was located made quite a name for itself in show business history. Throughout that section of New York were beer halls, burlesque houses, penny arcades, restaurants, and other vaudeville theaters" (DiMeglio, 126). Finally, but far from inconsequentially, another prominent vaudeville venue was located in the Bronx, the borough where

Bushmiller was born and where he lived with his family for much of his childhood. In the words of DiMeglio once again: "A very interesting neighborhood theater, played by headliners, was the Paradise in the Bronx" (128).

Growing up in an area saturated by vaudeville, Bushmiller as a young man also met several of its most famous performers. In what has become an oft-repeated biographical detail, the cartoonist got his professional start working as a copyboy in the art department at the *New York World* when he was fourteen. As a variety of past and present critics have pointed out, this newspaper published several landmark American comics, including Richard Outcault's *Hogan's Alley* and Rudolph Dirks's *The Katzenjammer Kids*. Indeed, Walker has written that "Bushmiller couldn't have found himself in a more stimulating environment. While at the *New York World*, he ran errands for, and eventually rubbed elbows with, some of the pioneers of the comic strip form" (16). Keir Keightley has documented how *Hogan's Alley* is filled with references to Tin Pan Alley, the music-making factory that cranked out most of the songs that were performed on the vaudeville stage: pieces of sheet music litter the streets, the Yellow Kid and gang sing Tin Pan Alley–esque songs, and they even attend vaudeville performances (29).

Reading installments of *Hogan's Alley* was not the only way that Bushmiller could have encountered vaudeville while working at the *New York World*. As Brian Walker said of the cartoonist, "His big breakthrough came when he was assigned to illustrate a Sunday feature of Harry Houdini's magic. The young teenager was treated to the thrilling experience of having the legendary illusionist demonstrate his latest tricks to him in Houdini's New York apartment" (15). Houdini, of course, was one of the biggest stars on the circuit. As Anthony Slide, in *The Vaudevillians: A Dictionary of Vaudeville Performers*, has discussed, the magician was a headlining performer who drew large audiences wherever he appeared (74–75).

Just before Bushmiller created the character Nancy, he had another chance to meet some well-known vaudeville performers. "In 1931, film comedian Harold Lloyd, after seeing Ernie's work in a newspaper, invited the cartoonist to come to Hollywood to work as a script writer" (Walker, 21). Although Lloyd had made a name for himself as an early silent film actor rather than a stage performer, he knew many vaudevillians and former vaudevillians in California. Bushmiller spent time in the company of some of these stars when he was working for Lloyd. The cartoonist and his new wife "spent the first year of their marriage socializing with Groucho Marx, Edward G. Robinson, and many other movie stars and attending fabulous parties at Lloyd's mansion" (21).

Finally, but far from inconsequentially, Ernie Bushmiller also had a familial connection to vaudeville. The cartoonist's father, Ernest Bushmiller Sr., was born in Germany and immigrated to the United States as a young man. As Walker has written, "Ernie Sr. was a talented artist and performed stand-up chalk-talks on the vaudeville circuit for a short time" (14). Unfortunately, though, he "couldn't support his family doing this," so he retired from the vaudeville stage and, "because of the language barrier, ... was only able to make a meager living bartending, selling insurance and working at various other odd jobs" (14). Although Ernie Bushmiller Sr. "never found a profitable livelihood that made use of his artistic and intellectual" abilities (14), he passed these interests on to his children in general and his son in particular. "Ernie Jr. inherited his father's love for literature and art," and his father encouraged him in these pursuits throughout his life (14). In this way, "Ernie's father was a major influence on his life" (14). The cartoonist credited his father with instilling in him not simply a strong work ethic but also a love for art. Commentators over the years have noted, in fact, that Bushmiller Jr. became the artist in many ways that his father had always longed to be.

Another aspect of the elder Bushmiller's biography may have shaped his son's life, interests, and career. While previous discussions about the cartoonist's father focus on his aptitude for drawing, his involvement with vaudeville may have been just as relevant and important. As numerous friends, interviewers, and fellow cartoonists noted, "Ernie always talked about his father with pride and admiration" (Walker, 14). One of the features that Bushmiller may have admired about, and even emulated from, his father was his fondness for vaudeville.

In *The Best of Ernie Bushmiller's "Nancy"*, Brian Walker remarks: "Although I have made an effort in this book to reveal the man behind the cartoon, the key to understanding *Nancy* is not in the personal life of its creator" (11). I would challenge this belief. Bushmiller's historical time period, life experiences, and family history are far from inconsequential background details in the creation of *Nancy*. Instead, they constitute an important and heretofore overlooked source of possible influence on the comic. As DiMeglio has written, "If it is considered that vaudeville audiences contained great numbers of young minds easily influenced by amusements, it is no wonder that the influence of vaudeville on America is still great" (197). Ernie Bushmiller, of course, was one of those "young minds" who lived and worked during the heyday of vaudeville. Accordingly, as DiMeglio suggests, it should come as no surprise that this performance mode may have shaped the cartoonist's imagination and influenced his creative work.

"A JOKE BOOK AND A SERIES OF RUBBER STAMPS": NANCY AS A VAUDEVILLIAN

In some ways, the newspaper strip that Ernie Bushmiller inherited and that would eventually become *Nancy* already had loose links to vaudeville. Not only was *Fritzi Ritz*—which Bushmiller began ghostwriting for its creator, Larry Whittington, in 1925 and officially took over in 1927—set in the geographic home base of vaudeville, New York City, but its title character was involved in the movie industry. Henry Jenkins has discussed how the decline of vaudeville in American theater during the 1920s did not result from a decline in audience enthusiasm. Rather, vaudeville left the live stage largely because it had taken up residence in a new medium: motion pictures. Many of the most commercially successful and critically acclaimed films from the 1920s and 1930s trafficked in aspects of vaudeville. These films featured some of the biggest stars from the vaudeville stage—such as George Burns, Eddie Cantor, and Charlie Chaplin—and also showcased plots, characters, and jokes taken directly from this performance mode. While Fritzi Ritz auditions for parts as the beautiful leading lady, not as a vaudeville-style performer, American motion pictures of all forms during the 1920s were strongly linked to vaudeville. As Jenkins notes, even movies that were dramas, biopics, and Westerns often borrowed vaudeville conventions for their aesthetic look, plot elements, and narrative structure (20–30).

Of course, only months after Nancy debuted in *Fritzi Ritz*, she herself became involved in show business. In the comic that appeared on September 19, 1933, the eight-year-old girl accompanies her aunt to a studio in Los Angeles. While there, Nancy catches the eye of the director and—much to her aunt's chagrin—is offered a part in the film. "Say—by the way," the man in charge of casting tells Fritzi, "we need a little girl like her for our new picture" (34).[1] Both on and off the movie set, Nancy engages in antics that epitomize what Susan A. Glenn, building on the work of Henry Jenkins, has identified as "'the vaudeville aesthetic': fast-paced wordplay, gags, and physical humor" (Glenn, 650). These elements, in fact, quickly became signature facets of Bushmiller's character and the strip that would soon be retitled in her name.

Nancy made her entrance on the newspaper comics page just as vaudeville was making its exit from the American theater stage. As DiMeglio has written, "by 1933"—the same year that Nancy debuted—"this show business giant would be nearly toppled. With the depression, talking pictures, and radio taking their toll, vaudeville was played in only a handful of theaters. Its day was over" (12). That Nancy engaged in facets of this performance mode was an asset, not a liability. Far from participating in an outmoded or even antiquated cultural form, Bushmiller's strip gave readers material that they already knew and loved. Andrew K. Erdman has written that, in the opening decades of the twentieth century, the United States was "thoroughly vaudevilized" (163). In what has been a long overlooked facet of *Nancy*, so, too, was Bushmiller's comic. In details ranging from the cartoonist's commitment to offering wholesome entertainment and Sluggo's tendency to lapse in and out of a heavy Bronx accent for comedic purposes to the way in which Nancy and Sluggo function as a male-female comedy team and Nancy's engagement in physical humor and even her frequent use of props, the strip is an extended vaudeville show.

• • •

One of the reasons that vaudeville became so popular and attracted such a wide audience was that it operated according to a strict code of morality. Vaudeville featured performers whose acts were respectable, decent, and suitable for all patrons, even those with the most delicate of sensibilities. As Erdman has written, "Vaudeville . . . had succeeded largely by having distinguished itself as a 'clean,' 'wholesome' entertainment, fit for the entire family" (2).[2] In what has become an oft-repeated remark, the theater mogul B. F. Keith operated his many vaudeville houses according to the following ethos: "I made it a rule at the beginning . . . that I must know exactly what every performer on my stage would say or do. If there was one coarse, vulgar, or suggestive line or piece of stage business in the act, I cut it out" (quoted in Erdman, 2). Countless other venues adhered to a similar policy. Keith's main rival in the vaudeville industry, Edward Franklin Albee, for example, "had a sign of his own attached to the backstage bulletin board of the Palace Theatre. 'Remember this theatre caters to ladies and gentlemen and children. Vulgarity will not be tolerated'" (DiMeglio, 50). This statement was far from hyperbole. Albee's code of performer conduct "went on to list forbidden words, among them 'hell, damn, devil, cockroach'" (50). The penalty for breaking any of these rules was both swift and serious. The "Notice to Performers" posted at the vaudeville theaters owned by B. F. Keith admonished: "If you are in doubt as to the character of your act, consult the local manager before you go on the stage, for if you are guilty of uttering anything sacrilegious or even suggestive, you will immediately be closed and will never again be allowed in a theater where Mr. Keith is in authority" (quoted in Erdman, 2–3). As these examples suggest, "Vaudeville's pride was in offering family entertainment, and by extension, morality of the highest order was to be practiced by its performers" (DiMeglio, 196).

Ernie Bushmiller conducted his professional life according to a similar code. As Brian Walker said of the cartoonist, "In private, Ernie could be described as 'a man's man,' and had a salty side to his personality. But he never let this enter into his strip" (224). The rules that Bushmiller established for the content of his comic were very similar to the ones outlined for vaudeville performers: *Nancy* never contained any vulgarity, profanity, or crass content. "'I don't like cruel humor,' [Bushmiller] once said. 'I don't like night club humor, insult humor, where you make fun of somebody. I like a gentle type of humor, a Bob Benchley type'" (Walker, 224). Even during the 1960s and 1970s, when comics were becoming increasingly risqué—and Bushmiller and his work were increasingly being ridiculed for being "square"—the cartoonist never wavered from this modus operandi. In the words of Walker once again, "*Nancy* was frequently praised for its wholesomeness by religious and educational groups, and that was the way Ernie wanted it" (224).

Together with being known for offering wholesome, family-friendly fare, vaudeville was also known for another aspect of its performance style: the simplicity of its sets. "Constance Rourke, writing in 1919, argued for the 'simplification of stage settings' to allow the vaudeville spectator greater concentration: 'Settings must not overshadow the performance'" (Jenkins, 77). Vaudevillians who delivered dramatic speeches or whose acts depended on wordplay had long followed this dictum. "Monologists and comic teams whose appeal was primarily verbal frequently played in front of the curtain with no sets or props whatsoever" (Jenkins, 77). Meanwhile, for performers who appeared on what came to be known as the "small-time" circuit of vaudeville houses in modest cities and large rural towns, limited budgets dictated that every act adopted a minimalist approach (77). Regardless of whether the sparse settings were freely chosen or circumstantially imposed, one detail was clear: minimalist sets became a hallmark of vaudeville shows. Many managers and performers believed that the sparse sets were an asset. "The absence of other stage effects sharpened the focus upon the performer," they routinely asserted (77).

Forming yet another link to vaudeville, *Nancy* has long been known for its simplistic drawing style and minimalist overall aesthetic. As Mark Newgarden and Paul Karasik have famously said about the strip: "Walls, floors, rocks, trees, ice-cream cones, motion lines, midgets and principals are carefully positioned with no need for further embellishment. And they are laid out with one purpose in mind—to get the gag across. Minimalist? Formalist? Structuralist? Cartoonist!" (98). Scott McCloud has echoed this observation, commenting how *Nancy* is "so simply drawn it can be reduced to the size of a postage stamp and still be legible" (McCloud, "Five Card"). This feature is especially true of the period when critics considered Bushmiller to be at the height of his creative powers: from 1944 to 1954 (Walker, 66). The settings of the strips from this era are sparse, and the shading is limited. Sometimes, as Newgarden and Karasik note, the only background detail is a simple ground line (98–100). Moreover, the only items depicted in the panels are the ones necessary to present the scenario and make the gag. In what has become an oft-repeated anecdote, "Art Spiegelman explains how a drawing of three rocks in a background scene was Ernie's way of showing us there were some rocks in the background. It was always three. Why? Because two rocks wouldn't be 'some rocks.' Two rocks would be a pair of rocks. And four rocks was unacceptable because four rocks would indicate 'some rocks' but it would be one rock more than was necessary to convey the idea of 'some rocks.' A *Nancy* panel is an irreducible concept, an atom, and the comic strip is a molecule" (McCloud, "Five Card"). For this reason, Bushmiller was known, both during his career and in the present day, for his "reduced-to-the-bare-essentials drawing style" (Editors, 6).

The similarities between *Nancy* and vaudeville go beyond a general shared aesthetic and an overarching commitment to offering respectable content. They also include some of the more specific features of Bushmiller's comic, as well as of this performance mode. While the lineup of acts featured in any given vaudeville show varied widely depending on the venue and on the talent available, one staple of all playbills was humorists. Every vaudeville show featured a comedian, and usually more than just one. Audiences came to performances to relax, have fun, and unwind—and there was no better way to satisfy these desires than with laughter (McLean, 50–60).

The type of comedy featured in vaudeville was specific. As Susan A. Glenn has discussed, the most popular and successful acts used "two primary comic forms—the physical abuse and violence of 'slapstick' (or 'knockabout') humor and the verbal barbs of satire, often delivered by punning, malapropisms, and twisted syntax" (651). These modes of humor had broad appeal and thus quickly came to dominate vaudeville comedy. Jokes of this nature transcended the boundaries of race, class, region, and ethnicity. Additionally, these comedy styles offered something for lowbrow as well as highbrow tastes, with the former demographic delighting in the slapstick humor and the latter group reveling in the clever wordplay.

The humor in *Nancy* reflects these elements. In language that is markedly similar to Glenn's discussion about the comedy style of vaudeville, Brian Walker observed: "Bushmiller's playfulness also extended to language. Puns, clichés, and slang were used as a source for jokes. But even these word gags usually ended with a visual punchline" (Walker, 178). This feature emerges in one of the first strips in which Nancy appears. In the comic that appeared on November 29, 1933—just a few months after her debut—Nancy is told by a crew member on the movie set, "The director wants you—he's ready to shoot a very important scene" (Bushmiller, 34). The next panel shows her standing in front of the camera and engaging in a bizarre dance: her eyes are crossed, she is flapping her arms like a bird, and she is hopping across the floor on one foot. The director understandably asks Nancy, "Are you cookoo—what's the idea?" (34). Her explanation in the closing panel combines the previous use of slapstick with that of wordplay. "Well—you said to me—'Get in there and act like you've never acted before,'" Nancy tells him matter-of-factly (34).

When Sluggo was introduced to the strip in 1938, Nancy acquired not simply a romantic interest but a comedy partner. Indeed, the two characters functioned as a vaudevillian comedy duo much like Joe Weber and Lew Fields, Eddie Cantor and George Jessel, and, of course, George Burns and Gracie Allen. As Brian Walker has observed, from the moment that Sluggo first appeared, "He lapsed in and out of a Bronx accent for no apparent reason" (66). Sluggo's working-class slang and especially his thick "New Yawk" pronunciation form the basis for many comedic scenarios. When Nancy first brings Sluggo home, for example, her aunt is horrified by his poor manners. "H'ya Lady!—Nice li'l joint y'got here!!" Sluggo says to her upon walking through the door (46). Determined to "get rid of that little lowbrow," Aunt Fritzi walks into the living room and gruffly asks him: "Er—before you *leave*, would you care for some milk or cocoa?" (46; emphasis in original). Because he lacks social refinement, Sluggo completely misses this verbal cue. "I'll take milk now . . . and cocoa before I leave!" he tells Aunt Fritzi in the punch line that appears in the final panel (46).

Bushmiller was still using Sluggo's heavy Bronx accent and lack of social graces for gags near the end of his career. In the comic on November 3, 1973, Nancy asks Sluggo how school went that day. "I loined how to spell new woids," he tells her (Bushmiller, 234). As she has many times before, Nancy corrects his pronunciation: "Don't say 'loined' and 'woids'—say 'learned' and 'words'" (234). Sluggo gets the last laugh, however. Pointing to a sign posted on the wall behind him that reads "No Loitering," he tells Nancy: "We better move—we're *lertering*" (234; emphasis in original).

Of course, this exact type of ethnic verbal punning permeated vaudeville. As Gavin Jones has written, "Vaudeville had the depiction of dialect at its heart" (161). While a variety of comedy teams engaged in it, "the vaudeville act of Joe Weber and Lew Fields, a dialect comedy and slapstick duo who performed under the names of Mike and Meyer," was arguably the most successful (Jones, 167). One of their most famous comedic routines contains strong suggestive echoes to the exchanges between Nancy and Sluggo.

> MEYER: Vot are you doing?
> MIKE: Voiking in a nut factory.
> MEYER: Doing vot?
> MIKE: Nutting.
> MEYER: Sure—but vot are you doing?
> MIKE: Nutting.
> MEYER: I know, but vot voik are you doing?
> MIKE: Nutting, I tole you. (Jones, 167–68)

As Jones has said about the work of Mike and Meyer, "The confusion, wordplay, and sudden shifts in pronunciation and accent that arose from the 'ethnic interfacings' of the Lower East Side became the foundation for its discourse-based humor" (168–69). The same observation applies to Nancy and Sluggo.

Even when Sluggo speaks without his thick Bronx accent, the similarities that he and Nancy possess to vaudeville comedy teams do not dissipate. In many of the strips where he converses in Standard English, Sluggo's interactions with Nancy resemble those of vaudeville's male-female comedy teams like George Burns and Gracie Allen. As Anthony Slide has said of this duo: "If the man in the street was asked to name one act which symbolized all that was great about vaudeville, an act that has endured in popularity for more than fifty years, there is no question that the answer would be Burns and Allen" (19). Burns and Allen did not simply deliver generic jokes. Their act "was a flirtation routine" (Staples, 206). Allen played the ditzy "straight man" to Burns's clever comments and sassy wisecracks. The following exchange is a well-known example of their onstage banter:

> GRACIE: Did you know that my brother was held up by two men last night?
> GEORGE: For how much?
> GRACIE: Oh, all the way home!" (Slide, 19)

Regardless of the specific scenario for the joke, one aspect of their act remained same: "Burns and Allen simultaneously exploited and transcended twentieth-century attitudes about gender, and I believe this largely accounts for their extraordinary success" (Staples, 5). Indeed, in a remark that few would contest, Slide asserted about Burns and Allen: "As a comedy team, they were unrivaled in the annals of show business" (19).

Nancy and Sluggo likewise engage in a flirtatious comedic routine that mirrors vaudeville's male-female comedy duos in general and Burns and Allen in particular. A famous Nancy and Sluggo comic that R. C. Harvey has discussed offers an excellent example. "In one daily installment that might well be the touchstone for the strip," Harvey writes, "we see Nancy in a rowboat in the first panel, muttering that she'll 'show' Sluggo and Trixie (Sluggo's current heartthrob, Nancy's perennial rival) that she doesn't care about their romance" (para. 17). Harvey continues: "In the next panel she disembarks the rowboat onto land, saying, 'I'll just ignore them like they don't exist'" (para. 17). The comic's final panel, which delivers what Harvey calls "the visual punchline," offers a surprising revelation (para. 18). "There we see Nancy ignoring Sluggo and Trixie. All three of them are on a tiny island by themselves, entirely isolated" (para. 18). In an action that could have been performed by Allen's ditzy onstage persona, "Nancy walks around and around the couple, pointedly looking away from them. The joke is that Nancy, in order to demonstrate that she is oblivious of them, has purposefully sought them out, thereby proving quite the contrary" (para. 18).

Whether appearing as a solo act or part of a team, vaudeville comedians engaged in a specific style of comedic delivery. As Henry Jenkins has observed, they "sought to build towards a 'Wow Finish' that would top all preceding gags" (79). The comedy routine of the vaudeville legend Eddie Cantor offers an illuminating example. As Jenkins explains, "Cantor viewed the story as an excuse for songs, dances, and gags, as a showcase for his performance skills" (102). Even when Cantor ceased performing live onstage and instead moved his act to motion pictures, "his lifetime commitment to the vaudeville aesthetic reinforced his tendency to stress gag over story" (102). Everything that Cantor said, did, and even wore in his routine served the punch line. His words, gestures, and facial expressions acted as lead-ins to, or buildups for, the joke. For this reason, "gags block and often derail narrative development" in vaudeville (105). These humorists participated in "a 'player centered' medium which placed a premium on 'personality,'" not on story (Glenn, 655). As Susan A. Glenn has observed, "It was joking for its own sake" (655).

Once again, this feature exactly mirrors that of *Nancy*. R. C. Harvey, in fact, has said of the title character: "Every day, her *raison d'etre* is to set up a situation that will lead to the visual punchline of the last panel in which the prop gets the laugh. She has no personality; she is a simple plot device" (Harvey, para. 14). Mark Newgarden and Paul Karasik agree. As they observed, "Characterization, atmosphere, emotional depth, social comment, plot, internal consistency, and common sense are all merrily surrendered in Bushmiller's universe to the true function of a comic strip—to provoke the 'gag reflex' of his readership on a daily basis" (98). Speaking about his creative process throughout his career, Bushmiller repeatedly said that everything that happened in his strip was in service of the punch line. In fact, he began the comic by coming up with the final panel, which he called "the snapper," and worked backward. "I start with a blank piece of drawing paper and just sweat and stew until I think of a subject that seems likely to produce a ludicrous situation," Bushmiller said. "I usually can visualize how the last panel will turn out, so I start to pencil in the finish of the strip very roughly. If it looks okay, I then work backwards toward the starting panels" (quoted in Walker, 90). Sometimes, of course, the idea for the joke didn't pan out, and he scrapped the idea. But Bushmiller's process always remained the same: "I always work my strips in reverse. In this way I can choose the best path leading to the snapper" (90).

• • •

Maurice Horn, in the 1976 edition of *World Encyclopedia of Comics*, infamously remarked that *Nancy* "was created by a syndicate staffer using a joke book and a series of rubber stamps" (Editors, 6). This observation, of course, was meant disdainfully, as "an act of cruelty toward the still-working Bushmiller" (6). Although Horn's comment was intended to deride the cartoonist and his work, it can also be seen as gesturing toward an important and long-overlooked influence on the comic: vaudeville. As Jenkins has discussed, many vaudeville comedians "kept an index file of potential jokes, frequently clipped from the humor magazines, comic strips, and joke magazines of the period; stored jokes could be quickly reworked and inserted into a new routine" (80). This observation was even true of the most famous comedy duo in vaudeville history, George Burns and Gracie Allen. As Shirley Staples has documented, in their early days on the vaudeville circuit, "George had an act, too, put together from joke books and the like, so they started with their act" (206).

Gavin Jones credited vaudeville's mass appeal to a single feature: its "simple stupidity" (176). Most acts lacked intellectual sophistication. Instead they offered fun, mindless, escapist entertainment, which was exactly what audiences wanted. In a comment that has been cited by many past and present critics, Bushmiller's "advice to young cartoonists was to 'Dumb it down'" (Walker, 11). As Brian Walker explained, Bushmiller "understood that a comic strip is a medium of mass entertainment.... Its success depends on communicating to the widest audience" (11). The elements of vaudeville that permeate *Nancy* add a new explanation for, along with significance to, the intellectual, artistic, and cultural simplicity that has long been associated with the comic. Ernie Bushmiller's *Nancy* has long been seen as "stupid." Indeed, R. C. Harvey once griped, in sentiments that have been echoed by many others, "His work, to me, seems aimed at simpletons" (para. 2). An awareness of the way in which vaudeville works in *Nancy* and, in turn, helps to make the comic work reveals that Bushmiller's strip was not simply "stupid"; it was smartly stupid.

"DON'T FORGET THIS IS SMILE WEEK": NANCY AND BLACKFACE MINSTRELSY

Together with featuring jugglers, operatic soloists, acrobats, and dramatic monologists, another staple on the vaudeville playbill was minstrel performers. As Robert Toll, Eric Lott, and David Roediger have all discussed, this performance mode, in which white actors blackened their faces with burned cork to lampoon blacks and black culture, first emerged in the United States during the 1840s and reached its apex of popularity during the 1880s. "Between the Civil War and the turn of the twentieth century," however, "minstrelsy was gradually supplanted by vaudeville" (Garofalo, 20). Vaudeville, however, did not replace minstrel shows as the most popular form of mass entertainment in the United States; it absorbed blackface, incorporating these acts into its offerings. Whereas minstrel shows had been their own independent, autonomous, and stand-alone theater events, they were now becoming one of the acts featured in vaudeville's lineup. Indeed, some of the best-known and beloved vaudeville performers were minstrel acts. Bing Crosby and Bob Hope regularly appeared in blackface on the vaudeville stage (Slide, 247–50). Meanwhile, other performers, including Al Jolson and Bert Williams, made a name for themselves doing minstrelsy almost exclusively.

Ernie Bushmiller's *Nancy* can be placed in dialogue with the tradition of blackface minstrelsy in the United States. While the title character never blackens her face with burned cork, she possesses a variety of physical, behavioral, and narratological traits that recall this popular performance mode.

Figure 2.1. Still image from *Gone with the Wind* (1939).

First, and perhaps most powerfully, is the young girl's appearance. Nancy resembles a diminutive "Mammy" figure in many ways. Often described as being "fireplug-shaped" (Harvey, para. 6), she is stocky in ways that recall the common representation of this known racial stereotype. In addition, the red bow in Nancy's hair recalls the kerchief that Mammy characters commonly wore, including one of the most famous visual renderings: the advertising icon Aunt Jemima. Finally, but far from insignificantly, Nancy's dark vest and white collar also echo the common way in which Mammies were dressed (fig. 2.1).

Nancy's distinctive hair extends her connection to blackface. Her signature frizzy coif is commonly described as looking like a Brillo Pad (Harvey, para. 6), but it also strongly resembles both the woolly wigs worn by minstrel performers and the highly minstrelized way that young black children were rendered in advertisements (fig. 2.2). Even the coloration of Nancy's face can be linked with the blackface tradition. The young white girl embodies a photo negative of minstrel performers: instead of possessing deep black skin that is contrasted with bright white eyes and an exaggerated mouth like those of performers such as Al Jolson (fig. 2.3), Nancy possesses bright white skin that is contrasted with deep black eyes and an exaggerated black mouth. Nancy's distinctive physical appearance assumes added weight, given that the young girl is drawn in a manner that differs greatly from her aunt. Whereas Fritzi Ritz is rendered in a more realistic style—with her almond-shaped eyes, Grecian nose, and curly bobbed hair—Nancy's appearance is highly

58 *Nancy* and the Vaudeville Aesthetic

Figure 2.2. Tin sign for Picaninny Freeze frozen treats, circa 1920s. Reproduction.

Figure 2.3. Al Jolson in blackface, circa 1920s.

Figure 2.4. Panel from *Nancy* comic strip, January 31, 1934.

Nancy and the Vaudeville Aesthetic 59

Figure 2.5. Panel from *Nancy* comic strip, November 16, 1941.

Figure 2.6. Mr. T. Rice as the original Jim Crow. New York: E. Riley, 1832.

simplified and stylized. While many past and present critics have argued that her appearance is cartoonish, it can also be seen as minstrelized.

Bushmiller's strip demonstrated its conversance with the conventions of minstrelsy at numerous points during its run. A black janitor who appears in the background of a *Fritzi Ritz* strip featuring Nancy from January 31, 1934, is drawn with the exaggerated mouth, bulging white eyes, and signature white gloves of minstrel performers (Bushmiller, 35) (fig. 2.4). Similarly, a neighborhood girl named Marigold, who serves as Nancy's nemesis at various points throughout the comic, is dressed in a manner that mirrors one of the most famous minstrel performers: Jim Crow. In the strip from November 16, 1941, in fact, Marigold dances in a fashion that mimics one of the best-known lithographs of this character (59) (figs. 2.5, 2.6). Finally, and far from insignificantly, Nancy herself darkens her face at several points during the strip. In the comic that appeared on February 25, 1946, she startles Sluggo when she walks out to greet him and her face is so black that it blends into the shadows, giving the impression that she lacks a head (85). When Nancy comes out into the light of the room, she offers an explanation for her appearance: "I'm trying Aunt Fritzi's Beauty Mud" (85) (fig. 2.7). Of course, as Frantz Fanon, Anne McClintock, and most recently Hershini Bhana Young have documented, blackness has historically been associated with dirt, grime, and mud. "Racial blackness is firmly coupled with dirt," Young writes (140). In examples ranging from nineteenth-century editorial cartoons that presented working-class Irish as "less white" because their faces and hands were often

Figure 2.7. Panel from *Nancy* comic strip, November 16, 1941.

Figure 2.8. Panel from *Nancy* comic strip, November 16, 1941.

physically dirty, to Victorian soap ads that depicted a seemingly black child becoming Caucasian after taking a bath, blackness was routinely associated with filth. For this reason, as Hershini Bhana Young has written, "Culturally specific practices of hygiene became a way of defining the body, with the blackness of dirt demarcating the African from the clean whiteness of the imperial [Anglo-European] self" (140).

Nancy's application of Aunt Fritzi's beauty mud is not the only time that she appears with a blackened face. The comic printed on Sunday, March 20, 1966, uses this element as the source of the gag. The strip opens with Nancy strolling down the street (Bushmiller, 143). After passing a sign that reads,

Figure 2.9. Title page to *Nancy Is Happy: Complete Dailies, 1943–1945*. Design by Jacob Covey.

Figure 2.10. Frontispiece to *Nancy Is Happy: Complete Dailies, 1943–1945*. Design by Jacob Covey.

"This Is Smile Week," she bursts into a big grin. Unfortunately, while she is walking, a bucket of black paint falls from a ladder and dumps its contents on her head. Immediately after getting doused in paint, she sees another sign announcing: "*Don't Forget* This Is Smile Week." The final panel shows her resuming both her walk and her big toothy grin. Since Nancy's face has been completely blackened by the paint, her visage now strongly resembles that of minstrel performers (143) (fig. 2.8).

A slightly modified version of this image—showing Nancy with a blackened face, wide white smile, and bright red bow in her hair—is the one that Fantagraphics Books chose to feature on the title page of the collection *Nancy Is Happy: Complete Dailies, 1943–1945* (fig. 2.9). Meanwhile, a variation on this visage—where Nancy is not smiling—adorns the page before it (fig. 2.10). Furthermore, this image is the only item on that page: there is no text and no other images. Nancy's blackened head and her red hair bow appear alone in the center against a white background. The end result of these choices is that when readers open the book, they are greeted with what can most accurately be described as a blackface version of Bushmiller's character. Then, when they turn to the next page, this blackface Nancy bursts into an exaggerated grin, akin to countless minstrel performers.

• • •

Nicholas Sammond, in his discussion of early cartoon characters like Felix the Cat, Mickey Mouse, and Bugs Bunny, classifies them as "vestigial minstrels" (3). These figures, Sammond explains, can be seen as "carrying the tokens of blackface minstrelsy in their bodies and behaviors yet no longer immediately signifying as such" (3). In details like Mickey Mouse's white gloves, Felix the Cat's facial coloration, and Bugs Bunny's tricksteresque behaviors, these characters "came to embody the conventions of blackface minstrelsy" and, in so doing, to reveal how "those same conventions became obscured, though never erased," in American popular culture (Sammond, 3). In the apt words of Daniel Goldmark, "Minstrelsy never died—it simply changed media" (quoted in Sammond, 69). Early animation was one such venue. In the words of Sammond once again: "Cartoons didn't borrow from minstrels; they joined minstrels" (18). Early American animation is a case study in "the durability of the blackface minstrel" (13).

Of course, comics are also a form of cartooning. Although static and not animated, these strips belong to the same artistic tradition. In the words of Sammond once again, "Film and media historians have long noted that American animation is indebted to blackface minstrelsy" (xi). The numerous physical, behavioral, and aesthetic connections that Bushmiller's strip has to minstrelsy extend this observation to comics. Akin to animated characters like Mickey Mouse and Felix the Cat, Nancy is a vestigial minstrel in many ways.

In *Playing in the Dark*, Toni Morrison traces what she calls an "American Africanist" presence in US literature. "White American fiction, [Morrison] states, has fabricated a black persona that is 'reflexive,' a means for whites to contemplate their own terror and desire without having to acknowledge these feelings as their own" (Steiner, para. 2). As Wendy Steiner summarizes Morrison's argument, "Such characters thus operate like vaudeville blackface, indicating 'the sycophancy of white identity'" (para. 2). Bushmiller's *Nancy* can be placed in dialogue with this phenomenon. Whether she is fighting with Sluggo, testing the patience of her Aunt Fritzi, or clowning with her cartoonist creator, she is also playing in the dark.

John DiMeglio, writing during the height of *Nancy*'s popularity in the mid-1970s, noted: "The vaudevillian is not dead, and neither is his America. It has transferred itself to radio, movies, and television" (198). The influence of vaudeville on these three forms of American entertainment has been widely documented. Given the way in which vaudevillian elements permeate *Nancy*, we could and even should add another medium to this list: comics. Although the strip, with its simple style, quiet tone, and minimalist cast of characters, seems far removed from the noisy, crowded, and chaotic world of vaudeville, it is deeply indebted to it. For nearly five decades in *Nancy*, vaudeville experienced not a curtain call but an encore.

Chapter 3

From Battling Adult Authority to Battling the Opposite Sex

Little Lulu as Gag Panel and Comic Book

• •

On February 23, 1935, a new cartoon made its debut in the *Saturday Evening Post*: *Little Lulu*. Drawn by Marjorie Henderson Buell, the wordless, single-panel comic featured the title character, Lulu Moppet, walking down the aisle as a flower girl at a wedding. Instead of spreading rose petals, she is dropping banana peels. Behind her, the bridesmaids are slipping and falling (fig. 3.1).

Little Lulu was an immediate commercial and critical success. Readers young and old, male and female, urban and rural, adored the title character's irreverence. The gag comic became a regular feature in the *Saturday Evening Post*, appearing in each weekly issue until December 30, 1944.

The history of Little Lulu does not end there, however. Buell, who was known both personally and professionally by the nickname "Marge," recognized the commercial potential that branding afforded. As Tom Heintjes notes, "She was one of the first American cartoonists to retain copyright to and licensing control of her characters" (Heintjes, para. 2). As a result, Lulu had a long and multifaceted existence in American print, visual, and material culture. From 1944 through 1960, for example, the character was a fixture in television commercials and print ads for Kleenex (Shutt, 33). Likewise, from the end of World War II until the end of the 1960s, Lulu appeared in a syndicated comic strip that ran in hundreds of newspapers across the country (38–39). In addition, from the 1940s through the 1990s, she starred in dozens of animated television shows, movie shorts, and feature-length films.

While each of these items was its own discrete entity, they also served to promote the veritable empire of Little Lulu–themed commercial goods and consumer products. As Craig Shutt has commented, "Today's merchandisers have nothing on Marge's acumen for licensing her character for supplemental

Figure 3.1. Little Lulu gag panel, by Marjorie Henderson Buell. *Saturday Evening Post*, February 23, 1935.

products" (39). Beginning in the 1940s and extending through the 1990s, Buell's character was featured on toys, dolls, clothes, dishes, stationery, bedding, games, cosmetics, glassware, hosiery, cleaning supplies, furniture, candy, and jewelry (39). The ubiquity of these objects remains evident today: "It can be difficult to avoid her smiling face while strolling through any toy show (or even flea market) in the country" (32).

Of all the material, visual, and print forms in which Little Lulu appeared over the decades, however, arguably none was more successful than the comic book series. Written by John Stanley and drawn by Irving Tripp and called *Marge's Little Lulu* to acknowledge the comic's creator, the series delighted untold numbers of children during its run from 1948 until 1984. Indeed, Steve Raiteri calls Stanley and Tripp's series "one of most widely acclaimed and fondly remembered children's comics" of the twentieth century (103). Given both Little Lulu's public visibility and her commercial success, she embodies one of the most important characters in American comics, male or female. As Tom Heintjes has asserted, both in telling the story of sequential art in the United States and "in tracing the evolution of marketing consumer products using comics characters, encountering Marge Buell and her moppet creation Little Lulu is inevitable" (para. 1).

While Little Lulu enjoyed a lively existence in many facets of American culture, this chapter addresses her life in print. More specifically, it spotlights the shift from her initial residence in the *Saturday Evening Post* during the 1930s and early 1940s to her appearance in a comic book series during the 1950s. This move precipitated an array of artistic, literary, and material changes to Buell's comic along with its central character. These modifications included the gender politics involved when *Little Lulu* went from being penned by a woman to being written by two men, the literary ramifications that accompanied the transition from a wordless single-panel magazine strip to a multipanel monthly comic book that relied heavily on word balloons, and the sociohistorical implications of the title character existing against the backdrop of the Depression era to that of the postwar economic boom. However, another and formerly overlooked change also took place. When Little Lulu moved from the weekly magazine to the monthly comic book, the object of her rebellion shifted. In the single-panel gag comics of the 1930s and early 1940s, Lulu was largely flabbergasting adults with her antics. Later, however, in the comic books by Stanley and Tripp, her sworn enemy—and thus the target of her pranks—is the gang of neighborhood boys.

The shift from intergenerational conflict in the prewar era to intragenerational ones postwar forms a compelling and previously unexplored facet of the literary, artistic, and cultural alterations that took place to this character across different print formats. These details shed new light on Lulu's place in American mass culture, as well as the role that she played in its popular imagination. At the same time, the change from plots that pitted children against adults in the 1930s to ones that pitted girls against boys in the 1950s reflects larger changes in American culture regarding the gendering of children and the sexual segregation of childhood. The postwar period was marked by the strong commercial expansion, as well as strict social enforcement, of "his" and "hers" children's goods and, by extension, childhoods. Consequently, whereas previous generations of young people in the United States had largely been united by their shared age, they were now increasingly separated by their differing genders. The print career of Little Lulu reflects this phenomenon. When this character shifted print formats in the 1950s, she also shifted social targets. I argue that this alteration did far more than merely permit the comic book version of *Little Lulu* to tell artistically new, socially different, and materially longer stories; it radically altered the aim and intent of Buell's original character along with the commentary on gender, childhood, and American culture that it offered.

FROM BOYS AND GIRLS TO BOYS VERSUS GIRLS: THE CREATION OF "HIS" AND "HERS" CHILDHOODS

Walk into any store in the United States that sells items for children, and the first feature that you will likely notice is the color coding: a blue side for boys' items and a pink side for those intended for girls. From clothing and bedding to diapers and especially toys, the children's aisles are "sharply divided into 'boys' and 'girls' sections" (Paoletti, 117).

This situation has not always been the case. As historians such as Eleanor Emmons Maccoby, Jeanne Maglaty, and Jo B. Paoletti have documented, US culture and, by extension, American childhood were not always bifurcated along the lines of gender. For many generations, children were seen as young people first and gendered beings second.

The clothing that young people wore provides a telling index of this condition. As Paoletti has discussed, for much of the nineteenth century, children of both genders in the United States wore the exact same attire when they were young: "simple, unfitted dresses, usually white" (22). The factors that gave rise to this sartorial situation were largely pragmatic: frocks of this type were easy to make during a time when most mothers sewed all their own baby clothes; their open bottoms made changing diapers convenient; and the white color provided a clear indication when the garment was soiled while also allowing it to be "boiled or bleached without fading" for ease of laundering (29). For these reasons, baggy white dresses for infants, toddlers, and young children were the standard. For generations, youngsters who were both male and female, from working-class as well as well-to-do backgrounds, and living in urban along with rural locals wore them.[1] Jeanne Maglaty, for example, discusses childhood photographs of Franklin Delano Roosevelt and Ernest Hemingway outfitted in white dresses (para. 1). As Paoletti explains, "It's not unusual to hear modern people describe Victorian babies as being dressed like girls; this is an error. To their own parents and grandparents, a child wearing the traditional white dress looked like 'a baby'" (26). The garment was the sartorial equivalent of today's plain white onesie: ubiquitous, utilitarian, and—most importantly—unisex.

Clothing was not the only aspect of American childhood that was gender neutral during this period. So, too, were many material goods, like toys, personal care items, and nursery decor. "Baby dolls were listed in the UCLA [archive of] baby books as common first-birthday gifts for boys as well as girls" through the 1920s (Paoletti, 38). Similarly, "Baby paper dolls before 1910 were sometimes identified by sex, but usually not, just as 'the baby.' In rare cases when paper doll infants are identified as boys, their appearance gives no evidence of any subtle gender markers; all wear white dresses, some plain, some fancy, but identical to those worn by baby girls" (29). Finally, and perhaps most surprisingly, the colors pink and blue were not gendered during this era (Maglaty, para. 6). Baby boys were commonly given pink blankets, bedding, and nursery room decor by their parents and relatives in the same way that baby girls routinely received these same items in blue (Paoletti, 91). Throughout the opening decades of the twentieth century, the color pink was associated with age, not gender. Echoing the etymology of the term, the shade was linked with "spring, health (as in 'in the pink'), and youth" (87). Consequently, "Young men and women might wear pink clothing; old men and women did not" (87).

These examples reveal a significant difference between cultural conceptions of children during the nineteenth century and in the present day. As Paoletti writes, "Long before clothing for the youngest children acquired gender symbolism, by far the most significant message it conveyed was age" (20). In marked contrast to current attitudes, Americans in the Victorian era believed that babies and young children occupied a realm outside the sex-gender system. In the words of Paoletti once again, "Pre-Freudian baby boys were not perceived as masculine, and to say otherwise was in very poor taste. 'Masculine' connoted 'manly,' in the adult sense, and only grown men were manly" (24). For this reason, children wore clothing that was appropriate to their age, not their gender. Dressing a little girl like a woman, or a little boy like a man, during the nineteenth century "was considered inappropriate for young children, whose asexual innocence was so often cited as one of their greatest charms" (26). In fact, Americans thought of children as sexless, in every sense of the word. "The makers of Mellin's baby food recognized the humor value of this in their 1905 guessing-game contest. Mellin's ad featuring twenty babies in the *Ladies' Home Journal* promised a generous reward to readers who accurately guessed the sex of the most babies" (26). When the results of the contest were published in a later issue, subscribers learned that not a single entrant "had correctly guessed the sex of all twenty babies" (26). As Paoletti aptly notes, "It is very hard to imagine twenty-first century parents submitting their child's photo to a nationwide magazine in the hope of 'stumping' readers on their baby's sex" (26). However, Mellin's contest—along with many others like it during the Progressive era—demonstrates "how different we are from our ancestors on the subject of infants' gender. Whereas modern parents work to eliminate gender ambiguity, their great-grandparents found it natural and amusing" (26). In the words of Paoletti once again, "It was much more important to observe age conventions than it is for us today: dressing a three-year-old boy in a man's suit would have been unthinkable" (21).

Of course, children were not dressed in androgynous clothing forever. Boys and girls did eventually grow up and were expected to assume their respective masculine and feminine gender roles, including the attire considered appropriate for their sex. But this phenomenon did not occur until they were on the brink of puberty. "Not until around the age of seven were boys 'breeched,' or put into their first pair of trousers" (Paoletti, 21). Typically "this transition in clothing accompanied a boy's first short haircut" (46). The attire that girls from white, middle-class families wore would also change around the same age. Francis B. Cogan has discussed how a girl's former wardrobe of loose-fitting dresses that had allowed free range of motion would be replaced with more formal, as well as more fitted, gowns that had boning, stays, or corsets (30–35). Likewise, her hairstyle would become more structured, stylized, and elaborate. Whereas her locks had formerly been allowed to fall naturally, they would now be pulled into intricate braids or fashioned into artificially created curls, often held in place by tight pins (56).

For many young girls—as well as for boys—such changes in their attire did not take place until early adolescence. Jo March, in Louisa May Alcott's wildly popular novel *Little Women* (1868), is permitted to jump fences, clomp around in her father's army boots, and behave like a "hoyden" until she is fifteen. Similarly, Caddie Woodlawn, in Carol Ryrie Brink's 1935 novel of the same name, is allowed to "run with the colts" and romp with her brothers until roughly the same age (Brink, 245). These fictional examples reflect factual practices in American life. Many mothers, especially from white, middle-class families, delayed transitioning their children from the loose-fitting garments of youth to the more formal, fitted, and gendered attire of adolescence for as long as possible: they wanted to spare their sons the stresses that came with joining the masculine world of work and let their daughters enjoy the physical freedoms of girlhood (Cogan, 30–50; Paoletti, 44–47). Consequently boys and girls were largely reared in an environment where rigid gender divisions were kept at bay. Sex roles were a matter for the adult world, not the realm of children.

This situation began to change around 1900. The dawn of the new century saw the dawn of new attitudes about childhood and, by extension, views about children's material goods. As a consequence, young people's clothing, toys, and bedding became increasingly more gendered at increasingly younger ages. As Jeanne Maglaty explains, "The march toward gender specific clothes was neither linear nor rapid" (para. 6). On the contrary, "The transition from ungendered to gendered clothing for toddlers and children between 1900 and 1930 . . . was primarily focused on boys' fashions. During this time, little boys' fashions gradually acquired more elements of adult male dress, while details once considered neutral and 'youthful'—including flowers, dainty trim, and the color pink—were relegated to girls and women" (Paoletti, xx).

These changes were largely the result of new social and scientific anxieties regarding adolescent masculinity and heteronormativity. These sentiments arose from a complex interaction of cultural events, including arguments from the nascent fields of sexology and psychology regarding the alleged childhood origins of adult sexual perversion; increasing fears about rising immigration and the possible attendant loss of white Anglo-Saxon racial hegemony; and the generational backlash against the fad of Little Lord Fauntleroy suits (Paoletti, 65–75). Taken collectively, they caused a paradigm shift in the way that both children and childhood were viewed in the United States. Whereas babies and young children were formerly regarded as "sexless cherubs," they were now seen as "nascent men and women" (Paoletti, xix). In this way, Maglaty explains, "What was once a matter of practicality . . . became a matter of 'Oh my God, if I dress my baby in the wrong thing, they'll grow up perverted'" (para. 5). To ease such concerns, three methods quickly emerged to make male infants and toddlers look more masculine: "hair length, bifurcated clothes such as trousers, and stylistic cues such as fabric, decoration, cut, and color" (Paoletti, 78). Not surprisingly, the first change to be implemented was the elimination of any feminine styling on boys' clothing: "lace, bows, ruffles, and other elaborate trims" (81). As these alterations reveal, being a boy became defined as *not* being a girl. Not only were children being exposed to gender roles at younger ages, but these gender roles were increasingly being framed as oppositional.

The economic deprivations precipitated by the Great Depression and then the rationing of consumer goods during World War II slowed this process.

Toys, bedding, and "clothes that could be handed down to the next child [were] more practical than gendered [items] through the restrictions of the Great Depression and World War II" (Paoletti, 56). But the decade of the 1950s—with its rigid adherence to traditional gender roles for men and women, widespread homophobia, and booming consumer economy, especially in the realm of items for children—would see this phenomenon return with new force and fervor. Indeed, the postwar period was when the color pink became firmly associated with girls, and blue with boys (Paoletti, 91). As a consequence, this period saw the rigid social sex segregation of children almost from birth. Young people were discouraged from identifying with, and in many cases even playing with, children of the opposite gender. Moreover, they were often socially ridiculed, parentally reprimanded, or even medically pathologized if they did so. As Gary Morris has commented, boys in the 1950s who enjoyed female playmates, toys, or activities were called "sissies" and became the cause of acute anxiety for many parents, especially fathers (para. 2–5). Within this climate, the formerly common practice of dressing a male infant, toddler, or child in a white dress became unthinkable.

These sociocultural changes precipitated changes in the way that young people viewed both themselves and each other. Rather than feeling a sense of kinship with their opposite-sex peers because of their shared status as children, boys and girls were increasingly encouraged to regard themselves as separate and even divided. To be sure, the increasingly feminized toys, clothes, and bedding intended for girls that began appearing in the 1950s encouraged young girls to identify adult women, not boys of their same age, as their peers. Likewise, in a detail that accelerated during the postwar era, boys were socialized to define themselves largely in opposition to femininity—a message that prevented boys from forging much of a bond with girls their same age or even seeing them as potential playmates. Taken collectively, these phenomena caused children to regard a peer who belonged to the opposite sex not merely as their antithesis but as their nemesis in many ways. The aversion that the popular comic strip character Dennis the Menace—who made his newspaper debut in 1951—had to girls epitomized this trend. Rather than cooperate, boys and girls must compete. Instead of fostering solidarity between the sexes, postwar American culture reinforced a firm separation.

Given the highly sex-segregated nature of modern American childhood, Eleanor Maccoby has characterized the condition of boys and girls since the postwar period as one of "growing up apart" (iii). Far from simply meaning that boys and girls play with different toys or wear clothes in different colors, styles, and cuts, Maccoby argues that this sharp sex division creates entirely "different childhood 'cultures'" (1). The firm segregation of children by gender encourages "preferences for same-sex, and avoidance of opposite-sex, social partners" (15). Whereas the period of youth had once been characterized by boys *and* girls, it was now preoccupied with whether a child was a boy *or* a girl—or, phrased in a slightly more accurate way, a boy *versus* a girl.

A BATTLE FOR THE AGES OF THE AGES: LULU'S CHALLENGE TO ADULT AUTHORITY IN THE GAG PANELS

Little Lulu was conceived, created, and released during a pivotal moment in the sex segregation of American childhood. Making her debut during the middle of the Great Depression, she appeared after the onset of more gendered clothing for young people, but before the complete bifurcation of childhood into the separate spheres of "his" and "hers." In the gag panels, Lulu, whom Buell would later identify in articles and interviews as being eight years old ("Little Lulu," para. 1), almost always wears the same attire: a short, simple dress. Indeed, with its bib collar and baggy cut, the garment resembles the simple frocks that young boys and girls wore throughout the nineteenth century, rather than the more formal and fitted gowns worn by grown women. In addition, Lulu's long, curly hair is allowed to hang free; it is not tightly pinned, heavily styled, or pulled back into some type of fashionable adult coif. Taken collectively, Lulu's dress and appearance readily identify her as female but clearly code her as a child. Her feminine appearance is not "adultified" in any way; it retains a youthful quality. The young boys who appear in the gag panels are dressed in similarly gender-normative ways. Not only do they all have short haircuts, but they also all wear unmistakably masculine garments: pants, blazers, and sometimes even ties. As these details indicate, by 1935, when the first *Little Lulu* gag panel appeared, the unisex clothing and androgynous garments that had typified young children's attire just a generation before had begun to wane.

That said, although Little Lulu is dressed differently from her male counterparts, she does not regard them in antithetical, let alone antagonistic, ways. From Lulu's first appearance in the *Saturday Evening Post*, she was known for her pranks, antics, and overall irreverence. As Craig Shutt has commented, "Her tricks were seldom vindictive or mean-spirited but often were designed to cause mayhem just for the fun of it" (32). These behaviors, however, were overwhelmingly directed at adults. From parents, teachers, and doctors to shopkeepers, neighbors, and passersby, Lulu consistently unsettles the grown-ups around her, not her opposite-sex peers. In a detail that suggests children during the 1930s experienced a stronger sense of intragenerational solidarity, Lulu often teams up with her male peers to carry out pranks on this "common enemy." Boys, far from being her nemeses, are her accomplices. Little Lulu's consistent challenge to adult authority forms as much of a signature facet to the narrative premise of the gag comics as other commonly identified aesthetic hallmarks, such as their appearance in a single panel or their wordlessness.

• • •

Marjorie Henderson Buell announced her central character's rebellion against adult authority in the very first gag panel that appeared in the *Saturday Evening Post*. Craig Shutt describes this now-famous comic: "She acted as a flower girl in a wedding, only she strews banana peels rather than roses, causing the following bridesmaids to go splat" (32). Lulu's antics also cause the adult guests at the wedding to gasp. The mouth of an older woman sitting in the aisle directly behind Lulu hangs open in amazement. Meanwhile, a distinguished gentleman in the pew in front of her is so flabbergasted that his monocle has popped out. As these details reveal, Lulu has turned the grown-up world not only figuratively but—in the case of the slipping-and-falling bridesmaids—literally on its head. Indeed, other than the main character herself, the wordless panel contains no other young characters. She is the sole child.

Far from simply a feature that appeared in this inaugural comic, Lulu's penchant for shocking, upsetting, and at times even outraging adults would form a recurring aspect of her character and the comic as a whole. Many of the early panels that were reprinted in the Rand McNally collection titled simply *Little Lulu* and released in 1936 reflect this trait. Moreover, because this collection contains some of the most popular comics, it indicates that this feature was one of the beloved aspects of Buell's series.

Lulu's interest in sparring with adults is showcased via the first panel from the Rand McNally collection (fig. 3.2). The comic presents the main character sitting in the lap of a public statue of the famed British writer and politician Edward Bulwer-Lytton. The venerated figure is holding an important document out in front of him: perhaps a poem, a page from one of his novels, or a piece of legislation. Lulu lampoons this entire scene. Her posture, demeanor, and behavior make it appear that Bulwer-Lytton is reading the serious civic paper aloud to her like a bedtime story. Not only is the young girl sitting on his lap, but she is licking a lollipop contentedly. An older man and woman

Figure 3.2. Little Lulu gag panel. In Marge, *Little Lulu* (Chicago: Rand McNally, 1936).

are standing on either side of the fenced green space containing the statue. Their body posture and especially their facial expressions indicate that they are shocked by Lulu's behavior. The man on the left side of the panel is leaning over to one side to better observe this unusual scene; his eyes are open wide in amazement, and his mouth likewise hangs open in disbelief. The older woman on the right side of the fence is even more startled. Not only has she halted along the path to observe Lulu's iconoclastic behavior, but she is so flabbergasted by what she sees that emanata—"lines drawn around the head to indicate shock or surprise" (Rhoades, 132; see also Walker)—appear on each side of her face.

The third comic in the Rand McNally collection is even more focused on Lulu's defiance of the manners, mores, and conventions of proper adult society. The panel shows Lulu walking behind a row of men and women who are seated at a formal dinner (fig. 3.3). The young girl is holding a large pair of scissors and, as she walks by, cuts off the tails of the men's tuxedos. While three of the adults are unaware of Lulu's antics, the woman on the right side of the panel sees what the girl is doing. In an expression that has appeared on the faces of several adults in previous *Little Lulu* panels, the woman's mouth is hanging open in shock, her eyes are open wide in astonishment, and emanata appear on each side of her head.

The next comic in the Rand McNally collection is the first one to show Little Lulu in the company of other children (fig. 3.4). The panel presents the main character at her desk in a classroom at school. She is seated in the front row and is surrounded by other boys and girls. However, the target of Lulu's prank is not her peers, either male or female. Instead it is her adult teacher. To better get the attention of the older woman, Lulu is not simply raising her hand but holding up a long stick with a white glove perched on the end. The woman is predictably taken aback by Lulu's gesture; her eyes are opened wide in amazement.

Very few of the *Little Lulu* comics that appeared between 1935 and 1936 and are reprinted in the Rand McNally collection show the title character in the company of other children. Moreover, on those rare occasions when she is depicted with fellow boys and girls, her behavior is designed to unnerve the adults, not her peers. The other children serve as either props or accomplices. For example, in one well-known panel, Lulu is being pushed by a toddler in a baby stroller while holding up a sign that reads: "i WiLL GLADLY MiND YOUR BABY WiLE YOU GO TO THE MOViES, 5 ¢ AN HR" (fig. 3.5). The little boy who is pushing her doesn't seem to mind the arrangement; on the contrary, he seems to delight in this rare moment of role reversal. But two older women who are observing the scene are horrified. Forming what might be called the typical countenance of adults in Little Lulu comics, their mouths are hanging open in shock, their eyes are bulging in disbelief, and they have emanata radiating around their heads.

As even this brief overview suggests, Lulu is consistently surprising, shocking, and startling adults by her behavior. Indeed, in the Rand McNally collection alone, she engages in antics such as horrifying her mother by shouting into a doctor's stethoscope; scandalizing a group of men by donning a fake mustache and standing in the "Men Only" line; upsetting an all-adult group of relatives by making a menacing face during a family portrait; and flabbergasting a group of men and women on the subway by hanging upside down on the grab handles.[2]

Little Lulu's interest in shocking adults would remain a signature feature of the comic throughout its nearly ten-year run in the *Saturday Evening Post*. Many of her most popular, successful, and oft-reprinted panels are the ones in which she is alarming adult neighbors, teachers, parents, and passersby with her antics. The collection *Oh, Little Lulu!*, which was released in 1943 and contains comics from the closing few years of the strip's run in the *Post*,

Little Lulu as Gag Panel and Comic Book 75

Figure 3.3. Little Lulu gag panel. In Marge, *Little Lulu* (Chicago: Rand McNally, 1936).

Figure 3.4. Little Lulu gag panel. In Marge, *Little Lulu* (Chicago: Rand McNally, 1936).

Figure 3.5. Little Lulu gag panel. In Marge, *Little Lulu* (Chicago: Rand McNally, 1936).

provides a compelling example. A multitude of the gag comics that appear in the book present the main character battling her longtime bugaboo: adults. In one of the opening pages, for example, Lulu shocks a man on the street when she uses the tail from an unknowing woman's fur stole to keep her warm while they both wait at the bus stop during a storm (fig. 3.6). A few pages later, Lulu startles a female factory worker when she dons overalls and stilts in an attempt to answer the "Help Wanted" sign at a local candy packing plant (fig. 3.7). Finally, in a comic that mirrors one of her early antics, she frightens four adults on the subway when she sits down with a cage containing her two pet mice (fig. 3.8). Even the comic chosen as the cover image to *Oh, Little Lulu!* showcases her penchant for shocking adults. The full-color image shows Lulu startling a male clerk in a shoe store when her big toe pokes through a hole in her sock.

Admittedly, Lulu is more often in the company of other children in general and boys in particular in these later comics. A panel from one of the opening pages of *Oh, Little Lulu!* shows the protagonist using a thread from her plump male playmate's shirt for her kite string, much to his dizzying disapproval (fig. 3.9). Later she punches him in the eye so as to try out her

Figure 3.6. Little Lulu gag panel. In Marge, *Oh, Little Lulu!* (David McKay, 1943).

new first aid kit. Finally, she takes this same character to get a haircut so that she can commandeer the lollipop that the barber gives him. That said, the boy is not her nemesis in the gag panels; she uses him as her sidekick, her accomplice, and, most often, her dupe. But she does not regard him as her enemy—and neither does he view her with any enmity. The primary target for Lulu's pranks, as well as the focus of her attention and energies, remains adults.

The way in which the gag panels pivot around intergenerational dynamics gives new meaning or added significance to the descriptor that Buell chose for character, "*Little* Lulu." This term is a diminutive, of course, that connotes not only size but also age. As such, the name "Little Lulu" calls attention to the character's youth. In so doing, it aptly announces her efforts to challenge, resist, and defy adult authority. Far from an endeavor that is unique to Little Lulu, this trait is one with which all children—male or female, rich or poor, urban or rural—could identify during the 1930s and early 1940s. In a phenomenon that would be exceedingly difficult, if not outright impossible, today, Buell's character may have been a little girl, but she functions as an Everychild in many ways.

Figure 3.7. Little Lulu gag panel. In Marge, *Oh, Little Lulu!* (David McKay, 1943).

Figure 3.8. Little Lulu gag panel. In Marge, *Oh, Little Lulu!* (David McKay, 1943).

Figure 3.9. Little Lulu gag panel. In Marge, *Oh, Little Lulu!* (David McKay, 1943).

"THERE'S A FULL-BLOWN GENDER WAR RAGING IN LULU'S NEIGHBORHOOD": SHIFTING PRINT FORMATS AND SHIFTING SOCIAL TARGETS

The year 1943 was a landmark for both Little Lulu and Buell. This date marked the beginning of her comic creation's long and lucrative life as a licensed commodity. As Craig Shutt has discussed, Lulu's public "profile skyrocketed in 1943, when Paramount Pictures released the first of eight Little Lulu animated cartoons, which were proudly announced in the *Post*" (Shutt, 33). By 1947, Paramount had produced more than two-dozen cartoons featuring the spunky figure, many of which were later "broadcast on television to new generations of kids" (33).

In the wake of the success of Little Lulu cartoons, more licensing deals followed. In 1944, Autograph Company began selling "framed pictures of Lulu and her friends" for youngsters to use as decoration in their rooms or as collectible items to trade with friends (Shutt, 33). In the same year, "Hall Bros. Inc., the makers of Hallmark greeting cards ... produced a wide line of Lulu cards, including for such occasions as birthdays, Valentine's Day, Easter, Christmas, get well and bon voyage" (33). The real watershed moment in Little Lulu's licensing life came near the end of 1944 when Buell "signed an agreement with Foote, Cone & Belding advertising in Chicago to feature Lulu in a major national advertising campaign for Kleenex tissues" (33). Written in both English and French, and appearing in print as well as on television, "the ads were prominent and ubiquitous" (33). Moreover, they were an immediate hit with the public. Commercials featuring Little Lulu as the Kleenex spokescharacter "were so popular that the campaign continue[d] through Dec. 1960, a run of 16 years" (33).

While Buell was thrilled with the way that her character was expanding into new cultural venues, the *Saturday Evening Post* had a different reaction. As Shutt has documented, the licensing deals "made the *Post* editors uncomfortable" (33). When Little Lulu first appeared in the magazine in 1935, she was their exclusive entity: drawn just for the *Post* and appearing only in their pages. Although Buell owned the copyright to the character, Lulu was—for all intents and purposes—the *Post*'s proprietary figure. Given this history, the magazine "didn't like having their exclusive cartoon character appearing in other publications" (Shutt, 33). By 1944, however, Lulu had become so popular that she was taking on a cultural life of her own. "Unable to rein in the irrepressible Lulu, they decided to replace her. Marge and the *Post* parted ways—amicably, she said," in late December 1944, when the final *Little Lulu* cartoon ran in the magazine (33).

Far from hindering Lulu's ability either to keep her current fans or to cultivate new ones, Buell's separation from the magazine only enhanced it. Freed from her obligation to the *Post*, "Marge quickly signed what she called a 'comprehensive' agreement with Western Publishing Co. for the publication and distribution of 'books, comics, magazines and other publications containing or featuring Little Lulu and various supplemental and subordinate characters which may, from time to time, become associates with Little Lulu in stories or in pictures or in any printed form" (Shutt, 33). What this business decision meant for fans of the comic series was simple: "a plethora of Lulu items in every shape, size and medium imaginable" (33). Within months after making the licensing deal, Western began publishing a veritable avalanche of Little

Lulu–themed products: "paint books, coloring books, paint-by-number books, punch-out books, cut-out books, novelty books, toy books and activity books, games, puzzles, sewing cards and many other items" (33). The arrangement that Buell had with Western was not limited to print items alone. "The agreement also included production of phonograph records with the Sandpipers and the Mitch Miller Orchestra" (33).

More deals would follow as the 1940s progressed. "A range of companies licensed the little girl and her ever-more-famous friends for a host of products from bean bags to cookies and dish towels" (Shutt, 33). Indeed, Shutt remarks that even by modern commercial standards, it was nothing less than a "breathtaking array of merchandise" (34). Between 1945 and 1963, in fact, Buell "estimated that at least 35 companies produced official Little Lulu merchandise" (34).

Of all the various print, visual, and material items that emerged during this era, however, one stands out: the comic book version. The series was "perhaps the best known and certainly the longest running" of those featuring Buell's character (Shutt, 34). "Published first by the Dell Publishing Co. starting in 1945, the comic began with a series of 10 issues intermixed in the publisher's quirky *Four-Color Comics* run (#74, 97, 110, 115, 120, 131, 139, 146, 158 and 165)" (Shutt, 34). In 1948, Lulu was given her own exclusive title and stand-alone series. The comic was called *Marge's Little Lulu* both to acknowledge Buell as the character's creator and to recognize that Buell still owned the copyright. The title "shifted to Western's Gold Key imprint in 1962, and around 1980 it moved to the Whitman imprint (with some issues appearing under both imprints during the changeover)" (34). *Marge's Little Lulu* "ran continuously until 1984, publishing 284 issues (making a full run of 278 Lulu issues, counting the *Four-Colors*)" (34).

Throughout this period, Buell neither wrote any of the stories nor drew any of the artwork for the Little Lulu comic books. As Janet Horowitz Murray has discussed, Buell had been asked to helm the project "but declined to do the comic book version" (13). A combination of Buell's growing aversion to the public spotlight, her need to oversee the licensing and merchandising end of her character's career, and the increasing responsibilities in her personal life as a wife and mother all factored into her decision (Heintjes, para. 7).

When Buell opted out of the comic book version of Little Lulu, Western tapped its own in-house talent. "Lulu's first two comics (*FC* #74 and 97) were both written and drawn by John Stanley, a Western staffer who had worked on a variety of the company's other series before Lulu showed up. Irving Tripp was brought on to draw the series with the next issue (*FC* #110), following a distinctive approach Stanley used for his scripts" (Shutt, 34).

Although Buell was not directly involved with either writing or drawing the series, she did oversee its origins. "Marge talked with Stanley while he worked on the first issue, going over do's and don'ts to ensure her little girl remained in character" (Shutt, 34). As Tom Heintjes notes, though, the bulk of these conversations were to ensure that Stanley "would steer Lulu away from participating in 'vulgar or crude ideas'" (para. 10). Moreover, after these initial discussions, Buell's involvement with *Marge's Little Lulu* was minimal. "Although she kept an eye on the comic, she didn't interfere with its direction, according to reports" (Shutt, 34–35).

Because Little Lulu was already such a popular and distinctive character, Stanley wanted to remain faithful to Buell's original creation. Accordingly, the author-illustrator maintained Lulu's signature personality traits: "nonconformity, proto-feminism . . . and blithe courage" (Murray, 13). However, Stanley did implement some changes. Reflecting postwar population shifts out of the cities and into the rapidly expanding suburbs, "he brought [Lulu] down the socio-economic ladder from a tuxedo-and-dinner-party New York to a semi-urban-middle-class-neighborhood full of baby-boom kids" (Murray, 13). In addition, Stanley added an array of supporting characters. As Shutt explains, "The requirements for a 52-page and later 32-page comic book were significantly greater than a one-panel cartoon or advertisements, requiring the injection of new elements. Stanley began rounding out her supporting cast quickly, giving her tubby boyfriend/nemesis the name Tubby Tompkins" (35). All told, Stanley either introduced or gave significant new detail to nearly a dozen characters. These figures included Alvin Jones, Annie Inch, Wilbur Van Snobbe, Gertie Greenbean, Iggy Inch, Edie Stimson, Willy Wilkins, Witch Hazel, Little Itch, Miss Feeny, Clarence McNabbem, the Westside Boys, George and Martha Moppet, and, of course, Thomas "Tubby" Tompkins (35–36).

In spite of having a large cast of diverse characters, *Marge's Little Lulu* overwhelmingly focused on just two figures: Lulu and Tubby. In the words of Shutt, "A few adults, including Lulu's mother, also showed up to serve as obstacles, but this was definitely a two-kid act" (35). The comic book's focus on Lulu and Tubby revealed another even more significant, and previously overlooked, shift in the central premise. Whereas the Little Lulu gag panels that had appeared in the *Saturday Evening Post* focused on the main character's ongoing battle with adult authority, the recurring theme of the comic book incarnation was her ongoing battle with her male peers. As Janet Horowitz Murray aptly summarizes about *Marge's Little Lulu*: "Mostly her enemies are little boys. There is a full-blown gender war raging in Lulu's neighborhood, and the comics are clear on one point: it's the boys who started it" (13). Whatever the specific plotline—Little Lulu's interactions with Tubby, her experiences while babysitting Alvin, her frustrations with the neighborhood "Clubhouse fellers," or her encounters with the Westside Boys—the overarching theme is the war between the sexes. "'Those awful boys,' as Lulu and Annie call them, are always turning up to put frogs into their pitcher on the girls' lemonade stand, steal their picnic lunch or sabotage their dog-walking business" (Murray, 13). Almost every story from the more than two hundred issues of *Marge's Little Lulu* confirms the veracity of this claim. In the words of Steve Raiteri, "Lulu is a smart, self-confident little girl who always seems to get the better of the boys who tease her and won't let her into their club" (103). Far from an exaggeration, "Their clubhouse bears the inscription: NO GIRLS ALLOWED. Being caught playing with a girl is grounds for expulsion—even for 'exekution' by snowball" (Murray, 13). That said, Little Lulu is far from either a pitiable victim or a weak damsel in distress. On the contrary, she retains her signature moxie. Lulu might be "tricked, chased, rained upon, tackled and beset by frogs in her attempts to earn a quarter, join a club, or eat an ice cream cone, but [she] wins out in the end because of perseverance, cleverness and sheer female superiority" (13). Indeed, Murray notes that whatever the specific story line, *Marge's Little Lulu* comics all have "a strong feminist charge" (13).

Some of the first, as well as most famous, issues from the comic book illustrate the veracity of these observations. In an early issue, for example, Lulu and Tubby attend a costumed birthday party together. When Tubby sees the dainty angel outfit that Lulu's mother has made her wear, he immediately makes fun of her. "Lookit Lulu! Ha! Ha! Ha!" he guffaws when she comes downstairs (Stanley, Tripp, and Marge, 7). The feisty Lulu, however, fights back. "How would you like a poke in the snoot?" she asks him menacingly (fig. 3.10). Far from making an empty threat, on the way to the party, Lulu shoves Tubby into an alley and steals the beard from his pirate costume. When they arrive at the party and the mother of their classmate asks them about their costumes, Lulu kicks Tubby so that he gives the response that she wants: "She's—OW!! Er—Blackbeard the Angel" (9).

A battle between the sexes likewise forms the focus for the well-known story "Little Lulu Enters a Contest" (Stanley, Tripp, and Marge, 41). The tale opens with Tubby building a model airplane. When Lulu wants to help, he promptly tells her: "Girls can't make nothin' but fudge!" (41). Of course, the spunky Lulu is not about to let this comment—or the challenge it contains—slide. She immediately vows, "You'll be sorry you didn't let me help you" (42).

Figure 3.10. John Stanley, Irving Tripp, and Marge, *Giant Size Little Lulu*, vol. 1 (Milwaukie, OR: Dark Horse, 2010), 41.

Figure 3.11. John Stanley, Irving Tripp, and Marge, *Giant Size Little Lulu*, vol. 1 (Milwaukie, OR: Dark Horse, 2010), 60.

Lulu not only begins building her own airplane but enters it into the local contest with all the boys. Although her model isn't the most aesthetically pleasing—the wings are bent and the body is crooked—it takes first prize for being able to stay airborne for the longest time. "Boys, the little girl's plane was in the air six minutes! So, she wins the five-dollars!" (50). The feminist message inherent in this victory, however, is quickly tempered: the final panel shows Lulu using her prize money to buy a much-coveted doll that she had seen in the toy store window.

Finally, a number of the stories in *Marge's Little Lulu* not only showcase the new emphasis on the battle of the sexes but also reveal the different relationship that the child characters have to adults and adult society as a result. In "Tubby's Travels," for example, Lulu's male playmate decides to run away from home. After a number of false starts, he finds a male hobo in the woods with whom he immediately feels an affinity based on their shared gender—and the sexist attitudes that accompany it. When the hobo chides Lulu, "Why don't you go home, little girl? This life is only for men," Tubby

Figure 3.12. *Little Lulu*, no. 45 (March 1952). Dell Comics.

is quick to agree: "Go home!" he shouts at her (Stanley, Tripp, and Marge, 60) (fig. 3.11). After Lulu is gone, the man explains to Tubby: "Th' secret of happiness is learnin' how to get along without women" (60). Once again, the young boy eagerly sides with the adult. "You said it!" Tubby replies with a big smile. Whereas in the gag panels, the young boy teamed up with Lulu to resist and rebel against adults, in the comic book version he forms an alliance with adult men against his peer largely because she is of the opposite sex. In this and numerous other stories, the loyalty that Tubby feels based on his gender identity is far stronger than any bond connected to his age group. Of course, the many plotlines in *Marge's Little Lulu* that present the "Clubhouse fellers" waging a veritable war against the title character—and vice versa—only further affirm this dynamic (fig. 3.12). Lulu and the boys are roughly the same age, but they have an antagonistic relationship because they belong to different genders.

. . .

The gender politics that form the recurring plots of the Little Lulu comic books may also help to account for their waning popularity in the closing decades of the twentieth century. As Craig Shutt and Tom Heintjes note, public interest in Buell's character began to fade in the late 1960s and diminished rapidly in the 1970s.[3] The syndicated newspaper strip of Little Lulu ceased production in 1969 after years of steadily declining subscriptions. By this point, "The strip was running in only about 65 newspapers, leaving little profit for many licensees, packagers and creators involved" (Shutt, 40). The comic book series was destined for a similar fate. In 1984, after many years of falling sales, Western ceased production of the long-running title.

Critics commonly attribute these events to the fact that the creative potential of Lulu's character had simply been exhausted by this point: after nearly fifty years, all the possible story lines, scenes, and scenarios were fully mined. Indeed, as one of Lulu's writer-artists, Arnold Drake, remarked in 1981, "The comic was running out of steam" (quoted in Shutt, 42).

While not discounting the creative fatigue that often accompanies such longevity, I contend that another more specific sociocultural issue may also have contributed: changing views about the gendered nature of children and the sexual segregation of childhood. After decades of children's clothes, toys, and household items being increasingly separated into "his" and "hers" varieties, the late 1960s saw a steady reversal of this trend. This shift arose from a combination of the gains made by the second-wave feminist movement, the rise of hippie counterculture, and the baby boomer generation, who had been dressed in highly gendered ways throughout their youth, now having children of their own and making different parenting decisions. Whatever the specific motivation, growing numbers of parents wanted to raise their sons and daughters in ways that did not perpetuate damaging sexist stereotypes. As a consequence, they increasingly sought out items that were gender neutral (Paoletti, xx–xxi). Accordingly, as Jo B. Paoletti notes, the period from 1965 through 1985 in the United States was marked by a move toward unisex clothing, toys, and activities. Rather than being required to adhere to rigid rules about how boys and girls should dress, play, and behave, young people were increasingly—in the words of a well-known song from 1972—"free to be . . . you and me."

The Little Lulu comic books by John Stanley and Irving Tripp were wholly out of step with this new social mind-set and growing cultural milieu. Rather than working to forge a partnership between boys and girls, the series focused on their separation. Instead of demonstrating ways that boys and girls could exist together, the Little Lulu comic books exploited their animosity and even enmity. Back in the 1950s, when American society was heavily invested in enforcing sex segregation, this feature appealed to readers. But now, a generation later, when the nation was moving toward more androgynous children and unisex childhoods, such attitudes seemed antiquated, narrow-minded, and even offensive. Surely, for at least some segments of the comic-book-buying public, this element was a contributing factor in the declining popularity of *Marge's Little Lulu* in the 1970s and 1980s.

WHEN GIRLS VERSUS BOYS BECOMES WOMEN VERSUS MEN: LITTLE LULU'S PROXY WAR

While the shift from intergenerational conflict to an intragenerational one in the Little Lulu comic book series certainly reflects changes taking place in American children and childhood, it also has ramifications that extend beyond this realm. In a detail that brings the Lulu comics' initial focus on adults full circle, the gender war that is taking place in the comic book series can be viewed as a thinly veiled commentary on the plight of adult women in the postwar period. The experiences of adult women in American society during the 1950s mirrored those of the comic book's fictional girl character. Akin to Little Lulu's struggles with the gang of neighborhood boys who routinely ridicule and exclude her, many women in postwar America were facing a similar economic, social, and political climate. After witnessing an unprecedented expansion of female gender roles during the Second World War—as women were encouraged to help the war effort by taking on an array of formerly male roles, responsibilities, and professional jobs—they saw these gains reversed in the years following the cessation of hostilities. Instead of women being urged to seek employment outside the home, they were being urged to go "back to the kitchen." Exemplified by cultural icons like June Cleaver, Donna Reed, and Harriet Nelson, women were not simply encouraged but—given the era's powerful conformity—even required to be "the quintessential white middle-class housewives who stayed home to rear children, clean house, and bake cookies" (Meyerowitz, 1). Akin to the boys' clubhouse in the *Little Lulu* comic books, much of the world outside the home for women in the 1950s had a "NO GIRLS ALLOWED" sign hanging from it.

When placed within this larger sociohistorical context, Little Lulu's war against boys in her comic book series can be viewed as a proxy war for the one that adult women were waging against postwar patriarchal culture. Indeed, the year 1948—when *Marge's Little Lulu* first appeared—played host to a presidential election in the United States. As historians have often noted, "The election of 1948 marked a turning point in American politics"—along with sociocultural life (Hughes, para. 50). Although the Democrat Harry S. Truman won the election, the year marked an unmistakable turn toward a more conservative national mood. From foreign policy to domestic attitudes, the election of 1948 saw the end of the liberal progressivism that had characterized the war years and the beginning of a period when tradition, convention, and even conformity ruled the day. *Marge's Little Lulu* was part of this phenomenon, both for the child protagonist in the comic and for the nation's adult women who inhabited the world outside of it.

Art Spiegelman and Françoise Mouly have commented on how child characters in early American newspaper comics like *The Yellow Kid*, *Little Nemo in Slumberland*, and *The Katzenjammer Kids* served a dual purpose. While these figures were literal juveniles who offered commentary on the social construction of children and public perception of childhood, they were also powerful metaphoric characters who served as stand-ins for larger and sometimes more allegorical entities: the actions of parents, the attitudes of adults, and the conditions within American society as a whole (Spiegelman and Mouly, 13). Little Lulu can be viewed in a similar manner. The intragenerational conflict that takes center stage in the comic book version has significance that extends far beyond youth culture. The main character may only be eight years old, but the gender-based difficulties that she faces are anything but mere "child's play." On the contrary, Lulu's struggles with the neighborhood boys are evocative of many of the most problematic, as well as entrenched, dynamics within the American sex-gender system.

• • •

The long print career and multigenerational success of Little Lulu has often been credited to the comic's "ahistorical" quality. Joe Sutliff Sanders, for example, in a 2010 review of a newly reissued collection of *Marge's Little Lulu* comics, asserted: "There is an elegance to the gags that drives these cartoons, a simplicity that makes them timeless" (69). Michele Gorman, discussing another reissued volume of the *Little Lulu* comic books, made a similar observation in 2006. Calling attention to the atemporal nature of the strips, she confidently predicted, "Lulu's antics and the funny dialogue in this collection of stories are sure to win over a new legion of fans" (22).

Understanding how the core premise of *Little Lulu* transformed from the gag panels to the comic books challenges this common critical assumption. The shift from plots that focused largely on intergenerational conflicts during the 1930s to ones that spotlighted intragenerational animus during the 1950s reveals that, far from existing outside of history, this character was heavily influenced by social, cultural, and political events taking placing during her specific time period. The battle of the sexes that pits young boys and girls against each other is such a central feature of American life today that it seems universal. Indeed, the gender wars are so ubiquitous and so heated that they seem to have always been raging. But this situation has not always existed, either in the Little Lulu comics or in American childhood as a whole.

Chapter 4

In Your Dreams

Little Audrey, Freudian Psychoanalysis, and Postwar Child Psychology

• •

The history of the *Little Audrey* comic book series begins not with the printed page but on the silver screen. In 1947, Famous Studios released an animated short starring their new cartoon personality, Little Audrey. As Jerry Beck has documented, this figure was hardly innovative: "Having had little luck creating its own homegrown stars, Famous Studios had to settle for licensing several children's book (Raggedy Ann) and comics characters (such as Snuffy Smith or Superman) to adapt to animation. Always hoping that one of these licensed characters would catch fire, in 1944 they succeeded, with Little Lulu" (Beck, 8). However, when the licensing agreement that Famous Studios' parent company, Paramount Pictures, had made with Little Lulu's creator and copyright holder, Marge Buell, expired, the studio was unable to renew it. Rather than scrap this successful feature, they decided to continue it in a slightly different form. "Famous decided to utilize several already commissioned storyboards using a substitute character, Little Audrey, who had made her first appearance as a supporting player in a Christmas-themed one-shot cartoon, *Santa's Surprise* (1947)," Beck reports (8).

From her name and her personality to her physical appearance and her behavior, Little Audrey was a clear imitation of Lulu. Like Buell's creation, Audrey was also an immediate commercial success: "Little Audrey soon became the biggest cartoon star the animation division had developed from scratch since Betty Boop, back in the 1930s" (Beck, 10). Beck documents, in fact, that "Audrey appeared regularly on screen for the next eleven years in the Paramount *Noveltoon* cartoon short subjects" (10). The character was featured in sixteen movie shorts during the 1940s and 1950s ("Little Audrey," para. 1).

Famous Studios did more than simply mimic the appearance, attitude, and antics of Little Lulu with Little Audrey; the studio also followed Buell's successful business formula. Echoing Marge's commercial savvy, Famous Studios capitalized on Audrey's popularity through merchandizing. As Beck explains, "Paramount made a hit of Audrey's theme song and sold sheet music, licensed dolls, [and] toys" (10). In addition, Audrey appeared in other cultural venues. Beginning in the early 1950s, for example, movie shorts featuring this character began being syndicated for television. In 1951 she starred in short-lived daily newspaper comic strip ("Little Audrey," para. 2). Finally, in yet another echo of the career of Little Lulu, Little Audrey received her own comic book in 1948. "Twenty-four issues of her comic book were published by St. John through 1952, when Harvey [Comics] took over the license" (Beck, 10). Founded by Alfred Harvey in 1941, the company was a mainstay in the American comic book scene during the postwar period, releasing titles like *Casper the Friendly Ghost* and *Richie Rich*.

Little Audrey was even more popular in print format than she had been as an animated movie character. Her comic book series ran for more than twenty-five years (Beck, 11). It was during the postwar years, however, that Little Audrey reached the height of her fame. During the late 1940s and early 1950s, she was a pop culture icon, readily recognized by children and adults alike. As Benjamin A. Botkin has commented, "Little Audrey jokes were in wide circulation" during the mid-twentieth century, and the character's catchphrase "She just laughed and laughed" became part of the American vernacular of that era (359).

While the *Little Audrey* comic books were a commercially independent and artistically autonomous creation, they retained a powerful link to one of the features from the cartoon movie shorts: her penchant for dreaming. "In common with many animated shorts of the period, childlike fantasy played an important role in Audrey's early cartoons, which often used dream sequences as the basis of the storylines" ("Little Audrey," para. 1). So, for example, "Audrey could ride the clouds with Mother Goose (*Goofy Goofy Gander*, 1950), attend a wedding in Cakeland (*Tarts and Flowers*, also 1950), or face an underwater tribunal of outraged catfish (*The Seapreme Court*, 1954)" ("Little Audrey," para. 1). Dream sequences frequently punctuate the comic book version of *Little Audrey*, as well. In numerous issues, she falls asleep and embarks on an imaginative adventure that constitutes the bulk of the story line.

While these dream sequences may be seen as a remnant of Little Audrey's days as a screen character, they had special resonance for the stories' original audience. The postwar period in the United States was marked by the ascendency of psychoanalysis in general and the theories of Sigmund

Freud in particular. Fueled by a combination of the well-publicized work of army psychologists to select soldiers who were "mentally fit" for combat and then, after the hostilities had ended, by the collective search for answers to horrific atrocities like the Holocaust, the practice of psychology moved out of the medical realm and into the mainstream. As Nathan G. Hale has documented, the period from 1945 to 1965 became known as "the golden age" of psychoanalysis in the United States (276). Americans—young and old, rich and poor, urban and rural—were fascinated with the workings of the mind, both conscious and especially unconscious. From the notion of repression and the origins of phobias to the role of the Oedipus complex and the interaction of the id, ego, and superego, the psychological root of human behavior engrossed the nation. Indeed, Freud's theories so thoroughly pervaded American culture during the late 1940s and throughout the 1950s that, as Bart Beaty has commented, they were the topic of "cocktail chatter" (43).

A key facet of Freud's exploration of the unconscious mind was the examination of dreams. In his groundbreaking *The Interpretation of Dreams* (1899), he argued that an individual's nighttime ruminations were not the meaningless ramblings of the slumbering mind; on the contrary, dreams were coded manifestations of a person's fears, hopes, and desires. This view "revolutionized the field of dream analysis" (Walden and Poch, 113) and also firmly linked psychoanalysis—both during Freud's own time and especially during the 1950s—with the process of scrutinizing dreams.

In this chapter, I place the Little Audrey comic books in general and the dream sequences that occur within them in particular back within this Freudian-infused postwar context. These story lines can be seen as a direct by-product of the era's fascination with the somnolent workings of an individual's unconscious mind. While the interest in Freudian theory and the practice of psychoanalysis during the 1950s were largely confined to the realm of adults, the dream sequences in *Little Audrey* invite child readers to participate as well. These frequent, lengthy, and detailed episodes encourage boys and girls to play the role of analyst for the title character: decoding symbols, detecting themes, and deciphering hidden content in an effort to determine the "true" meaning of her dream.

That said, the dream sequences in the Little Audrey comic books do more than simply allow young people to join the growing legions of armchair psychoanalysts during the postwar period. In an arguably even more important implication, they also challenge the era's prevailing views about child psychology. Freud believed that boys and girls experienced simplistic dreams that were mere wish fulfillments. However, the sequences in *Little*

Audrey paint a far more complicated portrait of the unconscious mind of its juvenile character. Freudian analysis of her dream sequences uncovers profound anxieties about an array of pressing contemporaneous sociopolitical issues, such as the threat of nuclear war and the fear of communist infiltration—concerns that would have been on the minds of the adults who created these sequences, and would also have been readily recognizable to the comic book's young readers.

In this way, the *Little Audrey* comic books did more than merely participate in the widespread interest in psychoanalysis during the postwar period; they offered a rare critique of it. The dreams that the comic book's child protagonist experiences resemble adult-style nightmares about a variety of postwar fears, problems, and anxieties. Accordingly, I explore what Freudian theory can reveal about the dream sequences in *Little Audrey* and, in turn, what the series' traffic in postwar psychoanalysis can tell us about the role that comics storytelling for young people played in efforts to question, resist, and challenge this climate.

"SATURATION OF POPULAR CULTURE AND EVERYDAY EXPERIENCE": POSTWAR AMERICA'S FIXATION ON FREUD

From the rise of the Cold War and the growth of the suburbs to the origins of the civil rights movement and the advent of modern mass consumerism, the postwar period in the United States was a complex and interesting era. While many past and present historical accounts focus on the elements of social conformity and political containment that typified the period, another equally important trend ran counter to these phenomena: the rise of Freudian psychoanalysis. Unlike the general atmosphere of restraint that ran through the era, "Psychoanalysis is about what happens when things spill-out from one place to another, even to places where there would seem to be little connection" (Thwaites, 2). In a seeming contradiction to the primacy that Americans placed on self-control and privacy, they were fascinated with psychoanalytic theories about the unpredictable workings of the unconscious mind. Accordingly, as Jack D. Pressman has remarked, "Freud was everywhere—in movies, plays, and magazine articles—as the elite bragged about their fashionable analyses" (479). The 1950s are routinely represented by a variety of iconic images, such as teenage girls in poodle skirts and crowds wearing 3-D glasses at the movie theater. However, another equally emblematic image also exemplified the era: the analyst's couch.

"If psychoanalysis was born in Vienna in the 1890s," Bart Beaty has aptly observed, "it grew strongest in the United States [in] the mid-twentieth century" (23). Although the work of Sigmund Freud had been gaining both professional esteem and public popularity since 1909, when the father of modern psychoanalysis delivered a series of groundbreaking lectures at Clark University, "the Second World War truly conferred legitimacy. Psychiatrists were drafted into service in an effort to weed out the psychologically unfit from the armed forces and to treat returning veterans suffering from war neuroses" (Beaty, 24). The much-publicized efforts of these individuals gave Freudian theory a cultural visibility that it had not experienced before. Mary Jo Buhle provides some revealing statistics: "At the close of World War II, there were only about a thousand psychoanalysts in the United States, an estimate that included the influx of European analysts who had fled the Nazis during the 1930s and early '40s. Over the next two decades, the number of psychoanalysts grew ten-fold" (para. 13). The reason for this dramatic uptick was simple. "Increasingly, psychotherapy was becoming the treatment of choice for dealing with mental illness, and psychoanalysis was becoming the dominant model of psychotherapy" (Beaty, 24). As Pressman has commented, by 1950, "The language and theory of psychiatry was suffused with Freudian doctrine; the best and brightest psychiatric students chose analytic careers; the leadership posts within the associations were held by fellow travelers; and the departments of psychiatry within the nation's medical universities were governed, almost as a rule, by avowed Freudians" (479).

This new level of esteem for psychoanalysis was accompanied by a new perception about its application. During the postwar years, Freudian psychotherapy was seen as beneficial not merely for mentally ill patients who were being treated within institutionalized settings but for all individuals. Freud viewed the unconscious as a rich repository of repressed memories, taboo thoughts, and forbidden desires that had a powerful influence over our daily actions (Hale, 293). By undergoing psychotherapy, men and women could begin to understand the subconscious motives that were fueling their behavior, shaping their identity, and influencing their lives. Given the many benefits that psychiatry had to offer the general public, the practice began "seriously shifting away from the mental hospital and toward private practice. In 1947, half of all American psychiatrists were affiliated with hospitals, but a decade later that number had dropped to 16 percent" (Beaty, 24). Whereas receiving treatment by a mental health professional had been highly stigmatized in previous periods, undergoing psychoanalysis now became desirable and even faddish. As Yale Kramer reflected, "Your friends were in it, going to be in it, or had been in it" (44). Indeed, popular fascination with psychoanalysis grew so strong that even individuals who had never sat on a therapist's couch played the role of analyst to friends, colleagues, and family members. Coworkers debated the possible meaning of their boss's "Freudian slip" during a business meeting. College students characterized an absentminded professor as being "neurotic." Finally, cultural commentators speculated on the role that repressed sexual desires played in the growing popularity of the new musical genre of rock and roll (Shumway, 124–43).

More than simply talking about psychoanalysis during the 1950s, Americans were reading about it. The psychoanalytic work of "writers such as Erik Erikson, Karen Horney, and Erich Fromm were on best-seller lists"; meanwhile, the paperback racks at the local drugstore held copies of Freud's *Civilization and Its Discontents* (Buhle, para. 10). Many other volumes both by and about Freud enjoyed tremendous popularity during this era. As Patrick LaPierre writes:

> The postwar years were ones of Freudian solemnization highlighted by Ernest Jones' three volume biography of Freud entitled *Sigmund Freud: Life and Work* (3 vols., 1953, 1955, 1957); James Strachey's *Standard Edition of the Complete Psychological Works of Sigmund Freud* begun in 1946 (funded in large part by the American Psychoanalytic Association); the 1954 publication of Freud's letters to Fleiss entitled *The Origins of Psychoanalysis*; and the tributes occasioned by Freud's centenary in 1956. (24)

Although many Americans read Freud's work, "far more men and women experienced Freud's legacy via popular culture" (Buhle, para. 14). Psychoanalysis permeated nearly every facet of the nation's print, visual, and entertainment media. These venues played a significant role in the cultural circulation of psychoanalysis during the postwar period. For example, many of the era's most popular novels were infused with Freudian elements. J. D. Salinger's *The Catcher in the Rye* (1951), about a disaffected young man's search for both identity and community, was a runaway best seller. The novel's central themes echo key psychoanalytic concepts, including alienation, loss, and rebellion. Furthermore, the main character, Holden Caulfield, visits a therapist during the course of the story. A myriad of other commercially successful and critically acclaimed books also pivoted around psychoanalytic issues, such as William Golding's *Lord of the Flies* (1954), Grace Metalious's *Peyton Place* (1956), and Vladimir Nabokov's *Lolita* (1955 in French; 1958 in

English). Psychoanalytic views were equally endemic to works of nonfiction from this era. The most popular parenting book of the period, Dr. Benjamin Spock's *The Common Sense Book of Baby and Child Care*, was "solidly rooted in Freud's concepts" (Hale, 285).

Freud also permeated American visual media of the 1950s. In the world of art, the innovative new mode of abstract expressionism was viewed from a psychoanalytic perspective. Jackson Pollock's drip paintings and Mark Rothko's color-block canvases were regarded "as an expression of the unconscious" (Halliwell, 200). The influence of Freud was even more evident in American cinema. Alfred Hitchcock was one of the era's most successful and acclaimed directors. Freudian themes permeated nearly all his feature-length films, including *Rear Window* (1954), *Vertigo* (1958), and *North by Northwest* (1959) (173–75). Hitchcock was not alone in his engagement with cinematic subjects that lent themselves to psychoanalytic interpretation. From individual titles like the multiple Academy Award–winning *All about Eve* (1950) to entire genres such as film noir, "psychotheraputic concepts circulated through . . . the movies" (Frost, 121).

Even American theater was not immune to the reach of psychoanalysis. "*Lady in the Dark*, which played on Broadway before becoming a Hollywood feature film in 1944, was publicized as the first Freudian musical" (Buhle, para. 11). Moreover, one of the era's most accomplished dramatists was Tennessee Williams. In plays such as *The Glass Menagerie* (1944), *A Streetcar Named Desire* (1947), and *Cat on a Hot Tin Roof* (1955), Williams explored characters, themes, and subject matters that easily lent themselves to psychoanalytic interpretations: dysfunctional families, repressed sexual desires, and sublimated aggression. Williams's productions were performed to sold-out playhouses around the country. Moreover, both *The Glass Menagerie* and *Cat on a Hot Tin Roof* earned Williams a Pulitzer Prize. Finally, many of his plays were made into equally popular feature-length films starring some of the era's most famous actors and actresses. Marlon Brando and Vivien Leigh, for example, headlined the movie version of *A Streetcar Named Desire* (1951), and Elizabeth Taylor and Paul Newman played the leads in *Cat on a Hot Tin Roof* (1958).[1]

Offering a final, but equally powerful, example of Freud's influence on American culture in the 1950s, the realm of commercial marketing and consumer advertising was largely driven by the principles of psychoanalytic theory. In the words of Andrea Carosso, "As consumption in post–World War II society no longer served to fulfill basic needs and purchasing became leisurely and discretionary, advertisers slowly learnt how to tap the human subconscious in order to make valid marketing decisions, by developing a three-level theory of the human consciousness loosely based on Freud" (46–47). This new approach drew heavily on what came to be known as "motivational research." "According to the theory," Carosso explains, "consumption-related decisions were mostly of a subconscious nature and success in advertising was based on probing the human psyche in order to understand what consumers really wanted, not what they said they wanted" (47). Consequently, Vance Packard argued in *The Hidden Persuaders* (1957) that, to sell products, companies needed to learn how "to tap what Packard described as the 'eight hidden consumer needs,' which were located in people's most crucial psychological drives: quest for emotional security, reassurance of worth, ego-gratification, need for creative outlets and love objects, sense of power, and sense of roots" (Carosso, 47). Drawing heavily on Freudian psychoanalysis, motivational research demonstrated that most consumers made purchasing decisions not on the basis of whether an item satisfied a practical need but on the basis of whether it filled an emotional one. As a result, marketing firms needed to employ psychologists to explore "what Packard call[ed] 'symbolic manipulators' and 'probers' to feel out 'our hidden weaknesses and frailties'" (Halliwell, 16). If advertisements were designed to satisfy one of those needs, they could "more efficiently influence our behavior" and sell more products (16).

In light of these trends, psychoanalysis experienced a "saturation of popular culture and everyday experience" in the period after World War II (Rose, 264). Within the realms of both licensed professionals and lay citizens, the United States witnessed the thorough "penetration of Freudian theory" (Hale, 285). Indeed, as Michael S. Roth commented, psychoanalytic concepts were "common cultural currency" in this era (quoted in Buhle, para. 16).

"ZZZZZZZZ": LITTLE AUDREY'S DREAM SEQUENCES AS FREUDIAN NIGHTMARES

Although the *Little Audrey* comic book series ran until 1976, it experienced its heyday during what has come to be known as "the long decade of the 1950s" (Carosso, 11). Commencing in 1945 with the end of the Second World War and concluding with the assassination of President John F. Kennedy in 1963, this period, many historians contend, more accurately encapsulates a cohesive time of national social circumstances, political policies, and cultural conditions (11). After all, as Andrew J. Dunar reminds us, "Decades are useful but artificial divisions of time" (1).

The long decade of the 1950s also marks the period when the *Little Audrey* comic books reached the apex of their creative, literary, and cultural powers. As Leslie Cabarga has commented in a volume that reprints many of the comics featuring Little Audrey—along with her playmates and spin-off characters Little Dot and Little Lotta—from 1952 to 1962: "Although we were limited to presenting mainly the early years of Audrey, Dot, and Lotta's adventures, the stories of this period happen to comprise much of the trio's finest work" (Cabarga, 15). This observation is especially true for Little Audrey. Not only did she have her own popular comic book series during this era, but in 1951 she was featured in another print venue: as a national newspaper strip (Harvey Comics). Moreover, the spunky female protagonist continued to appear in Paramount movie shorts; beginning in 1956, many of these cartoons were syndicated for television (Harvey Comics). Finally, the long decade of the 1950s saw the release of a wide variety of Little Audrey merchandise, from dolls, purses, and games to cookie jars, Halloween costumes, and activity books. Taken collectively, these elements indicate that this character reached the apogee of her popularity in this period. Little Audrey never had a larger cultural footprint or national fan base than during the postwar.

Of course, the golden age of Little Audrey was also the golden age of psychoanalysis in the United States. While Freud remained popular throughout the long decade of the 1950s, some facets of his work enjoyed more social traction than others. After all, as Tony Thwaites reminds us, "Freud's output is huge: the Standard Edition in English, which includes only the psychoanalytic papers, takes up 24 volumes, and on top of that there are almost a dozen volumes of letters" (xii).

One of the key texts of Freud's oeuvre, as well as with regard to the popularization of psychoanalysis in the 1950s, was *The Interpretation of Dreams*. First published in 1899, the book articulated many of "the primary insights about the unconscious that founded the discipline of psychoanalysis" (David, 2). *The Interpretation of Dreams* was such an influential work that two year later, in 1901, Freud released a condensed edition. Called *On Dreams*, this version abridged Freud's original tome—which ran for more than 500 pages—to roughly 40 pages. An expanded edition of *On Dreams* was issued in 1911 and encompassed around 100 pages of discussion.

Because *On Dreams* presented Freud's ideas in a more direct, succinct, and understandable way, it enjoyed wide circulation, especially among the general public. If a lay reader during the 1950s was going to examine Freud's writings on dreams at all, *On Dreams* was likely the version he or she would peruse; it embodied a far more accessible text. Thus, when it comes to discussing popular views about Freud, this volume is arguably a more pertinent source than *The Interpretation of Dreams*. Giving further credence to this observation, *On Dreams* was released by W. W. Norton in 1952 and then again in 1963. Issued in paperback, the book could be found for sale in newspaper stands, drugstores, and airport terminals throughout the nation.

The core claim in both *The Interpretation of Dreams* and *On Dreams* is simple: "Using the evidence acquired from the analyses of his own dreams along with those of his patients, Freud claimed that all 'dreams really have a meaning and that a scientific procedure for interpreting them is possible'" (LaPierre, 6). Freud regarded dreams in much the same way as he did neurotic symptoms, verbal slips of the tongue, and jokes: as "a (disguised) fulfillment of a (suppressed or repressed) wish" (Freud, *Interpretation*, 160). Akin to these other behaviors, dreams were the product of a "disjunction between wanting to express deep-seated wishes (some tied to intense anxiety) and the social prohibitions inhibiting their expression" (LaPierre, 6). As a result, dreams were far from the inconsequential workings of an individual's mind during slumber. Rather, they were rich psychological puzzles that could be solved through psychoanalysis. As Freud would assert, "The dream is a *sort of substitution* for those emotional and intellectual trains of thoughts which I attained after complete analysis" (*On Dreams*, 18).

For Freud, the key to interpreting dreams involved understanding the relationship between what he called a dream's "manifest content" and its "latent content" (*On Dreams*, 19). "I contrast the dream which my memory evokes with the dream," he explained, "and other added matter revealed by analysis: the former I call the dream's *manifest content*; the latter, without at first further subdivision, its *latent content*" (19; italics in original). Accordingly, psychoanalytic consideration of a dream must involve two key questions: "(1) What is the psychical process which has transformed the latent content of the dream into its manifest content? (2) What is the motive or the motives which have made such transformation exigent?" (19). As Freud goes on to elucidate: "The process by which the change from latent to manifest content is executed I name the *dream-work*. In contrast with this is the *work of analysis*, which produces the reverse transformation" and reveals the true meaning of the dream (19; italics in original). Using this approach, Freud asserts that the analyst can decipher the meaning of even the most bizarre, incoherent, and seemingly inscrutable dream.

Freud created a three-tiered classification system for dreams that were experienced by adults—arranged from the most simplistic to the most enigmatic—but he did not feel that the dreams experienced by children possessed the same depth or diversity. Instead they fell exclusively into "the more readily intelligible dreams of the first class where, the manifest and latent content being identical, the dream work [thus] seems to be omitted" (Freud, *On Dreams*, 24). The dreams of children, Freud believed, were mere wish fulfillments: "They completely satisfy wishes excited during the day which remain unrealised. They are simply and undisguisedly realisations of wishes" (27).

To illustrate, Freud offered "some examples of dreams which I have gathered from children" in both his professional practice and his personal relationships (*On Dreams*, 25). "A girl of nineteenth months," he recorded, "was made to go without food for a day because she had been sick in the morning, and, according to nurse, had made herself ill through eating strawberries. During the night, after her day of fasting, she was heard calling out her name during sleep, and adding: '*Tawberry, eggs, pap*'" (25; italics in original). Freud explains that both the cause of the dream and its meaning are clear: "She is dreaming that she is eating, and selects out of the menu exactly what she supposes she will not get much of now" (25). The other examples follow a similar pattern: "A girl of three and a half years had made during the day a sea trip which was too short for her, and she cried when she had to get out of the boat" (25–26). Not surprisingly, Freud goes on to explain, "The next morning her story was that during the night she had been out on the sea, thus continuing the interrupted trip" (26).

To Freud, this dream, akin to all the nighttime ruminations of children, "is nothing else than a wish realised" (*On Dreams*, 27). Indeed, as he asserts at the end of his discussion: "The desires which are realised in these dreams are left over from the day or, as a rule, the day previous, and the feeling has become intently emphasised and fixed during the day thoughts" (28). Accordingly, the dreams of children require little, if any, interpretation. As Freud would repeatedly insist, their meaning is "obvious" (27). In fact, he referred to all dreams of this nature as "infantile" (29).

The *Little Audrey* comic book series traffics in the Freudian fascination with dreams during the 1950s. Many issues contain a lengthy and vivid episode that takes place in the character's mind while she is asleep. Moreover, the comic wants its child readers to be aware of this fact. The series uses a variety of both verbal elements and visual clues to demonstrate that the title character is dreaming. For example, the dream sequences in *Little Audrey* are routinely preceded by a panel showing her drifting off to sleep: her eyes are often closed, and in many cases, she is yawning or even openly commenting about how tired she feels. Then the dream sequence typically commences by showing a stream of "zzzzzz's" above her head, as well as a thought bubble with the beginning of her somnolent ruminations. The remaining panels change the focalization, shifting the dream from the background to the foreground of the comic. The image of a sleeping Little Audrey disappears, and the dream episode moves from her thought bubble into the main space of the panel, allowing the events that are taking place to occupy center stage. That said, the comic wants its child readers to remember that these occurrences are part of a dream: the borders to these panels do not have square corners like the others but are cloud shaped to indicate that they are occurring in the title character's unconscious.

The *Little Audrey* comic books do more than simply contain the title character's dream sequences; they also challenge prevailing Freudian views about the nature of children's dreams. Although the initial impetus for Audrey's dream is some direct event from her day, it quickly moves far beyond this issue. In so doing, these episodes paint a far more complicated portrait of the slumber-time workings of the child character's mind. Contrary to Freud's view about the "transparent" and "obvious" nature of children's nighttime ruminations, the dream sequences in *Little Audrey* encourage, reward, and even necessitate psychological interpretation. Far from mere wish fulfillments, many of these episodes represent coded anxieties about some of the most pressing social, cultural, and political issues of the 1950s.[2] Using the postwar psychoanalytic techniques that these sequences invite reveals that Little Audrey's dreams are actually Freudian nightmares.

・・・

The story "Carpet Bagger" from the February 1953 issue of *Little Audrey* provides a vivid example of the treatment of dreams in the comic book series. The narrative begins when a carpet from the "Arabian Rug Co" falls off a truck and lands on the title character and her friend Tiny. As Tiny chases after the driver, Audrey engages in the arduous task of rolling up the large carpet. "This rug may not be valuable, but it sure is *heavy!*" she remarks, beads of sweats emanating from her face (61; emphasis in original). Once Audrey has completed the difficult task, she sits down next to the carpet and reflects: "Now if it had been a *flying carpet*, I wouldn't have had all this trouble!" (61; emphasis in original). With the tired girl's eyes now fully closed, she repeats: "Yeah—a flying carpet! That would be swell" (61).

Figure 4.1. Panel from "Carpet Bagger," *Little Audrey*, February 1953.

The next panel shows Audrey fast asleep. A thought cloud emanating from her head presents what is taking place in her mind while she slumbers (fig. 4.1). The scene echoes Freud's view that children's dreams are a form of wish fulfillment. The bubble shows the carpet magically unrolling by itself and revealing that it is indeed capable of flight, just as Audrey had hoped right before falling asleep (fig. 4.2). "Golly! A real modern *flying carpet!* With a plastic windshield, *a cockpit*, steering wheel and controls!" she says excitedly once the carpet has unfurled itself completely (61; emphasis in original). The series of panels that follows shows Audrey gleefully enjoying this experience: she turns loops in the air like a stunt pilot; she swoops down low over her friends on the ground, giving them both a thrill and a scare; and she chases a jet airplane, waving to the astounded pilot in the cockpit as she races by (61–62). But the dream sequence quickly moves beyond merely satisfying a child's fantasy. Instead the episode introduces events that reveal deep-seated anxieties within Audrey's psyche—anxieties that can be examined, decoded, and understood via psychoanalysis in general and Freud's approach to dream interpretation in particular.

Freud believed that the dreams of adults are highly symbolic, semantically rich, and psychologically complex manifestations of the unconscious. Accordingly, everything that takes place during a dream—from the biggest events to the tiniest details—reveals information about our repressed hopes,

Figure 4.2. Panel from "Carpet Bagger," *Little Audrey*, February 1953.

fears, and desires. As W. Leslie MacKenzie explained in his introduction to Freud's *On Dreams*: "Take a remembered element of a dream, track it back and back by free association or other method, and you will find that, at one or two removes, the remembered element stirs up forgotten elements, and ultimately brings coherence out of incoherence" (xxiv–xxv). When a patient conveys to a therapist all the events that occurred during a dream and then explores what these details recall or evoke, psychoanalysis can decipher the dream's true meaning. To use Freud's own terminology for this process, it will illuminate the relationship between the dream's manifest content and its latent content. The unconscious mind employs a wide array of strategies to encode the dream's underlying or latent meaning from its outward or manifest content, including condensation, displacement, dramatization, subversion, and transference (Freud, *On Dreams*, 34–91). But the end result is the same: symbolic cohesion and semiotic unity. As Freud explains, "The thoughts themselves fit beautifully together into chains logically bound together with certain central ideas which ever repeat themselves" (16). In this way, no aspect of a dream is insignificant, inconsequential, or meaningless. Instead, as he asserts, "If the chain of associations be followed up which proceeds from one element of the dream one is soon led back to another of its elements. The thoughts evoked by the dream stir up associations which were not noticeable in the dream itself" (13).

Figure 4.3. Panel from "Carpet Bagger," *Little Audrey*, February 1953.

The dream that Little Audrey experiences in "Carpet Bagger" can be viewed in this way. The transition from mere wish fulfillment to symbolic commentary on anxieties in her waking life occurs in the fifth panel. The plane that Audrey races with her flying carpet is not a commercial jet, as one would expect and which would be a far more common sight in the sky above her suburban neighborhood. Instead it is a military fighter plane (fig. 4.3). The presence of the fighter jet is not merely puzzling but ominous: it introduces the specter of war into this peaceful and even halcyon civilian environment, evoking both the recently concluded conflict in Korea and the looming possibility of future military threats to the nation and its citizens via the Cold War. Moreover, affirming Freud's view that no aspect is too small or event too insignificant in a dream, the fighter plane has a number written on its side. In both of the panels that depict the jet, we see "521" clearly emblazoned below the cockpit. Moreover, the second panel zooms in on the plane's nose, thereby calling added and, I would assert, unmistakable attention to it (fig. 4.4). In a detail that seems too evocative to be merely coincidental, the US Air Force had a 521st Air Defense Group in the postwar era. Although the unit had been disbanded after World War II, it was reactivated in 1953, the same year that this comic appeared. Moreover, in yet another feature that resonates with this dream sequence being a product of Little Audrey's anxieties about the Cold War, the 521st Air Defense Group consisted largely

Figure 4.4. Panel from "Carpet Bagger," *Little Audrey*, February 1953.

of fighter-inceptor squadrons comprising small, speedy aircraft (US Air Force Historical Division, 299). The squadrons were stationed in Sioux City, Iowa, and tasked with intercepting enemy aircraft—especially bombers and reconnaissance planes—to prevent them from carrying out their missions over civilian airspace (299). Therefore, echoing the presence of this plane in the skies over Little Audrey's suburban neighborhood, the 521st was primarily concerned with domestic air defense.

As Little Audrey's dream progresses, the concern about military threat and even invasion continues. After beating the fighter jet in a race, Audrey breaks through the sound barrier and enters the earth's atmosphere. Upon doing so, she encounters an alien spaceship. The physical appearance of the flying saucer mirrors the geometric circles that form the pattern on her flying carpet, suggesting that the object is another manifestation of her psyche. The moment that Audrey sees the spaceship, she attempts to run from it. As Freud would likely argue, though, such attempts to escape from herself are futile: the young girl is immediately caught in a tractor beam and pulled aboard. "Consider yourself captured by the *flying sorcerers!*" a robot-like space alien informs her on the deck of the spaceship (62; emphasis in original). Immediately after uttering this statement, however, the aliens erupt into laughter. A full panel shows the aliens doubled over in hysterics, with the words "HO-HO-HO" and "HAW-HAW!" in large capital letters

Figure 4.5. Panel from "Carpet Bagger," *Little Audrey*, February 1953.

above their heads. When Audrey asks the aliens what is so funny, their reply resonates powerfully with the atmosphere of conformity during the postwar era: "You—you're the *funniest* looking creature we've ever seen! Ha-Ha-Ha-Ha!" (62; emphasis in original).

On the next page, Audrey slyly escapes the aliens' clutches by blowing a giant bubble with a piece of gum that she finds in her pocket. When the bubble pops, the aliens become trapped in the sticky mess. As they struggle to get free, Audrey hops back into her flying carpet and departs. In her haste to return to earth, though, she flies too fast and loses control. "My gosh! I can't get out of this spin! . . . O-O-Oh—I'm going to *crash!*" she exclaims in a panel that shows her hurtling uncontrollably to earth (64; emphasis in original). Audrey crashes to the ground, and the depiction of her impact and its aftermath is highly symbolic of another prevalent fear during the 1950s: both she and her carpet explode in a giant mushroom-shaped cloud (fig. 4.5). Not only is the cloud featured in its own stand-alone panel, but the plume is so massive that it dwarfs the city beside it, a detail that makes it look even more like a nuclear bomb. Finally, lest the magnitude of the explosion is not already apparent, the word "BOOM" is superimposed on it. This event is so dramatic and frightening that it jolts Audrey awake, ending her dream. "*Help! Help me!*" she cries, as Tiny tries to comfort her (64; emphasis in original).

Although the dream has ended, one final Freudian facet remains to this sequence: Audrey has developed a phobia as a result of the experience. After she returns the lost carpet to the driver of the delivery truck, he tries to give her a small rug as reward for her honesty. Audrey does not simply decline but becomes frightened. "A rug? Oh no, thank you!" she replies nervously, a halo of worry lines emanating from her face (64). "It might *fly!*" Audrey anxiously explains in the following panel while running swiftly away (64; emphasis in original). Both the truck driver and Tiny are completely baffled by this behavior. The story's closing panel shows them standing on the sidewalk looking dumbfounded; large question marks appear above their heads. While Audrey's phobic behavior may be puzzling to these two characters, it is perfectly understandable to the comic's juvenile readers after their foray into the young girl's unconscious.

Many other dream sequences in the *Little Audrey* comic book series can be viewed in a similar manner. Although these episodes are initially precipitated by an event from her immediately previous waking experience, they quickly morph into something much more complicated and more psychologically telling. In so doing, they reveal coded anxieties about the social, cultural, and especially political circumstances of the postwar era. The story "Midsummer Day's Dream," from the August 1953 issue, forms a poignant example. The comic opens with a splash panel depicting the title character reading a book while floating in an inner tube in the shallow ocean surf. "'Aloha,' said the handsome stranger to the island girl," Audrey reads aloud to herself (96). Her friends Melvin and Tiny attempt to get her attention—waving to her and asking if she wants to play—but Audrey is so engrossed in her book that she does not see them. "'This is the isle of Bali-Hoo,' said the island girl," Audrey recites as she walks out of the surf and right past her friends, the book blocking her view (96). Audrey returns to her beach chair, continues reading, and muses aloud, "Gee, I wish *Melvin* was a handsome stranger!" (96; emphasis in original). Audrey drifts off to sleep in the following panel: her eyes are closed, and a thought balloon above her head shows her dreaming of a small, beautiful tropical island. The first event to transpire in her dream is a wish fulfillment: just as she had hoped before falling asleep, Melvin has indeed become a powerful tribal king, and Audrey is his love interest.

With the young girl's first wish satisfied, the events of the dream grow progressively more bizarre—and more Freudian. First, a crocodile threatens to eat the pair. But when its mouth opens, a Melvin doppelgänger inexplicably climbs out (97). Rather than being a wealthy member of the royalty, this new Melvin is a poor peasant. Audrey becomes enamored of him, and

King Melvin grows jealous. He decrees that the new Melvin can only remain on the island if he extinguishes the fire emanating from the mouth of the volcano. However, as peasant Melvin and Audrey carry buckets of water up the mountain in an attempt to do so, the volcano promptly erupts, causing the characters to flee. Luckily, in the next panel, rain starts to fall. But this happy development quickly turns tragic when the rainstorm turns into a monsoon. A panel shows Little Audrey and peasant Melvin struggling to walk in driving wind and drenching rain.

The duo's troubles are still not over: the monsoon next evolves into a hurricane. "It's getting *worse!*" island Audrey rightly says to her companion as the storm rips their clothing to pieces (100; emphasis in original). Once again, though, the conditions further deteriorate: a tidal wave appears on the horizon. The giant wave crashes into the beach, sweeping both Audrey and peasant Melvin out to sea. The dream ends here as Audrey wakes, startled by the experience. "Wake up, Audrey!" the real Melvin tells her as he helps her out of her beach chair, which is now sitting in the water. "The *tide's* coming in!" (100; emphasis in original). While the dream's conclusion may be seen as a reaction to her current conditions—Audrey gets wet as the water rises around her, and so she dreams that a tidal wave has struck the beach—the events that have preceded it suggest another, more Freudian interpretation. The progressive sequence of the dream—with a crocodile delivering a doppelgänger who had to climb a volcano that caused an eruption that sparked a monsoon that developed into a hurricane and that finally resulted in tidal wave—resonates with an important political policy and widespread social fear during the postwar era: the domino theory. In its most basic form, "The domino theory, which governed much of U.S. foreign policy beginning in the early 1950s, held that a communist victory in one nation would quickly lead to a chain reaction of communist takeovers in neighboring states" ("Domino Theory," para. 1). Not only does Audrey's dream depict a chain reaction, but—echoing actual US military actions in Southeast Asian locales like Indochina during the 1950s—it takes place in a setting that is reminiscent of the South Pacific. "By early 1950, makers of U.S. foreign policy had firmly embraced the idea that the fall of Indochina to communism would lead rapidly to the collapse of other nations in Southeast Asia" ("Domino Theory," para. 3). In fact, "The National Security Council included the theory in a 1952 report on Indochina"—the year before this issue of *Little Audrey* was released (para. 3). The domino theory received widespread attention in the national media and, consequently, was a concept with which most Americans (including children) were familiar.

Figure 4.6. Panel from "Who Killed Cock Robin," *Little Audrey*, August 1953.

One final, but equally illuminating, example of the psychologically rich and symbolically complex dreams that occur in the *Little Audrey* comic book series appears in the story "Who Killed Cock Robin." Appearing in the August 1953 issue and offering a variation on the classic English nursery rhyme, the comic opens with Audrey enjoying a mystery novel in bed. "As Detective Sam Snide followed the clues, twenty crooks leaped out of the dark alley!" she reads aloud in the first panel (126). When Audrey sprays water at her pet bird with a squirt gun in imitation of Sam Snide, her mother hears the commotion and shouts at her from the hallway to turn off the light and go to sleep.

The next panel shows Audrey with her eyes closed and a stream of "zzzzzz's" floating above her head. She dreams that a talking bird dressed as a newsboy appears on her windowsill, offering her a paper and making an extremely Freudian announcement: "*Wuxtra! Wuxtra! Cock Robin killed in Woodland Night-Club!* Read all about it!" (127; emphasis in original). Freud believed that the dreams experienced by adults often emanated from "repressed erotic desires" (*On Dreams*, 101). As W. Leslie MacKenzie summarized it: "That the emotions of sex should play an enormous part in the process of analysis is to be expected; for the sex emotions are among the deepest, if not the deepest, of our nature, and color every experience" (xxix). Echoing this observation, many of the events that occur during Audrey's dream can

Figure 4.7. Panel from "Who Killed Cock Robin," *Little Audrey*, August 1953.

be viewed in a sexualized way. First, a male turtle sheds his shell and watches television in his boxer shorts (127) (fig. 4.6). Then an ostrich has thrust its neck into a hole in the floor and refuses to pull it out (128). Finally, Audrey threatens the wooden bird from a cuckoo clock with a phallic-looking ear of corn (129). Furthermore, after she heats it with a match, the cob shoots kernels of popcorn (129) (fig. 4.7).

"Who Killed Cock Robin" can be viewed as more than merely a sexualized dream from a Freudian perspective. Akin to all the character's other nighttime ruminations, it encodes fears about postwar cultural conditions. Little Audrey, in her attempt to solve the case, impulsively accuses and mercilessly interrogates many characters. "*You* look suspicious, Mister Turtle!" she proclaims menacingly when he crawls by (127; emphasis in original). "I've got some *questions* I want to ask you!" she continues, pointing a condemnatory finger at him (127; emphasis in original). Poor Mr. Turtle is taken aback by these actions: his mouth hangs open in disbelief, his eyes are opened wide in amazement, and beads of sweat emanate from his brow.

When Audrey is unable to obtain any incriminating evidence from Mr. Turtle, she turns her suspicions—and her hard-boiled tactics—to the next animal she sees. "Hey there, Mister Ostrich! You're looking *mighty suspicious!*" she shouts while barging into the room (128; emphasis in original). Although

Audrey tears up the floorboards to interrogate the ostrich, who has buried his head in a knot in the woodwork, she once again obtains no evidence.

The next suspect in the Cock Robin case is the wooden bird from the cuckoo clock in the same room. Convinced of his guilt, Little Audrey chases him through the house, into a field, and up a tree until he confesses to the crime. But when she hauls the cuckoo bird back to her room to be punished, a surprising development takes place: Audrey learns that he has given a false confession under duress. The young girl's canary flies in the window and reveals that Cock Robin hasn't been shot with an actual arrow; instead he was harmlessly hit with one of Cupid's arrows in anticipation of Valentine's Day. Unlike in the original English nursery rhyme, Cock Robin is not actually dead. Consequently, no murder has been committed, and thus no murderer needs to be found.

After this detail has been revealed, Audrey's behavior recalls the postwar efforts to root out communists from government agencies—actions that would culminate six months after this comic book issue appeared, with the Army-McCarthy hearings in April 1954. Indeed, the hysteria that Audrey exhibits about finding the murderer is highly reminiscent of the hysteria during this period about finding communists.

Freud and his theories of psychoanalysis were not merely popular during the 1950s; they were revered. As Yale Kramer has written, the postwar period "raised Freud to the status of a cultural hero in America" (44). Bart Beaty, writing about the ascendency of psychoanalysis during the 1950s, noted that American culture absorbed, adopted, and applied these views largely without intellectual scrutiny or interpretive analysis. "The new popularizers were generally uncritical of Freudian thought" (Beaty, 24). Rather than interrogate any of Freud's psychoanalytic theories—by questioning his contentions, examining his methodology, and challenging his conclusions to ensure they were scientifically sound—people commonly accepted them. Beaty argues that this practice led to cultural misunderstandings about, and intellectual misuses of, Freud's work during the 1950s, while they also contributed to the era's atmosphere of conformity: "As a consequence, some observers have argued, the United States became more conservative, orthodox, and Freudian than even Freud ever was" (24).

The dream sequences that Little Audrey experiences break from this trend. These comic book stories offer not only a rare critique of Freudian psychoanalysis but one that serves a progressive purpose. *Little Audrey* makes a case that the psychological processes of children are more complex, more complicated, and more coded than the era's popular theorists contended. Like adults, young people are profoundly affected by the social, cultural, political, and economic conditions of the world in which they live. Moreover, they experience the same diverse range of hopes, fears, and anxieties as adults. *Little Audrey* may have been notorious for her penchant for dreaming, but these sequences suggest that it was popular psychology's views about the inner lives of children that were the true fantasies.

FROM PATIENT TO PRACTITIONER: RETHINKING THE RELATIONSHIP BETWEEN COMICS AND PSYCHOANALYSIS IN THE 1950S

Comics and psychoanalysis were certainly no strangers to each other in the United States, especially during the postwar era. Around the same time that Little Audrey was experiencing the dream sequences in "Carpet Bagger," "Midsummer Day's Dream," and "Who Killed Cock Robin," cultural commentators were using Freudian theory both to demonstrate the benefits of comics and, paradoxically, to call for their suppression. As Bradford W. Wright has discussed, defenders of comic books argued that these stories in general and the ones focused on crime and horror in particular embodied important avenues for young people to indulge in fantasy, to explore their instinctual impulses toward violence, and to release aggression (88–92). By contrast, figures like Fredric Wertham used Freudian theory to make the opposite claim. Rather than seeing comic books as therapeutic and thus beneficial, Wertham saw them as corrupting and therefore pernicious. In numerous lectures, books, and magazine articles, he asserted that comics did not assuage youth violence, aggression, and delinquency but rather encouraged such behavior. His viewpoint would prove persuasive. In what has become a well-known episode in the history of comics in the United States, in September 1954 growing concern about "the ten-cent plague" prompted a US Senate hearing that, in turn, prompted the creation of the Comics Code (Nyberg, 77–80). This strict system of guidelines for both the written content and the visual images in comic books effectively eliminated the crime and horror genres while imposing great limitations on all publications intended for children (Wright, 145–60).

Whether psychoanalysis was being employed to defend comic books or to condemn them during the 1950s, it was regarded as a valuable interpretive tool. The dream sequences in the *Little Audrey* series demonstrate that postwar Freudian theory was not simply being applied to comics; it was also being used by them. At the same time that the postwar popularity of psychoanalysis was affecting comics, comics were also making an impact on psychoanalysis. Placing the dream sequences in *Little Audrey* back within their original 1950s context reveals that the relationship that postwar comics had with popular psychology was not unidirectional. During the same time that Fredric Wertham was pushing against comics with psychoanalysis, titles like *Little Audrey* were pushing back with their own critique of Freudian theory.

Kenneth B. Kidd, in *Freud in Oz: At the Intersections of Freud and Psychoanalysis* (2011), points out: "Children's literature has spent decades on the psychiatrist's couch, submitting to psychoanalysis by scores of scholars and popular writers alike" ("Freud in Oz," para. 1). In *Freud in Oz*, however, Kidd "turns the tables, suggesting that psychoanalysts owe a significant and largely unacknowledged debt to books ostensibly written for children" (para. 1). Drawing on an array of past and present classics—including *Peter Pan*, *Alice's Adventures in Wonderland*, *Where the Wild Things Are*, *The Catcher in the Rye*, *Winnie the Pooh*, and *The Wizard of Oz*—Kidd illuminates the many psychological insights that have their genesis in books for young readers.

The *Little Audrey* comic books echo this phenomenon while also expanding on it. Kidd draws on an array of literary schools, aesthetic styles, and narrative formats for young people—from picture books to young adult novels—but he does not include comics. Especially during the postwar era in the United States, comics are often framed as being the passive targets of psychoanalytic theory. As the dream sequences in the *Little Audrey* series attest, however, they were also active critics of it, resisting, revising, and even rejecting some of its foundational views and cornerstone beliefs.

Little Audrey's signature phrase was "She just laughed and laughed." However, her comic book's insightful commentary on the psychoanalytic complexity of children's dreams was far from a joke. The series encouraged its child readers to examine the workings of their unconscious minds, and in so doing, it encouraged the adult field of postwar psychoanalysis to reexamine its views about children and childhood.

Chapter 5

"From the Top, Stupid!"
The *Li'l Tomboy* Comic Book Series, Female Juvenile Delinquency, and the Comics Code

• •

In October 1956, Charlton Publications introduced a new comic book character: Li'l Tomboy. Making her debut in volume 1, issue 11, of *Li'l Genius*, she is the cousin of the title figure and comes to visit one sunny summer afternoon.

Although Li'l Tomboy appears only briefly in one three-page story, titled simply "Li'l Genius and Li'l Tomboy," her presence is significant. The figure's main function in this vignette is not to serve as a counterpoint to her cousin's character but to establish her own. The story introduces five-year-old Li'l Tomboy to readers, gives them a sense of her personality, and—most importantly—announces the impending release of her own comic book series.[1] "Li'l Genius and Li'l Tomboy" ends with the spunky female character looking directly at the reader, winking, and saying, "S'long Folks. See ya soon in my own book! Look for me on the stands, won't ya?" Far from a false promise, the first issue of *Li'l Tomboy* appeared in late October 1956. In this way, the comic was a spin-off of a spin-off: *Li'l Genius*, which was called *Super Brat!* for its first five issues, was itself a copycat of the popular *Dennis the Menace* newspaper strip.

While Li'l Tomboy's literary lineage may have been derivative, the cultural and commercial impetus fueling her character was not. Charlton Publications launched the *Li'l Tomboy* series in an attempt to appeal to female consumers. As Bradford W. Wright has commented, "While surveys suggested that females read comic books only slightly less than males did, there were few titles aimed principally at girls and young women" (128). With Li'l Tomboy, Charlton sought to reach this lucrative and largely untapped market. "*Publishers Weekly* reported that the American public in 1953 spent over $1 billion on comic books. Surveys suggested that over 90 percent of boys and girls under 18 read them" (Wright, 155).

Li'l Tomboy did more than simply contest the masculine gendering of comic books during the Silver Age. The series also challenged traditional gender roles for white, middle-class girls in the postwar period. The title character does possess a conventionally feminine appearance. She is routinely depicted with shoulder-length hair, freshly pressed dresses, and even frilly underskirts, but her behavior does not match her appearance. As her name implies, Li'l Tomboy eschews traditional notions of proper female comportment: she abhors dolls, gets into frequent fistfights, and enjoys rough-and-tumble sports like football. Consequently *Li'l Tomboy* introduced a new type of female personality to mainstream American comic books during the 1950s. From her attitude and appearance to her demeanor and penchant for mischief, she differed radically from extant female comics characters like Margaret in *Dennis the Menace*, Betty and Veronica in the *Archie* series, and the superheroine Wonder Woman.

Charlton's presentation of an alternative female comic book character appealed to readers. *Li'l Tomboy* ran from October 1956 through December 1959. Moreover, this feisty female character also gave rise to her own spin-off series: the *Li'l Rascal Twins*, which featured Li'l Tomboy alongside her cousin Li'l Genius. *Li'l Rascal Twins* debuted in September 1957, and its final issue was released in January 1960.[2]

In spite of both the commercial success and iconoclastic content of the *Li'l Tomboy* comics, little has been written about them. To date, no books, essays, or articles exploring the series from a social, material, literary, aesthetic, or commercial perspective have been published. Likewise, *Li'l Tomboy* is not mentioned in any past or present discussions about the origins, history, and evolution of comic books in the United States.

In this chapter, I offer a corrective to this trend. I explore the *Li'l Tomboy* comic book series from a social, cultural, and historical standpoint. I examine this feisty five-year-old figure both in the comic books that bore her name and in issues of the *Li'l Rascal Twins* series, where she appeared alongside her cousin Li'l Genius. *Li'l Tomboy* embodies an important cultural intervention in the history of American comic books. She marks an early but illuminating moment when the industry attempted to break out of established commercial and literary formulas. More than merely a marketing experiment, *Li'l Tomboy* offers an important counterpoint to the cultural conservatism and social conformity that permeated this era. This spirited female character demonstrated to her young readers that alternative forms of identity not only existed for white, middle-class girls but were rich, liberating, and rewarding.

In so doing, Li'l Tomboy contributes to what Joel Foreman has identified as the "other fifties"—or the elements of social resistance and even cultural subversion lurking beneath the decade's smiling conformity. This character offers a compelling commentary on the complex feedback loop that existed between American popular culture during the 1950s and its prevailing social anxieties. The comic book career of Li'l Tomboy takes place against the backdrop of growing national concerns about youth rebellion in general and the rising rates of juvenile delinquency in particular. This feisty female figure engaged in behavior that went far beyond simply defying postwar notions about appropriate feminine conduct; it could often be seen as delinquent. In her debut story "Li'l Genius and Li'l Tomboy," for example, she throws a rock through a window and then trespasses through a locked gate into a private junkyard. Moreover, in many subsequent issues, she engages in other delinquent acts like petty theft, the intentional destruction of property, and sassing adult authority figures, including police officers.

Li'l Tomboy engages in these activities not simply under the watchful eye of the Comics Code Authority but with their official seal of approval. The morality-based literary standards that were enforced by this office had been implemented just two years earlier, largely in response to growing societal fears that comic books were responsible for the rising rates of juvenile delinquency or, at least, youth rebellion. During a time when the censors employed by the Comics Code Authority were at their most powerful and restrictive, Li'l Tomboy engaged in antics that far exceeded those that had been forbidden in other publications.

Much has been written in recent decades about the figure of the "bad girl" in the 1950s. As Leerom Medovoi reminds us, in examples ranging from the femmes fatales who populated film noir to the female juvenile delinquents who filled pulp fiction and the teenage girl renegades who appeared in mainstream Hollywood movies like *Rebel without a Cause*, iconoclastic women "played a much larger imaginative role in postwar American culture" than historians and cultural commentators have commonly credited (Medovoi, 266). The *Li'l Tomboy* comic books, with their mischievous title character, extended notions of female "badness" to an entirely new demographic: white, middle-class girls who were still in early elementary school. In a compelling paradox, however, the series used the figure of a "bad girl" as the means to attract "good" female consumers. Accordingly, this chapter tells the story of how, with the creation of Li'l Tomboy, Charlton Publications demonstrated that postwar gender conformity could be resisted and, even more significantly, so too could the Comics Code.

"WE LOVE HER JUST AS SHE IS": CHALLENGING POSTWAR GENDER NORMS

Perhaps no other decade in American history has been so heavily romanticized as the 1950s. While individuals venerate many aspects of this era—the booming postwar economy, the strong sense of patriotism, and the widespread confidence in national leaders—its clear and distinct gender roles are often the subject of admiration or, at least, nostalgia. As Joanne Meyerowitz has written, "Most of us are familiar with the well-entrenched stereotype of American women in the post–World War II era. Domestic and quiescent, they moved to the suburbs, created the baby boom, and forged family togetherness" (1). Exemplified by figures like June Cleaver, Donna Reed, and Harriet Nelson, the prevailing image of women during the 1950s was the "the quintessential white middle-class housewives who stayed home to rear children, clean house, and bake cookies" (1).

Although the redomestication campaign during the 1950s was a powerful sociocultural force that compelled many women to embrace—either by choice or by force—the image of June Cleaver, the phenomenon was not absolute. As Meyerowitz puts it, "While many women fit the stereotype, many others did not" (2). In examples ranging from the young women who affiliated themselves with the bohemian Beat Generation and those who defied the era's compulsory heterosexuality by living as lesbians to the figures who fought against the era's de facto and de jure forms of racial inequality by participating in the burgeoning civil rights movement and those who resisted the era's "back to the kitchen" movement by working outside the home in professional careers, "the postwar public discourse on women was more complex than often portrayed" (2). Contrary to prevailing popular perceptions that the 1950s were a time of widespread gender conformity, the actions, activities, and identities of many women during the 1950s "point to pockets of resistance" and call attention to individuals "who questioned and loosened postwar constraints" (4). As Joel Foreman has written, these women offered a portrait "of nascent rebellion and liberation" (3–4). The choices they made and the lives they led point to the small cracks in the wall of sociocultural conformity that, in the decade that followed, would widen into gaping fissures. Indeed, Susan Lynn has commented that while the feminist movement of the 1960s is commonly seen as emerging in reaction to the gender restraints of the 1950s, it can more accurately be regarded as amplifying sentiments that were already extant. "The efforts of women in the 1940s and 1950s provided an important bridge between earlier

Figure 5.1. Cover image to the first issue of *Li'l Tomboy*, October 1956. Charlton Publications. Photograph by Michelle Ann Abate. From the collection of Michelle Ann Abate.

generations of women activists and those involved in social movements of the 1960s" (Lynn, 121).

The figure of Li'l Tomboy forms an important, but previously overlooked, site of resistance to postwar gender and social conformity. Although this new character appears conventionally feminine—she has long hair and wears nice dresses—she does not behave in a conventionally feminine way. Li'l Tomboy, as her name suggests, enjoys rough-and-tumble activities like football and boxing. While her unconventional behavior elicits shock, dismay, and even aggravation in many adults, it provides her with increased physical freedom, a greater range of emotional expression, and, perhaps most important, the opportunity for social individuality. Even more radically, the comic book clearly maps out the benefits of defying traditional white, middle-class gender roles and adopting an alternative identity to its young female readership. Gender nonconformity during the 1950s was socially stigmatized and even medically pathologized, but Li'l Tomboy makes the subversive argument that it ought to be practiced and praised.

• • •

The way in which Li'l Tomboy poses a direct challenge to postwar gender stereotypes is evident even before juvenile readers open the debut issue. The cover image to the inaugural October 1956 edition depicts the title character gleefully standing atop a high flagpole (fig. 5.1). She is balancing on one foot and happily—not to mention fearlessly—reaching up into the air as if to catch a passing bird or, given the extreme height, perhaps an airplane. Small stick figures can be seen in silhouette on the ground far below. Presumably adults, they are all in a state of panic: several are waving their arms wildly, one is pointing up into the air in the general direction of the flagpole, and a third is running frantically toward the scene. A fire truck, which has presumably been called to "rescue" the girl, is parked off to the side. Although the truck's ladder is fully extended, it is nowhere near long enough to reach Li'l Tomboy. Nevertheless, with her large smile and buoyant body language, she is unconcerned.

Although the scenario depicted on the cover is not portrayed anywhere else in the issue, it aptly encapsulates Li'l Tomboy's character. It reveals her daring, her pluck, and—perhaps most importantly—the fact that she neither wants nor seemingly even needs to be rescued. The young girl has decided to climb up the flagpole; after she is done having her adventure, she will confidently climb back down.

When readers open the cover and encounter the first story in *Li'l Tomboy*, these first impressions are confirmed. Titled "The Sleepwalker" and appearing on the inside cover, this wordless tale shows the young girl being scolded by her mother for punching a boxing bag in the basement. Admittedly, since there is no dialogue, it is unclear whether Li'l Tomboy is being chastised because it is past her bedtime or because boxing is not an appropriately feminine activity. Whatever the reason, she is clearly angry that she must stop: the next panel shows her marching upstairs with a grumpy expression on face and wavy lines streaming from her head to indicate her resentment. But in a powerful suggestion that Li'l Tomboy's interest in rough-and-tumble activities like boxing is innate or inherent, she rises from her bed in the middle of the night and—as the title of the story indicates—sleepwalks back down to the basement and resumes jabbing the punching bag. As soon as she does so, a warm smile spreads over her face. While Li'l Tomboy's sleepwalking could be seen as a rebellious prank by a willful child, several panels depict a stream of "zzzzzz's" floating above her head. They indicate to readers that Li'l Tomboy is not pretending to be asleep; she is actually slumbering, and thus her actions stem from her unconscious desires.

The next full-length story develops these qualities further. The tale begins with Li'l Tomboy's father chatting with a male neighbor over a fence about parenthood. In his first comment, the neighbor gives voice to stereotypical postwar beliefs about gender by commenting how much easier it is to raise a daughter than a son. Although Li'l Tomboy's father insists, "That daughter of mine is plenty active!" the neighbor dismisses him: "You can't compare a sweet, gentle girl with a boy!" At that moment, Li'l Tomboy makes her entrance and debunks his preconceived notions about how a girl behaves. First she knocks over the neighbor while leaping the fence with her pogo stick. Next she body-slams him with a wrestling move when he offers to shake her hand. Finally, she snaps him in the posterior with one of his suspenders in an act that may or may not have been an accident.

While Li'l Tomboy's father is accustomed to his daughter's rambunctiousness and thus takes these events in stride, her mother is alarmed. "I think we should do something about Li'l Tomboy.... The child just doesn't do things that other little girls her age do!" she tells her husband. Recalling the way in which gender nonconformity was not simply socially punished during the postwar period but medically pathologized,[3] the mother suggests taking Li'l Tomboy to a doctor. Of course, the moment that the little girl is alone with the physician, she begins wreaking havoc: she zaps him with a hand buzzer when they first shake hands, she pins him to the ground to demonstrate some of her wrestling moves when he asks her what games she enjoys, and then, when he presents his mannequin for practicing CPR as "a doll" for her to play with, she flings it across the room and uses it as a football tackling dummy. Exasperated, the doctor informs Li'l Tomboy's parents that he cannot help her; the case is hopeless. Rather than being saddened or even alarmed by this news, they are content with it. "Guess there's nothing else to do but go home now. And I think we're just stuck with a tomboy for a daughter," Li'l Tomboy's father remarks with a smile. In a comment that makes an even more powerful argument for accepting female gender iconoclasm, her mother adds: "And do you know what I think? ... We love her just as she is!" To call further attention to the importance of this viewpoint, the mother's final comment serves as the story's title.

This message echoes an argument made by the prominent postwar psychiatric Robert Lindner in an article that appeared in *McCall's* magazine in February 1956, just nine months before the release of *Li'l Tomboy*. Under the attention-grabbing title "Raise Your Child to Be a Rebel," Lindner asserted: "For many families *You Must Adjust!* has virtually become the Eleventh Commandment. In every area of our life today individuals are forced to conform. They are commanded to distort their personalities, sacrifice their personal freedoms and fit themselves into a prevailing pattern" ("Raise," 102). In remarks that aptly describe Li'l Tomboy's mother, Lindner goes on to talk about how otherwise calm, reasonable, and intelligent parents

> panic when their children don't seem to "fit in with the group." Aware that in our society the nonconforming person is suspect, that the failure to adjust is regarded in some quarters as sinful, in others as criminal and in still others as perverse or abnormal, most mothers and fathers are appalled and unnerved by the spectacle of the child who stands out in any way from the crowd. ("Raise," 102)

As Lindner goes on to assert, however, such reactions are not only unwarranted; they are harmful. "The truth of the matter is [that] conformity is not a good but an evil. It represents a travesty on human nature, and our insistence on it today is responsible for a good deal of the distress of our time" ("Raise," 102). For this reason, he encourages parents, teachers, and other adult authority figures to allow young people to question the status quo.

> The world will not be saved by the submissive, the meek. Humanity's fate is bound to the instinct of rebellion, that bright flame at the core of being which cannot be gutted. To raise your child to be a rebel, to rear and instruct him in the uses of his natural capacity for resisting and overcoming the suppressive forces—man-made or otherwise— that conspire to dehumanize him, is to fulfill in the highest sense the obligation of a real parent. (Lindner, "Raise," 104)

As Lindner's choice of pronouns indicates, the psychiatrist was largely thinking about white, middle-class boys. But as the story "We Love Her Just as She Is" in *Li'l Tomboy* demonstrates, such attitudes could also be applied to their female counterparts. In several subsequent tales, in fact, the title character's tomboyish antics reveal how the gender-conformist behavior of several of her older adult female relatives is neither enjoyable nor authentic. Instead it is a false facade that they present for the sake of maintaining a socially acceptable public appearance. In the story "Vacation Bound," which appeared in the March 1959 issue of *Li'l Tomboy*, the central character's parents are horrified when they learn that their daughter has mailed her grandmother her collection of live lizards as a Christmas present. But the closing panels reveal a surprising twist. When the elderly woman opens the package, she is not horrified but delighted: "Lizards! Well, what do you know about that!" she remarks with warm smile. In the dialogue balloon that forms the closing lines to the story, Li'l Tomboy's grandmother goes on to explain: "I kept my lizard collection out of sight when they were here for fear that they wouldn't approve! Now I have these to join them!"

A variation on this phenomenon takes place in the tale "A Visit with Aunt Penelope," which appears earlier in the same issue. Li'l Tomboy's Aunt Penelope offers to have her niece visit for a few days with the intention of taming some of her tomboyish ways. After spending a week with Li'l Tomboy, however, Aunt Penelope does not convert her niece to femininity; instead she herself is converted to tomboyism. When she brings Li'l Tomboy back home, Penelope has forsaken her formerly prim and proper dresses and now wears a baseball uniform. Moreover, she tells her sister, "Come on out! We'll bang a few balls around the lot! Li'l Tomboy sure taught me how to have fun!"

Of the many Li'l Tomboy stories that call into question the naturalness, goodness, and uniformity of postwar notions about gender, perhaps the most poignant is "A Girl on the Team." Forming the penultimate tale in the first issue, it is also the most complex, detailed, and lengthy. The narrative does far more than simply attempt to expand the possible range of white, middle-class female gender expression by presenting the main character happily and skillfully engaging in an array of activities that are stereotypically coded as masculine. Instead the text openly and repeatedly challenges the era's essentialist beliefs and sexist attitudes. As the title "A Girl on the Team" suggests, Li'l Tomboy wishes to join the neighborhood football team and is predictably rebuffed by the boys who comprise it. To do so, they repeat an array of postwar platitudes about femininity: little girls are weak, they lack gumption, and, as one boy matter-of-factly asserts, they "cry when they get hurt." For these reasons, the boys tell Li'l Tomboy to "go play with your dolls."

As readers have likely come to expect by this point, the mischievous Li'l Tomboy subverts such gender expectations. She returns with her dolls, which she begins throwing at the boys. Several panels show the boys wincing and ducking as a hail of these items pelts them in the head at high speed. When the boys complain about getting hit, Li'l Tomboy replies with a smirk on her face: "Ya told me to play with my dolls—didn't ya?"

Li'l Tomboy's strong arm and pinpoint accuracy, however, still do not convince the boys to let her join their football team. "So what if she can throw? Girls can't tackle," remarks the boy whose yellow T-shirt reads "CAPTAIN." Somewhat predictably, immediately after he has finished this statement, Li'l Tomboy tackles him, flattening him to the ground. The word "*THUMMPP!*" appears above the image of the title character diving on him from behind (emphasis in original). To further illustrate the power with which Li'l Tomboy tackles him, the following panel shows the boy sitting on the ground with his eyes pointing in opposite directions and interlocking ovals swirling above his head representing his disorientation—even a possible concussion. Indeed, the symbol used to convey this condition loosely resembles Rutherford's model of the atom, suggesting that Li'l Tomboy's tackle was so powerful that it was nothing short of nuclear.

In a telling index of the entrenched nature of postwar gender stereotypes, the boys are still unsure whether they are willing to let a girl join their football team. They call a meeting at their private clubhouse to discuss the issue. Ironically, the boy with the yellow "CAPTAIN" shirt, whom Li'l Tomboy had first pelted with dolls and then flattened with her powerful tackle, is the most vocal opponent. "I say no! All that stuff she did before was just a fluke! Maybe she could do those tricks once or twice," he argues, "but she can't have enough strength to play a whole game!" Li'l Tomboy has been standing outside the clubhouse, eavesdropping on their conversation. When the issue is finally brought to a vote ("All of those in favor of letting Li'l Tomboy play—go over to that side of the club-house!"), she does something not simply impressive but nearly superhuman: she physically lifts one side of the clubhouse to move all the boys to the side of the room that indicates their belief that she be permitted to join the team. This tactic works; her feat of strength frightens the boys into finally letting her join the team.

Even so, when the day of their first football game arrives, the boys insist that she not let the other team know that she is a girl. Indicating the powerful social policing of the gender line during the 1950s—and the punishments doled out to those who crossed it—her male teammates assert, "It would be awful if they found that out!" and "We'd never live it down!" In a gesture that demonstrates the artificial nature of gender while simultaneously anticipating Judith Butler's famous later argument that masculinity and femininity are merely performative, Li'l Tomboy successfully hides that she is a girl simply by tucking her long hair under her helmet.

Unsurprisingly, Li'l Tomboy is the team's star player. A series of panels that occupy one full page show her single-handedly winning the game: she scores exciting touchdowns, skillfully evades opponents, and makes key tackles. To celebrate their victory, all the players take off their helmets and throw them in the air—an act that, of course, reveals that Li'l Tomboy is a girl. Her teammates are convinced that they will be ridiculed by their opponents. "We're (groan) ruined!" "We'll (sniff) never be able to hold our heads up again!" "Here they come! Betcha they (sob) start right in callin' us sissies!" three different boys fret in the same panel. But something far different and completely unexpected happens: the players from the opposing team try to convince Li'l Tomboy to play for them. "We'll make ya captain if ya want!" promises one boy. "We'll even make ya coach!" implores another. When her current teammates hear these offers, they protect their star player. "Anybody who tries to steal Li'l Tomboy away will hav'ta fight us first!" declares one of the boys who had earlier argued vehemently that girls can't play football. The story's closing line offers a final critique of the era's derogatory views about women. In a thought bubble that appears above Li'l Tomboy's head, she muses about the boys' adamant assertion that she remain on their football team: "Hmpf—and they say girls are the ones that keep changin' their minds . . . !"

By offering a direct and detailed challenge to postwar gender roles, Li'l Tomboy extends the site of social resistance during the 1950s to a new and even younger demographic: preadolescent girls. While the work of historians like Joanne Meyerowitz, Wini Breines, and Joel Foreman has called attention to the ways in which white, middle-class female adults, teenagers, and adolescents pushed back against the gender conformity of the 1950s, these scholars say nothing about elementary-aged girls from the same demographic. Indeed, this demographic group has historically been seen as lacking the personal agency, social power, and even cultural awareness to question the status quo. The absence of preadolescent girls from discussions about the "other fifties" seems to confirm that they did not participate in it. The comic book character of Li'l Tomboy suggests otherwise. Alternative and even iconoclastic models of middle-class white girlhood did exist during the 1950s. Moreover, beginning in October 1956, one compelling example was available at any local newsstand for the extremely affordable price of only ten cents.

"FROM THE TOP, STUPID!":
LI'L TOMBOY AS A LI'L JUVENILE DELINQUENT

In many issues, Li'l Tomboy engages in behavior that goes beyond being merely daring or iconoclastic; it can be seen as delinquent. As Thomas Doherty, Rachel Devlin, and Ramona Caponegro have all discussed, juvenile delinquency was a major cultural concern during the 1950s. In the best-selling book *1,000,000 Delinquents* (1955), Benjamin Fine examined how the social, economic, and especially familial disruptions precipitated by World War II had left a generation of young people restless and discontent. Especially in urban areas, unsupervised youths roamed the streets either individually or in "gangs" and engaged in an array of illicit and sometimes illegal activities, ranging from smoking, drinking, and racing cars to fighting, robbery, and vandalism. As a result, delinquency rates skyrocketed. Fine warned that "an FBI survey of two hundred cities showed a rise in the crime rate of adults in 1953 of 1.9 per cent as compared with an increase of 7.9 per cent in the crime rate of boys and girls under eighteen" (18).

These figures prompted President Dwight D. Eisenhower to ask Congress in 1954 for three million dollars "with which to attack the problem of juvenile delinquency" (Fine, v). In the following year, the Senate convened a special subcommittee to explore the social causes of, as well as possible solutions to, what they termed this "major American problem" (v). Thomas Doherty has documented that, in the minds of many politicians, juvenile delinquency was as serious an internal threat to the integrity of the United States as the external one of communism (40). Moreover, it was a crisis for which there was no end in sight. As the journalist Virginia Held wrote, "Juvenile Delinquency, particularly in the United States, has come to be considered one of the most urgent social problems of the day, and the epidemic . . . seems to be spreading so fast that it obliterates the best efforts society can make to control it" (quoted in Fyvel, 255). For this reason, discussion of the subject was not merely limited to the nation's political and scientific circles; it permeated the mainstream. In best-selling books like Willard Motley's *Knock on Any Door* (1950) and popular Hollywood films like *Blackboard Jungle* (1955), the growing problem of juvenile delinquency received widespread attention. While some of these portrayals framed the issue in highly raced and classed ways—as a problem among minority youth in the nation's cities—juvenile delinquency permeated all strata of US society.

Li'l Tomboy was written and released amid this atmosphere of cultural anxiety, social fixation on, and even political panic about, juvenile delinquency. Moreover, the comic book series reveals its awareness of this phenomenon. In the story "Baby Sitter First Class" (*Li'l Tomboy*, March 1958), the central character, who has been entrusted with watching a neighbor's toddler, shouts at her recalcitrant ward: "Come back, you delinquent!"

In numerous issues, Li'l Tomboy herself engages in an array of activities that could be seen as delinquent. As discussed at the start of this chapter, the character's penchant for partaking in behavior that is not simply mischievous but even criminal is showcased from the series' beginning. In the vignette "Li'l Genius and Li'l Tomboy" (*Li'l Genius*, October 1956), Li'l Tomboy intentionally throws a rock through a plate-glass window and then deliberately trespasses through a locked gate into a junkyard. Lest any doubts remain whether she is intruding into private property, the sign on the fence outside clearly reads "Keep Out."

Far from a misleading presentation of Li'l Tomboy's personality, this introductory portrait is accurate. At numerous points in both the comic book series that bears her name and the issues of *Li'l Rascal Twins* where she appears alongside her cousin, she engages in behaviors that can easily be described as delinquent. In keeping with her antics in "Li'l Genius and Li'l Tomboy," by far her most common form of misconduct is trespassing. In the story "At the Zoo" (*Li'l Rascal Twins*, September 1957), for example, the cousins wish to visit the animals but lack the money to buy a ticket, so they sneak into the zoo by climbing over a wall. A similar scenario appears in the story "Are You for Real?" (*Li'l Rascal Twins*, January 1958). Here, the cousins slip into a local playhouse without paying admission because Li'l Tomboy longs to see a beloved movie star appear in a drama. The bulk of the story depicts the pair evading capture by running from ushers, security guards, and ticket takers.

Together with trespassing, Li'l Tomboy and her cousin engage in frequent acts of petty—as well as not-so-petty—theft. The cover image to the September 1957 issue of *Li'l Rascal Twins* shows the pair stealing a monkey from the zoo; in the background, readers can see that they have locked the zookeeper in the cage. In the story "Let Us into the Ballgame" (*Li'l Rascal Twins*, November 1957), Li'l Tomboy snatches a baseball that has been hit out of the park from the hands of the sewer worker who found it so that they can gain free admission to the game. The vignette "Lost and Found," which appears on the final page of the same issue, reinforces the title character's distorted sense of right and wrong. Li'l Tomboy happily reports to her mother that she found a dollar bill by a tree. When her mom asks, "Are you sure somebody lost it?" Li'l Tomboy replies gleefully: "Of course, I'm sure, Mom ... I saw the man looking for it!"

Adding to the way in which Li'l Tomboy embodies many of the defining traits of juvenile delinquents during the postwar period, at one point she even joins a gang. In the story "Making like a Lady" (*Li'l Tomboy*, October 1959), she expresses interest in an array of conventionally feminine activities not because she is beginning to slough off her tomboyish ways—as her mother hopes—but because it is part of a pledging process. "I had to go through *initiation* by *acting* like a *sissy girl*," she announces to her parents while pulling off her frilly bow and taking down her perfectly coiffed hair (emphasis in original). The name of the group to which Li'l Tomboy has just gained admittance suggests that it is not merely a social club or play group but a gang. "I've just been elected a member of the *City Dump Rat Killer's Society!*" she gleefully announces (emphasis in original).

Ramona Caponegro, Rachel Devlin, and Grace Palladino have observed that one reason why the delinquency rate among young people rose so sharply during the postwar period was that the definition of what constituted delinquent behavior expanded. While a young person engaging in clearly criminal acts such as stealing and trespassing would have been deemed aberrant in any historical era, delinquency in the 1950s also encompassed a myriad of behaviors that were simply rebellious, disobedient, or insolent. During a time of intense social conformity and the powerful social policing of personal behavior, any conduct that did not adhere to conventional manners and mores was demonized. As Grace Palladino has commented about the postwar period, "The interpretation of delinquent behavior was in the eye of the beholder" (161). She goes on to explain that "delinquency ranged from talking back and refusing to share in household tasks to going steady, staying out late, and taking the family car across state lines in order to buy beer" (161). Consequently, as Rafiel York explains, "Juvenile delinquency became any act of youthful rebellion, any expression of adolescent freedom, or any behavior of which adults disapproved" (105). This observation was especially true for young girls. Ramona Caponegro has discussed how the delinquency laws for minors in some states included the following offenses: "incorrigibility; being beyond parental control; engaging in immoral, indecent, or disorderly behavior; and displaying sexual irregularities" (314). Indeed, Rachel Devlin documents cases of female juvenile delinquency where the girl's chief offense was talking back, defying curfew, or breaking household rules. According to Ruth Shonle Cavan, in many states during the 1950s and 1960s, a juvenile

Figure 5.2. Panel from "The Hair Raiser," *Li'l Tomboy*, June 1957. Charlton Publications. Photograph by Michelle Ann Abate. From the collection of Michelle Ann Abate.

delinquent was regarded as "any child or youth whose conduct deviated sufficiently from normal social usage to warrant his [or her] being considered a menace to himself, to his future interests, or to society itself'" (17).

When postwar juvenile delinquency is understood to include behavior that was not criminal but simply defiant or disobedient, Li'l Tomboy's antics become even more rebellious. To be sure, much of her behavior can be seen through the lens of "incorrigibility," "being a menace," and deviating "sufficiently from normal social usage," especially for young girls. For instance, when Li'l Tomboy's mother takes her for a haircut in the June 1957 issue of *Li'l Tomboy*, the barber asks how she would like it cut, and she replies, "From the top, stupid!" (fig. 5.2). Similarly, in the story "Goes Shopping" (*Li'l Tomboy*, September 1957), she crashes into the grocery store manager while racing a cart around the store and sassily demands, "Can you '*manage* to get outta the way?'" (emphasis in original) (fig. 5.3).

Whether juvenile delinquents during the 1950s engaged in activities that were outright criminal or merely incorrigible, one key part of this rebellious identity for white youth was their traffic in elements from black culture. As historians like Wini Breines and Joel Foreman have written, white, middle-class young people announced their rejection of the white, middle-class

Figure 5.3. Panel from "Goes Shopping," *Li'l Tomboy*, September 1957. Charlton Publications. Photograph by Michelle Ann Abate. From the collection of Michelle Ann Abate.

status quo by appropriating elements from black culture, such as possessing a love of jazz music, professing an emotional affinity to the plight of black people, and adopting slang terms from black culture like "daddy-o," "dig," and "cat" (Breines, *Young*, 18, 22; "Postwar," 53–77; Foreman, 1–23). This phenomenon was especially true for middle-class white girls during the 1950s. As Breines has discussed, the Beat Generation, the jazz scene in Harlem, and the new musical genre of rock and roll formed powerful and appealing alternatives to the consumerism and conformity of the white suburban existence ("Other," 382–408).

Li'l Tomboy participates in this phenomenon. The young Caucasian girl frequently constructs her mischievous identity via elements of various racial and ethnic minority groups. As I have written elsewhere on this topic, white tomboyism has a long but hidden history as a racialized construct. Not only did this new code of female conduct emerge during the mid-nineteenth century in the United States as a eugenic practice that was a means to help ensure white racial supremacy, but it also incorporated numerous facets of blackness or, at least, nonwhiteness (Abate, *Tomboys*, xxiv–xxviii). Authors repeatedly described ostensibly Caucasian tomboys as having "brown" skin tones and "dark" physical features. Moreover, in fashioning their rebellious, rambunctious, and rough-and-tumble behavior, these narratives drew on elements such as blackface minstrelsy, modernist white fantasies about primitivism, and the racialized language of white feminism. In so doing, white tomboyism trafficked in various forms of symbolic, performative, and co-opted blackness for generations in the United States (xii–xiii).

In a variety of stories, Li'l Tomboy's "wild," "uncivilized," and "unruly" behavior is created via a link to racial and ethnic minority groups that have historically been characterized as "wild," "uncivilized," and "unruly" by the white hegemonic powers. The vignette "Monkey Business," which appeared on the inside cover of the January 1958 issue of *Li'l Rascal Twins*, offers a poignant example. The opening splash panel shows the two cousins wearing loincloths and swinging through the house like Tarzan. "Oo-ee-oo-ee-oo! I'm an ape man!" shouts Li'l Genius. "I'm an ape-girl!" adds Li'l Tomboy. In response, Li'l Genius's mother implores them: "Now act dignified."

In the tale "That's Show Business" (*Li'l Rascal Twins*, August 1959), this theme recurs. Li'l Tomboy dresses up as "Dangerous Dot, the Wild Girl," when she and her cousin open their own free circus in their neighborhood. In an image that recalls the long-standing practice, not only at circus sideshows but also at public fairs and even museums of natural history, of displaying racial and ethnic minority groups ostensibly for the edification of white audiences but really for their amusement,[4] a panel depicts the young girl wearing only a leopard-print bodysuit. She is hunched over, so that her knuckles are nearly dragging on the ground. She has an angry look on her face, and one of her legs is roped to a stake. A large bone is lying in the grass in front of her, and she is grunting, "Grrrr Grrrr Grrrrr."[5]

"NASTY POLICEMAN!": CIRCUMVENTING THE COMICS CODE

While passages depicting a young girl engaging in delinquent behaviors such as trespassing on private property and stealing other people's possessions would be daring for a comic book released in any era, they were especially radical given the sociocultural backdrop to Li'l Tomboy: this character debuted just two years after the historic Senate hearings about the pernicious influence of comic books on young people and the implementation of the Comics Code. In one of the most significant episodes in the history of comics in the United States, the psychiatrist Fredric Wertham spearheaded this infamous crusade against what David Hajdu has called "the ten-cent plague." While working with juvenile delinquents during the postwar era, Wertham discovered the widespread prevalence of comic book reading among young people and blamed the violent, lawless, and sexually charged content contained in many of these publications for the rising rate of youth rebelliousness, truancy, and even criminality. As Bradford W. Wright has discussed, in popular genres ranging from the seemingly innocent young romance comics to the grisly tales about crime and criminals, "These stories and many others like them invited young readers into a world where parents, teachers and other adult authority figures were clearly unwelcome. They stood as a challenge to consensus entertainment and marked a major stride towards the autonomy of youth culture" (149). For Wertham, it was clear that "comic books ... flaunted defiance of traditional values and common notions of middle-class morality" (Wright, 156). Consequently, in his view, "They were tangible evidence of a youth culture slipping out of parental control" (149).

Wertham decided that it was time to take action. In a series of articles that appeared in academic journals, national newspapers, and popular magazines beginning in the late 1940s,[6] and then via the publication of his book *Seduction of the Innocent* in 1954, he "called comic books 'the greatest book publishing success in history and the greatest mass influence on children'" (Wright, 96). Wertham "insisted that comic books brought out violent tendencies in maladjusted children and even harmed normal children by fostering low self-esteem, sexual deviance, and disrespect for the rules of society" (158). To illustrate this claim, Wertham pointed to numerous instances in which young people had directly mimicked events that they had seen in comic books: "children who hanged themselves after seeing a hanging in a comic book, kids who jumped off of rooftops as if they were Superman, and boys who hit girls because they saw gangsters hit women in the comic books" (159). As Wertham stated matter-of-factly in *Seduction of the Innocent*, "Comic books and life are connected. A bank robbery is easily translated into the rifling of a candy store" (Wertham, 96).

That said, a child did not need to directly emulate the happenings in a comic book to be negatively influenced by its content. In Wertham's view, "Comic books poisoned the minds of children in a more sinister manner than even these incidents suggested. He argued that comic books amounted to a 'distillation of viciousness' that indoctrinated children against the accepted rules of decency, much as propaganda had done in totalitarian nations" (Wright, 159). While the bulk of Wertham's clinical work was with boys, he insisted that comic books had just as damaging an effect on girls. He "contended that female superheroes like Wonder Woman were 'always a horror type.' Physically powerful, assertive, and cruel, they dominated and tortured men, thus presenting 'an undesirable ideal for girls, being the exact opposite of what girls are supposed to be'" (Wright, 160).

For this reason, Wertham devoted his career to making the public aware of the perniciousness of comics. He "charged that the comic book industry exploited the innocence and insecurities of children for the sake of profit. They gave children a distorted and unhealthy image of the world and impeded their social adjustment" (Wright, 158). Wertham's opinions reached a wide and welcoming audience. As Wright has documented, "*Seduction of the Innocent* became a much talked about book in 1954. *Reader's Digest* and the *Ladies' Home Journal* printed excerpts from it, eliciting uniformly favorable letters which the magazines reprinted in response" (163–64). The publicity that the book received prompted the Senate Subcommittee on Juvenile Crime to call a public hearing to investigate the issue in April 1954. While the hearings considered the role of many different forms of mass media on youth behavior, comic books were its main focus. Not surprisingly, "The key witness at the Senate hearings . . . was Wertham" (Nyberg, ix). The psychiatrist's testimony largely repeated his previous arguments about the dangers of comic books. As Amy Kiste Nyberg has written, Wertham told the subcommittee that "children who were exposed to a steady diet of comic books and other violent material learned that such behavior was socially acceptable and put those lessons into practice" (Nyberg, 97). Indeed, in both *Seduction of the Innocent* and his testimony, Wertham asserted that the rude, rebellious, and disrespectful characters in comic books "normalized delinquent behavior in the minds of children" (97). For this reason, he reiterated "his call . . . [for] national legislation based on the public health ideal that would prohibit the circulation and display of comic books to children under the age of fifteen" (Beaty, 157).

The Senate subcommittee opted not to recommend the passage of any laws concerning the content or consumers of comic books, given their awareness that such statutes would violate First Amendment rights (Nyberg, 79). However, the negative publicity generated by the hearings, coupled with the threat of possible legislative action, prompted the comic book industry to begin regulating itself. In fact, as Nyberg has commented, "The intention of the hearings from the beginning was to force (or frighten) the publishers into adopting a self-regulatory code" (79). To that end, in September 1954, they created the Comics Magazine Association of America (CMAA).[7] The CMAA had a purpose similar to the organization after which it was modeled, the Motion Picture Association of America (MPAA). As Jean-Paul Gabilliet has written, the CMAA was a "trade association whose primary mission was to issue a self-regulatory code that would keep comic books from falling back into the excesses that had led to their public demonization" (42). These standards were known as the Comics Code, and the office in charge of enforcing them was the Comics Code Authority. In the same way that the CMAA was fashioned after the MPAA, the Comics Code was based on the Hays Code that had regulated the motion picture industry since the 1930s. In the words of Nyberg, "The 1954 comics code was a hasty rewrite of the Film Production Code, adopted in the 1930s when the film industry faced similar criticism.... The comics code retained much of the language of [the] film code" (54). Moreover, the process worked in much the same way. As with the MPAA and the Hays Code, publishers would voluntarily join the CMAA and then submit their unpublished comics to the Comics Code Authority for review. This office would evaluate the plot, text, and images to see if the comic conformed to the Code's standards. The document's preamble made the mission of this endeavor clear: "To make a positive contribution to contemporary life, the industry must seek new areas for developing sound, wholesome entertainment" ("The Comics Code"). The Authority identified elements in comic books that violated the Code, flagging those areas in blue pencil for removal or, at least, revision. Conversely, "When a comic book met the office's standards, it received the seal of the Comics Code Authority. Parents would know that this comic book had passed the stringent requirements of [CMAA's] office" (Wright, 173).

In a move that demonstrated the industry's commitment both to the Code and to rehabilitating its public image, the CMAA asked Fredric Wertham to run the Authority office. However, he turned down the position, believing that federal legislation, not industry self-regulation, was needed (Nyberg, 85–100). Instead Judge Charles F. Murphy "was appointed as the 'comics czar'" (Wright, 173). As a longtime legal crusader against juvenile delinquency, a devout Catholic, and a husband and father, Murphy was regarded as "a perfect choice to act as moral guide to the publishers" (Gabilliet, 42).

The Comics Code was ratified in late October 1954. As Wright has commented, "Even by the conservative standards of the time, the code was extremely restrictive. Indeed, spokesmen for the code boasted that it 'imposed restrictions far greater than any in force against competing media'" (173). Moreover, Murphy proved to be a far more strident enforcer of these already stringent standards than the CMAA had imagined or even intended. When the organization appointed Murphy to the position, "Publishers intended for him to ignore all but the most obvious code violations. Instead, Murphy had his staff review the material carefully and demand changes for any infraction of the code, however minor" (Nyberg, 111). The two primary subjects that the Authority office censored were sex and violence. To that end, it especially targeted criminality, lasciviousness, gore, and the use of weapons. David Hajdu, for example, describes one comic that was submitted to the Authority office:

> An emphatic "Bang" appeared above the head of the victim, who groaned "Ugh" as he shot a pistol in the air. In the same story, revised for publication in the January 1956 issue of *Penalty Comics*, the machine was whited out, giving the attacker empty hands. There was no "Bang," no "Ugh," no gun blast. (307)

In another issue, the artist "had to white out the dagger in a villain's hand, while the slash in his victim's chest was permitted to stay, giving the impression that the bad guy had stabbed the other fellow with his fingers" (Hajdu, 309). As Hajdu has discussed, some of the "dangerous weapons" that the Authority office identified as unacceptable were questionable at best. "Dick Ayers was a regular artist on *The Rawhide Kid*, a character named for the bullwhip he always carried; under the Code, the Rawhide Kid lost the whip and took up farming" (309).

The power of Murphy's office was not simply limited to identifying officially forbidden items like sex and violence. The censors at the Authority could, and often did, deem an array of ostensibly innocuous plot points objectionable. As Nyberg has written: "The comics also left a loophole for the code administrator with this catch-all provision: 'All elements of techniques not specifically mentioned herein, but which are contrary to the spirit and intent of the Code, and are considered violations of good taste and decency, shall be prohibited'" (113). This statement "gave the code administrators broad powers of censorship that went far beyond the explicit prohibitions" (13). The Authority office, especially under Charles F. Murphy, used this provision frequently. David Hajdu describes the environment:

> Everyone working in comics during the first years of the Code seemed to come away with a pet story about the Murphy office and its rigid, seemingly arbitrary demands. The artist Russ Heath submitted a drawing of a baseball player at bat, taking a hard, full swing, and he was ordered to remove the sweat from the batter's brow. (Hajdu, 308–9)

As Herb Rogoff, a longtime writer and illustrator for Ziff-Davis Publications, asserted about the CMAA: "They blue-penciled everything. You could find anything objectionable if you're looking for it" (quoted in Hajdu, 309). Offering a powerful indication of the sheer volume of comic book material censored, "In a press conference held in December 1954, Murphy said that the staff had excised more than 5,656 drawings and rejected 126 stories during the short time that the code had been in effect" (Nyberg, 114).

All five of the trained reviewers employed by Murphy's office were women. As Amy Kiste Nyberg has written about this phenomenon:

> It is interesting that comic book censorship was judged to be a woman's task. Certainly the idea was tied in with notions of motherhood and the fact that in postwar America, caring for children was primarily a mother's responsibility. Enforcing standards in children's reading material was an extension of a mother's role. Also, women could be expected to be more stringent in their censorship duties, since women were judged by society to be the weaker sex, more emotional, and thus more easily upset by objectionable content. In addition, the code could be seen as an effort to feminize and domesticate the unruly world populated by comic book characters. In place of violence and rampant sexuality, there would be order and respect. (Nyberg, 115)

No matter how petty or even ridiculous the objections from the Authority office seemed, publishers had little choice but to comply with them. A conversation that Herb Rogoff, an editor at Ziff-Davis, recounted exemplified the situation: "Why don't we just tell them to go foof themselves?" he suggested to his supervisor after receiving yet another absurd request from the CMAA office concerning the content of one of their publications (quoted in Hajdu, 310). Rogoff went on to relay the remainder of their discussion: "'Oh,' the big boss said. 'The printers won't print.... No, they're scared. They won't print without the seal, and the distributors won't ship without the seal, and the newsstands won't sell without the seal. Without the seal, we're out of business'" (quoted in Hajdu, 310).

The methods of the Comics Code Authority may have been draconian, but they were effective. As Bradford W. Wright has discussed, "Although it did not become clear until 1956 the code had indeed 'cleaned up' comic books" (175). In direct response to Fredric Wertham's main concern about the pernicious content of these publications, for example, "Crime and horror comic books were gone entirely, while those that remained were of the most innocuous sort" (176). Some comic book titles did continue to depict crimes, but these acts "were rarely violent, never bloody and always punished with swift and sure legal justice" (175–76).

Unfortunately the Comics Code did more than simply sanitize the subject matter of comics; it also sanitized the literary creativity, artistic ingenuity, and social commentary that these publications contained. For generations, comic books had been a site of youth culture and experimentation. "Generally fashioned for an adolescent audience by creators often little older, comic books have spoken to youths' concerns and sensibilities with a consistency and directness that few, if any, other entertainment media can claim" (Wright, xvi). Comic books were a venue where young people could experience life outside the realm of adult authority. Both the act of reading these publications and the stories that were featured in them provided youngsters a means to escape into imaginative fantasy worlds; encounter new people, viewpoints, and ways of life; and explore otherwise forbidden feelings and subject matters. "Like rock-and-roll, comic books responded to the emergence of adolescents as a discrete market with tastes and preoccupations of its own, sometimes in direct conflict with mores of mainstream adult culture" (Wright, xvi).

The Comics Code Authority, however, with its highly restrictive standards and despotic methods of enforcement, changed the long-standing social role and even psychological purpose that comics had served. These publications were no longer permitted to serve as a venue for youth to explore unconventional issues, encounter taboo subjects, and contemplate alternative sociocultural structures. With the passage of the Comics Code in 1954, comic books were required to reinforce the status quo, not question it. "Reflecting a bland consensus vision of America, comic books now championed without criticism American institutions, authority figures, and middle-class mores. The alternative simply disappeared" (Wright, 176).

Li'l Tomboy embodies a notable exception to this situation. This character, both as she appeared in the comic book series that bears her name and as she was portrayed in the issues of *Li'l Rascal Twins* alongside her cousin Li'l Genius, offers a powerful site of resistance to the seeming uniformity of comic book content during the late 1950s, as well as to the seemingly inviolable power of the Authority. This mischievous character made her debut during the closing months of Charles F. Murphy's appointment as "comics czar." Both the vignette in *Li'l Genius* that announces the impending release of her own comic book series and the first issue of *Li'l Tomboy* itself are dated October 1956, which is the month that Murphy's appointment ended.

As Amy Kiste Nyberg has written, Murphy's departure from the Authority office was neither unexpected nor unwelcome. "His strict enforcement of the code set him against the publishers. His zeal was one reason that his contract was not renewed by the association at the end of two years" (Nyberg, 110). Murphy insisted that the split was mutual. In various articles and interviews, he complained that the CMAA did not provide him with either sufficient financial resources or sufficient staffing to properly carry out his duties. So rather than remain in his post and do a poor job, he resigned his position at the Authority office in October 1956 when his contract expired (130). Mrs. Guy Percy Trulock was hired as the new head of the Comics Code Authority. She was far less zealous than Murphy. Under her leadership, the seemingly arbitrary and even wholly absurd requests like removing the beads of sweat from a character's brow all but disappeared. However, Trulock was anything but a lax administrator. She took her duties as a guardian of the nation's young people seriously, and her office made sure that none of the comic books that appeared on newsstands contained objectionable content. Indeed, as historians like Nyberg have documented, the requirement that all publishers strictly abide by the Comics Code did not ease until 1971, when Marvel Comics engaged in its now-historic act of defiance in a special three-issue story of *Amazing Spider-Man* that, at the request of the US Department of Health, Education, and Welfare, addressed the growing problem of drug addiction (Nyberg, 139–44).

The comic book career of Li'l Tomboy has its origins in Murphy's office and its finale in Trulock's. Although the vignette in *Li'l Genius* that announces the impending release of this new comic book series and the first issue of *Li'l Tomboy* itself are dated the month that Murphy's appointment expired, this detail does not mean that they were spared the persnickety scrutiny of his office. As Wright notes, however, "To prolong the shelf-life of their comic books, publishers have traditionally post-dated their issues by several months. Thus, a comic book with a cover date of March 1941 likely appeared on newsstands just before the end of 1940" (xviii–xix). Of course, before even being released, all stories featuring Li'l Tomboy would have had to be reviewed by Murphy's office. Issues published during the later years of *Li'l Tomboy* and *Li'l Rascal Twins*, of course, would have passed through Trulock and her staff. This mischievous female character embodies a daring challenge to, and ostensibly direct violation of, numerous aspects of the Comics Code, whether it was being enforced by Murphy or Trulock. Li'l Tomboy ridicules police officers, brandishes weapons (including firearms), and engages in an array of bad behavior that is more often rewarded than punished. Not only were these elements permitted to remain in *Li'l Tomboy* and *Li'l Rascal Twins*, but the issues in which they appeared were given the official seal of approval.

• • •

In the same way that *Li'l Tomboy* acknowledged the burgeoning problem of juvenile delinquency, it was equally aware of the Comics Code Authority—and realized that its readers would be aware of it as well. Many issues of both *Li'l Tomboy* and *Li'l Rascal Twins* not only bore the well-known emblem "Approved by the Comics Code Authority" but included the following statement at the top of the opening page:

> This seal of approval appears only on comic magazines which have been carefully reviewed prior to publication by the Comics Code Authority and found to have met the highest standards of morality and good taste required by the Code. The Code Authority operates apart from any individual publisher and exercises independent judgment with respect to Code-compliance. A comic magazine bearing its seal is your assurance of good reading and pictorial matter.

Although clearly addressed to parents more than children, the statement calls attention to the fact that the issue contains content that is decent, wholesome, and even uplifting. As the announcement asserts, the seal indicates that the publication meets "the highest standards of morality and good taste." Moreover, to give added weight to these remarks, whenever they appeared in an issue, they were also signed by the executive editor of Charlton Publications.

While Charlton wanted the parents of its readership to know that issues of *Li'l Tomboy* and *Li'l Rascal Twins* had met the stringent standards of the Comics Code Authority, they simultaneously wished to give the impression to their juvenile audience that their stories were anything but innocuous. Instead, they contained daring, dangerous, and even forbidden content that had been subjected to the Authority's infamous blue pencil. In a variety of vignettes, speech bubbles that are being uttered by angry or exasperated adults and which presumably contain curse words have been replaced with a rectangular black box that says "CENSORED" (fig. 5.4). This feature, in fact, appears in the first full-length story of the first issue of *Li'l Tomboy*. After the title character has zapped a male doctor with a hand buzzer, flattened him with a wrestling move, and used his CPR dummy for tackling

Figure 5.4. Panel from "Menu," *Li'l Tomboy*, January 1958. Charlton Publications. Photograph by Michelle Ann Abate. From the collection of Michelle Ann Abate.

practice, he exclaims in frustration: "Why you little CENSORED." Of course, this element is not the actual hand of the Code made visible in the comic. Rather, it indicates that the character used a profane word and the writers replaced it with "CENSORED." Similar passages appear in a variety of other stories from both the *Li'l Tomboy* series and the *Li'l Rascal Twins* series. These "CENSORED" boxes gave juvenile readers the thrilling impression that the comic book that they were reading was much more subversive than adults, who saw the Authority seal but likely did not examine all the issue's content, realized.

In spite of such attempts to make issues of *Li'l Tomboy* and *Li'l Rascal Twins* appear as though they strictly conformed with the Comics Code, numerous tales from each series contain elements that diverge from and even openly defy these standards. First, and perhaps most noticeably, is the graphic design for the title to the *Li'l Tomboy* comic. In what forms both an eye-catching visual and an accurate representation of the title character's personality, the middle letter in the word "Li'l" is formed not by a lowercase *i* but by a stick of dynamite. Moreover, in some issues, the fuse has been lit: sparks can be seen emanating from the tip. Given that some postwar comics were being chastised by the CMAA for including firearms, it is difficult to imagine how this feature either escaped the notice of the Authority's censors or was met with their approval. At best, the dynamite suggests socially destructive mayhem; at worst, it encourages violent youth insurrection. Of course, anxiety over what one prominent psychiatrist called "the mutiny of the young" during the 1950s (Lindner, "Mutiny," 3) had prompted Fredric Wertham's campaign against the "ten-cent plague" and the regulation of the comic book industry via the Code in the first place.

Comics featuring Li'l Tomboy violate other taboos of the Comics Authority. Whereas numerous other publications were forbidden from presenting weapons of any kind, especially guns, the series often featured firearms. The tale "Reel Robbery," from the November 1958 issue of *Li'l Rascal Twins*, for example, depicts a seedy gang of criminals pretending to film a movie at a local bank: they dress up as security guards and then hold the tellers up at gunpoint. Similarly, in the story "Ghost in the House" (*Li'l Tomboy*, October 1959), Li'l Tomboy wanders into an abandoned house that is being used as a hideout for a husband-and-wife crime team. Not only does the man have a revolver, but at several points he threatens to discharge it to defend himself. Firearms assume an even more vivid presence in the tale "Sign Happy" (*Li'l Tomboy*, August 1959). While her parents are away one afternoon, Li'l Tomboy decides to make some extra money by renting out rooms in the house to tourists. Her first guests are two crooks, and her second set of patrons is a wealthy older couple. As one might expect, the two con men quickly rob the affluent wife, holding both the woman and Li'l Tomboy at gunpoint. In two separate panels, readers see the title character and the elderly lady with their arms up in the air and a frightened look on their faces. Finally, and most astoundingly, given the Comics Code's previous zero-tolerance policy about firearms, in the tale "All Bankers Beware," Li'l Tomboy herself brandishes a gun. In the January 1958 issue of *Li'l Tomboy*, the title character inadvertently walks into a bank during an armed robbery. The young girl's disruptive behavior quickly foils the crime. At one point, she mischievously sticks out her foot and trips one of the criminals. He drops his weapon, and Li'l Tomboy picks it up, detaining the criminals at gunpoint and preventing them from running away until the police arrive. In a passage that seems shocking when viewed in dialogue with the Code's generally timid tastes, a panel shows the five-year-old girl confidently pointing the firearm at the two robbers. She has a look of fierce determination on her face, and she informs the crooks when they remark that they might be able to get away: "No, you're not . . . **I caught your guns!**" (emphasis in original) (fig. 5.5).

Figure 5.5. Panel from "All Bankers Beware," *Li'l Tomboy*, January 1958. Charlton Publications. Photograph by Michelle Ann Abate. From the collection of Michelle Ann Abate.

Closely connected to the prohibition against "excessive and unnecessary knife and gun play" ("The Comics Code") were the Code's equally strict guidelines regarding the portrayal of crime and criminals. The first point in Part A of the General Standards states: "Crimes shall never be presented in such a way as to create sympathy for the criminal, to promote the distrust of the forces of law and justice, or to inspire others with a desire to imitate criminals." This statement was far from the only remark on the subject. Four additional points in Part A discuss the portrayal of criminality. The second point, for example, asserts: "No comics shall explicitly present the unique details and methods of a crime." Similarly, the fourth point decrees: "If crime is depicted it shall be as a sordid and unpleasant unactivity." On a related note, the fifth point offers the following admonition: "Criminals shall not be presented so as to be rendered glamorous or to occupy a position which creates the desire for emulation." Finally, and somewhat redundantly, the sixth point asserts: "In every instance good shall triumph over evil and the criminal punished for his misdeeds."

Li'l Tomboy is involved in situations that repeatedly violate these standards. In the story "Roped" (*Li'l Rascal Twins*, November 1958), for example, Li'l Tomboy and her cousin Li'l Genius interfere with the work of a police detective and, in so doing, allow a criminal to get away. The story begins by showing the two cousins having fun playing with a lasso. To test their roping skills, Li'l Tomboy wants to see "if we can lasso a *desperado!*" (emphasis in original). Almost immediately, the pair witnesses what appears to be an armed robbery: a man in a brown suit is pointing a gun at another man in a blue suit; the latter figure has a frightened look on his face, and his arms are raised in surrender above his head. Seeing what they believe is a crime in progress, Li'l Tomboy and Li'l Genius attempt to stop it: they sneak behind a fence, lasso the man with the gun, and tie him to a sturdy tree. When the duo comes around the fence to view their handiwork, the man in the brown suit exclaims: "I'm a **detective** . . . I was searching that guy. **He's** a crook! Let me down!" (emphasis in original). Meanwhile the man in the blue suit can be seen in silhouette in the background, running away down the street. Of course, upon learning that the man in the brown suit is a detective, Li'l Tomboy and Li'l Genius untie him. However, in marked contrast to the Code's insistence that "in every instance good shall triumph over evil and the criminal punished for his misdeeds," they are never punished for their interference in a police investigation. On the contrary, the final panel of the comic presents a very different outcome. Li'l Genius is annoyed that the officer didn't compliment them on either their roping skills or their attempt to be good Samaritans: "You'd have thought he'd praise us for trying!" Li'l Tomboy is even more indignant, grousing, "Yeah . . . and the language he used! I'm going to tell the police chief about **him!**" (emphasis in original) (fig. 5.6).

Numerous other stories depict Li'l Tomboy not only engaging in bad behavior—some of it criminal in nature—but also avoiding punishment. On the contrary, her antics are often rewarded. In the tale "Office Pest" (*Li'l Tomboy*, March 1958), the young girl wreaks havoc at her father's place of business when she visits him for the day: first Li'l Tomboy smashes the boss in the face with the carriage of a typewriter; then she activates one of the indoor sprinklers, soaking everything in the room; afterward she turns on a fan to help dry the place out and promptly blows a stack of important papers around the room; next she hits an important client in the head with the drawer of a filing cabinet; and finally she knocks down the same potential customer while sliding down the banister. Rather than ruining the company's business that day because of her poor behavior, her actions serve as a boon to their sales. "I'm glad to buy . . . vitamins from you! I can see how lively they make your daughter!" the client happily informs Li'l Tomboy's father.

Figure 5.6. Panel from "Roped," *Li'l Rascal Twins*, November 1958. Charlton Publications. Photograph by Michelle Ann Abate. From the collection of Michelle Ann Abate.

The story "Let Us into the Ballgame" (*Li'l Rascal Twins*, November 1957), which I discussed earlier, takes this phenomenon even further. Not only are Li'l Tomboy and Li'l Genius not punished by any adults for taking the baseball from the sewer worker who is its rightful owner, but their actions are rewarded: the stolen ball allows the kids to meet their favorite ballplayer, Home Run Dolan, who slugged the big hit. Moreover, he gives them a season pass to the ballpark for returning the memento to him.

In the same way that the Comics Code insisted that crime and criminals be presented in a negative light, it was, unsurprisingly, equally adamant that agents of law and order were presented in a respectful manner. The third point in Part A of the General Standards of the Code states: "Policemen, judges, government officials, and respected institutions shall never be presented in such a way as to create disrespect for established authority." As before, *Li'l Tomboy* repeatedly violates this standard. On numerous occasions,

Figure 5.7. Panel from "At the Zoo," *Li'l Tomboy*, November 1957. Charlton Publications. Photograph by Michelle Ann Abate. From the collection of Michelle Ann Abate.

the title character's sass and insolence are directed not merely at barbers and grocery store managers but at police officers. While riding in the car with her father in the story "At the Zoo" (*Li'l Tomboy*, November 1957), she shouts from the window to a plump motorcycle cop, "Move over fatso!" (fig. 5.7). Admittedly, Li'l Tomboy, or more accurately her father, is punished for this remark. The officer hears her comment, is predictably shocked and offended, and pursues their vehicle. "Hey, Pop! Fatso is following us!" she informs her father. While the officer writes out the ticket, he tells Li'l Tomboy's dad: "This will teach you to discipline that pest!" Punishment is doled out in this story, but it is the father, not the daughter, who is reprimanded for this insolence.

Li'l Tomboy's lack of respect for the police is even more evident in "Driving Lesson." Appearing in the September 1957 issue of *Li'l Tomboy*, the tale depicts Li'l Tomboy's father attempting to teach her mother how to drive. Predictably, everything goes wrong: her mother changes lanes erratically, drives too fast, and narrowly misses running down a pedestrian. When a traffic cop, whom she also nearly hits, pulls her over, Li'l Tomboy unleashes a string of insults in defense of her parents. When the officer threatens to "throw the book at" her father for letting a student driver out in heavy traffic, Li'l Tomboy vows, "I'll punch you in your big fat nose!" Then, while

Figure 5.8. Panel from "Driving Lesson," *Li'l Tomboy*, September 1957. Charlton Publications. Photograph by Michelle Ann Abate. From the collection of Michelle Ann Abate.

the policeman writes out citations for "reckless driving, no license, [and] exceeding speed limit," Li'l Tomboy points at him from the sidewalk, jumps up and down, and shouts: "Nasty Policeman!" Finally, when the cop reminds Li'l Tomboy's father that he is the one who needs to drive the car home, she retorts, "Aw, go blow your whistle!" (fig. 5.8). Although her father is embarrassed and the officer is offended by these comments, the young girl is not punished for them. The police officer tells her parents, "I'd like to have that kid of yours just for one day!" but he does not act on this threat. Likewise, if Li'l Tomboy's parents punish her for her insolence, this event is not shown to readers.

Li'l Tomboy likewise violates other legitimate, but arguably less serious, aspects of the Comics Code. As Nyberg has discussed, "The film code forbade the use of obscenity and profanity. The comics code went one step further, adding a warning about the use of slang, since it was felt that good grammar should be used in comic books in order to promote the medium's educational value" (113). Indeed, Part C of the General Standards asserted, "Although slang and colloquialisms are acceptable, excessive use should be discouraged and, wherever possible, good grammar should be employed." Although Li'l Tomboy hails from a solidly middle-class family who reside in a comfortable suburban neighborhood, she frequently uses working-class speech patterns. In "The Hair-Raiser" (*Li'l Tomboy*, January 1957), for example, she howls at the barber who is about to cut her hair: "I don't wanna lose my beootiful black locks!" In "Can't Tell a Book by Its Cover" (*Li'l Tomboy*, September 1957), she utters statements such as "Aw, wot fun is that!" "I want sum books with pitchers!" and "Don't be 'fraid Mom, I'll pertect ya!" Finally, and most vividly, is the story "First Movie." Appearing in the March 1957 issue of *Li'l Tomboy* and documenting the title character's trip to see a movie in a theater for the first time, the story is filled with slang terms, grammatical constructions, and pronunciations that recount stereotypical notions of working-class speech patterns. When her father delights in finally finding a parking spot, for example, Li'l Tomboy corrects him: "You didn't find it, Pop.... It wiz there alla time!" Similarly, when her dad asks the lady at the ticket booth, "May I have two big and one small, please?" Li'l Tomboy interjects: "Wotta ya askin' permission for, Pop. You're payin' for 'em!" Likewise, when her father hands the tickets to the usher, she says, "Hey Pop, ya just bought 'em, wotta ya givin' 'em away for?" As they pass the concession stand, Li'l Tomboy begs, "Kin I have sumthin, Pop?" Then, as she is selecting her candies and treats, she tells the attendant: "I'll have som' o' those, nd som' o' those, 'n ..." Such remarks continue after they get inside the theater. "Xcuse me too!" she says while climbing over a man to her seat, and "I don't like this pitcher. I wanna see Howdy Doody," soon after the movie starts.

• • •

The way in which the comics featuring Li'l Tomboy were able to elude the objections of the CMAA office offers a compelling window onto popular perceptions about age, race, and gender in the postwar period. Li'l Tomboy not only belongs to, but is being made and marketed for, a demographic that was commonly seen as existing outside the realm of sociocultural suspicion during the 1950s: young, white, middle-class girls in early elementary school. I would contend that this mischievous figure and, by extension, her creators used these prevailing attitudes to their advantage. Postwar beliefs that middle-class preadolescent white girls were not participants in the era's youth rebellion allowed this character and the comic in which she appeared to engage in—as well as get away with—a surprising amount of mischievous behavior. In fact, the vignette from the October 1956 issue of *Li'l Genius* that introduces Li'l Tomboy and announces the impending release of her own comic book series nods in this direction. When Li'l Genius's mother informs her son that his cousin will be coming for a visit, she admonishes him "to act a li'l gentleman." "Gee, Mom, the way ya talk, someone would think I'm a mean little boy!" Li'l Genius grumbles, hurt and offended by her presumption of his bad behavior.

From the moment the duo meet, however, it is Li'l Tomboy, and not Li'l Genius, who possesses a powerful penchant for mischief. Moreover, this rascally female figure uses popular perceptions that little boys, not little girls, are the ones who are naughty to give license to her behavior and, more importantly, to escape being punished for it. For example, when Li'l Tomboy picks up a rock and contemplates throwing it through a window, Li'l Genius implores, "Don't, I'll get blamed for it!" She replies, "Gee, Ollie, I didn't think of that," and promptly pitches the rock through the plate glass. As such passages indicate, rather than regarding being both young and a girl as drawbacks that restrict her actions and her identity, Li'l Tomboy—and, of course, the creators at Charlton Publications—recognized that these aspects could be used to her advantage. Being a five-year-old white girl opened up loopholes both in the rules about expected social conduct and in the rules of the Comics Code. Li'l Tomboy did not just capitalize on those loopholes to forge her own unique identity; she used them to circumvent these entire sociocultural institutions.

Of course, the aesthetic style in which Li'l Tomboy is rendered contributes to this phenomenon. Drawn by the cartoonist Frank Johnson, Li'l Tomboy is presented in a cartoonish style that visually links her with comics that were seen as culturally innocuous. These titles included *Dennis the Menace* (1951–present), *Archie* (1942–present), and *Richie Rich* (1960–91). The main characters in these titles might get into scrapes, but they did not engage in any truly bad behavior that would be seen as violating the Comics Code. Given both their aesthetic depiction and their personal conduct, figures like Dennis the Menace and Li'l Tomboy can be placed in dialogue with what Gary Cross has termed the "mischievously cute" child that emerged during the early twentieth century (43–44). As Cross explains about this new cultural trope, "The cute child is naturally a little naughty but always nice, radiating not a naïve look of youthful beauty but energy, spunk, and friskiness" (44). For example, "The cute [child] can steal cookies from the cookie jar but do it without malice or greed" (44). Instead, the actions of these children are seen as adorably naughty or charmingly impish. In this way, "Cuteness takes both the child and the adult to the edge of acceptable, even across the line of self-control, to a playful, unserious anarchic moment" (44). Li'l Tomboy exemplifies this condition. She embodies a powerful case study of how traits that were commonly seen as disempowering liabilities during the 1950s could actually be used as advantageous benefits. Li'l Tomboy's status as an elementary-aged feminine white girl from a middle-class family who is rendered in a highly cartoonish style does not circumscribe her behavior; instead, these elements allow her to circumvent restrictions.

"AINTCHA GLAD I CAME?": RETHINKING COMIC BOOKS DURING THE SILVER AGE

The impact that the creation of the CMAA and the implementation of the Comics Code had on the comic book industry cannot be overstated. As David Hajdu has documented, "Between 1954 and 1956, more than half the comic books on the newsstands disappeared; the number of titles published in the United States dropped from about 650 to some 250" (326). Not surprisingly, given the tremendous restrictions that the Authority imposed on plot, artwork, and dialogue, many companies decided to pull out of the comics business. A number of publishers who opted to remain went bankrupt. "Between 1954 and 1956, eighteen publishers exited the field, and none entered" (Wright, 179).[8]

Even for the publishers that managed to survive, the situation was grim. EC Comics, which had previously dominated the field, now limped along: "By the end of 1955, when EC discontinued all of its comics (retaining only *Mad*), five other publishers went out of business" (Hajdu, 326). The industry had enjoyed steady growth and expansion for decades, but the creation of the CMAA marked the end of comics' Golden Age. "Never again would the comic book industry enjoy the kind of mass circulation and readership that it had commanded before the code" (Wright, 179).

That said, the creation of the Comics Code did not spell financial disaster for everyone. As Wright has discussed, a handful of "established publishers who had rarely looked outside that market anyway remained unaffected by the code, and some, no doubt, welcomed the opportunity to purge the glutted industry" (181). Dell Publications, for example, formed a poignant example. Holding the comic book licensing rights to characters like Mickey Mouse, Porky Pig, Donald Duck, and Bugs Bunny, the company's publications had never contained the "sadistic torture," "sexy, wanton images," and "vulgar and obscene language" that had prompted Wertham's crusade and were the main target of the Comics Code (Wright, 103). For this reason, Dell never joined the CMAA, and its publications were largely unaffected by the Authority office's rules and regulations.

For the majority of comic book companies, however, continuing to do business under the Code necessitated implementing major editorial shifts. For most companies, this process translated into discontinuing all titles aimed at teenagers and focusing instead on the "kiddie market" of readers in early elementary school. In the words of Wright, "The code essentially dictated that comic books ought to be produced only for young children" (181). The story of Harvey Publications provides a representative example. After the enactment of the Code, the company "dropped its horror titles and introduced a number of characters aimed at a very young readership, including Baby Huey, Little Dot, Hot Stuff, Casper, and Richie Rich" (Nyberg, 127).

Charlton is another publisher commonly cited as having found ways to maintain profitability under the Code. As Jean-Paul Gabilliet has written, "Charlton was a jack-of-all-trades of comic books. This family-owned publishing house, for which comics were just one type of periodical amongst all others, was probably the most visible publisher of illustrated magazines with Dell and DC during the second half of the twentieth century" (51). Charlton's secret to commercial success was multifold. The company "had survived the recession of the late 1950s partly because it owned and operated its own distribution system and published other entertainment magazines in addition to comics" (Wright, 194). In fact, while other comic book publishers were scaling back their efforts under the Code, Charlton was expanding its offerings. "In the mid-to-late 1950s, as other publishers went out of business or curtailed their production," Randy Duncan has written, "Charlton aggressively recruited talent and acquired titles, mostly romance, Western and horror from a number of defunct publishers, including Fawcett Publications, Superior Comics and Joe Simon and Jack Kirby's Crestwood/Mainline Comics" (94). Through this combination of controlling its own distribution and being highly selective about the type of comics that it offered, the company was able to weather even the grimmest periods of the Code. "Charlton never won an especially large or lasting audience, but it enjoyed consistent, if modest, sales and carved out a niche for itself in nonsuperhero genres like romance, sci-fi, and, especially, war comics" (Wright, 194).

Remembering and recouping the character of Li'l Tomboy changes the portrait both of Charlton Publications and of the comic book industry in the years directly following the implementation of the Code. For nearly fifty years, the widespread belief among comic book historians has been that the Authority "confined comic books to a supervised, puerile level and enforced the very kind of conformity that millions of young people were beginning to reject" (Wright, 179). Indeed, Wright claimed that "by forbidding challenges to established authority and many varieties of conflict, the code ran counter to emerging trends in youth culture at a time when the market for young consumers had never been greater or the competition more intense" (181). As a result, Wright and other scholars claim that comics ceased to be a vehicle for cultural iconoclasm, social subversion, and political dissent. Instead, after 1954, they became "a strictly preadolescent pastime at best or an outmoded nostalgic curiosity at worst" (179).

Charlton Publications has commonly been viewed in a similar manner. The company has long been regarded as a conventional and conservative one that released equally conventional and conservative comic books that did not question the status quo. In their history of Charlton, for example, Jon B. Cooke and Christopher Irving commented that "the comics output [at the company in the late 1950s] settled down to pretty standard Comics Code–approved fare of genre material—romance, war, westerns, kiddie, science-fiction" (3–4).

Li'l Tomboy challenges this assessment. When the company debuted this mischievous character in October 1956, it made a bold departure from its previous publishing fare; even more significantly, it also successfully resisted and circumvented the CMAA. Li'l Tomboy did far more than merely defy the era's codes of conventional social conduct and notions about proper female decorum. This character defied the Comics Code itself. From her repeated insolence to police officers and engagement in petty crimes to the stick of dynamite in her name emblazoned across every cover and the fact that her bad behavior was rarely punished and usually rewarded, Li'l Tomboy was hardly "pretty standard Comics Code–approved fare."

The iconoclastic nature of *Li'l Tomboy* is even more radical when the title is placed back within the context of its own publication history. The first issue of this new comic book series is not labeled as no. 1; instead it is no. 92. Before becoming *Li'l Tomboy*, the series had been Fawcett's *Funny Animals*. Charlton acquired *Funny Animals* when it bought up a number of Fawcett's comic book properties in 1954 (Gabilliet, 49). More than simply the title of this specific publication, "funny animals" was actually the name for an entire type or category of comic book. As Wright has written, funny animal comics were one of the most popular comic book genres among elementary-aged children of both sexes, and they were also the most innocuous. As the name implies, funny animal comics featured mischievous mice, curious cats, and all manner of barnyard hijinks. Fawcett's *Funny Animals* adhered to this formula. The comic featured stories about talking pigs, goofy dogs, and a myriad of other silly creatures.

Charlton acquired *Funny Animals* in the same year that the CMAA was created. Rather than continuing to publish this already established and clearly Code-friendly comic, the company made the unexpected and far more risky decision to replace it with *Li'l Tomboy*. The new series was targeted not to a general elementary-aged audience but to the slightly more niche one of elementary-aged girls. In a nod to the comic's previous readership, though, it still included an occasional "funny animal" story interspersed with those featuring the title character. That said, *Li'l Tomboy* was also radically different. Whereas *Funny Animals* was devoid of any socially objectionable plotlines or culturally iconoclastic scenarios, the premise for this new character was predicated on challenging social norms and breaking established conventions.

In the October 1956 issue of *Li'l Genius* where Li'l Tomboy makes her debut, she greets her cousin by squirting him in the face with a water gun. "Hi Ollie, ainchta glad I came?" she says sassily as he stands there dripping. While Li'l Genius may not have been too thrilled with the arrival of his cousin on that sunny autumn afternoon, young female readers then and cultural critics now are delighted that Li'l Tomboy appeared on the scene. This feisty female figure embodies an important aspect of the forms of social resistance that existed during the 1950s, of the history of Charlton Publications, and of the nature of comic books during the Silver Age.

Epilogue

From Li'l to Big
The Legacy of Classic American Comics Starring Girls

• •

In the apt words of Jerry Robinson, "The world of children has been one of the most enduring themes in the comics" (94). The commercial history of the art form in the United States begins with a serial that featured a young boy as its central character. The Sunday supplement *Hogan's Alley* debuted in the *New York World* in 1895. Created by Richard F. Outcault, the comic contained a large cast of ragamuffin kids living in an urban tenement, but it also had a clear protagonist: a mischievous little imp named Mickey Dugan—but better known by his nickname "the Yellow Kid." As Mary Wood has said of this figure, "With his jug ears, two buck teeth, beady blue eyes, and yellow nightdress, the Yellow Kid hardly looks like an icon for comic and commercial success, but that's exactly what he became in late nineteenth-century America" (para. 1).

The impact that *Hogan's Alley* in general and the Yellow Kid in particular had not simply on American comics but on American society as a whole is difficult to overestimate. Although Outcault's strip ran for only three years, it would shape national print, popular, and material culture for generations. In the words of Wood, "The Yellow Kid was a sensation: he inspired theater and vaudeville shows across the country and was used to sell products directly licensed by Outcault and even used to attract shoppers to stores" (para. 2). The Yellow Kid appeared on "billboards, buttons, cigarette packs, cigars, cracker tins, ladies' fans, matchbooks, postcards, chewing gum cards, toys, whiskey and many other products" (Wallace). For this reason, *Hogan's Alley* is commonly credited "with being the first comic strip," and the Yellow Kid is identified as "the first commercial success of a comic strip character" (Robinson, 18, 21).

In the years that followed, a variety of subsequent comics followed in the aesthetic, literary, and cultural footsteps of *Hogan's Alley*. These serials adopted many of the formalist elements employed by Outcault, which would quickly come to be seen as hallmarks of the genre. For example, such comics included "a narrative told in a sequence of pictures, a continuing cast of characters, [and] the inclusion of dialogue and/or text within the picture frame" (Horn, *100 Years*, 15). In addition, they routinely engaged with sociopolitical issues in a humorous or satiric way (Inge, 5) and sought to capitalize on licensing, branding, and merchandising opportunities (Gordon, 37–58). Finally, and most importantly for the purposes of this discussion, they also featured a young boy as their protagonist. In examples such as Rudolph Dirks's *The Katzenjammer Kids* (1897–present),[1] Winsor McCay's *Little Nemo in Slumberland* (1905–14; 1924–26),[2] and Lyonel Feininger's *The Kin-der-Kids* (1906–7), these strips reflected the male-dominated nature of American culture during this period by showcasing central characters who were young boys. Although the precise age of the youngsters was not always specified, they were—akin to the Yellow Kid—preadolescent. Stephen Becker, for example, has made the following observation about McCay's protagonist: "Nemo himself was a tousle-haired boy somewhere between six and eight" (22). Similar comments could be made about Hans and Fritz of *The Katzenjammer Kids*, as well as about Strenuous Teddy and Pie-Mouth of *The Kin-der-Kids*. Indeed, while the stars of Feininger's strip have somewhat adultlike heads, which are disproportionately large for their bodies and also feature ample forehead wrinkles, they are all the size of toddlers.

Of course, Outcault himself would go on to pen another hugely influential comic strip that starred a young boy: *Buster Brown* (1902–23).[3] As Richard Marshall has written, the Yellow Kid and "Buster Brown were brothers under the skin. Buster was more than mischievous; he was a congenital prankster. Buster wrecked his parents' ballroom, terrorized the help, sabotaged dinners, frightened elderly neighbors, and reveled in every moment of scheming and execution" (quoted in Goulart, 13–14). In the same way that Buster Brown mirrored Outcault's earlier protagonist, he also rivaled the Yellow Kid in terms of success. The comic inspired a myriad of imitation characters, including Perry Winkle from the strip *Winnie Winkle* (1920–96) and the eponymous figure in the *Bobby Bumps* animated shorts (1915–25). In addition, as a licensed property, "Buster Brown proved even more lucrative than the Yellow Kid. There were stage shows and books, and Buster's image was used to sell clothes, including the 'rich, stylish' Buster Brown Suit, candy, bread, postcards, coffee, games, rugs, and Christmas cards" (Goulart, 15). Of all these ventures, "the longest lasting licensing enterprise was the Buster Brown Shoe Co. A type of little girls' shoe is still called Mary Janes because of Buster's girlfriend" (15). For this reason, Ian Gordon has argued, "'Buster Brown' cannot be understood solely as a comic strip. All of his incarnations contributed to the makeup of his character, and each reinforced or advertised the others" (26).

The period directly following the release of *Buster Brown* is commonly identified as the first golden era of comic strips starring children. Stephen Becker, Brian Walker, and Jerry Robinson have all discussed how, beginning in the 1910s and extending through the 1920s, "Everyday life, viewed through the eyes of comic strip kids, was another thematic preoccupation on the funnies page" (Walker, *Comics*, 166). Many of the most commercially successful comics from this era featured young people. Some of these strips, such as Gene Byrnes's *Reg'lar Fellers* (1918–49), Merrill Blosser's *Freckles and His Friends* (1915–73), and Ad Carter's *Just Kids* (1923–56), fell into the category of what Robinson terms "kid gangs" (96). These comics featured an ensemble cast of child characters, always from the same neighborhood and often living on the same street. Other strips, such as James Swinnerton's *Little Jimmy* (1904–58), C. M. Payne's *S'matter Pop?* (1911–40),[4] and Percy Crosby's *Skippy* (1925–45), could more accurately be categorized under Brian Walker's label of "child stars" (*Comics*, 166). While these comics routinely featured a collective of kids, they also had a clear protagonist. Whatever the specific classification for these comics, they collectively affirmed Becker's observation that "kids, particularly, proliferated" in the funny pages during the 1910s and 1920s (70).

This vibrant genre of "kids' comics" during the opening decades of the twentieth century has largely been synonymous with "boys' comics." While the basic premise and specific plots of strips like *Reg'lar Fellers*, *Just Kids*, or *Skippy* varied, they all had one trait in common: they featured boys as their central characters.[5] In *The Funnies: 100 Years of American Comic Strips*, Ron Goulart mentions a bevy of additional strips from the 1910s and 1920s that featured kids as protagonists. Examples range from Gene Carr's *Chub's Big Brother* (1918–19), A. C. Fera's *Just Boy* (later titled *Elmer*, 1914–56), and Jack Farr's *Bringing Up Bill* (1919–30) to Tom McNamara's *Us Boys* (1910–28), Al Zere's *Buttons and Fatty* (1909–34), and Walter Bishop's *Muggs and Skeeter* (1928–74) (Goulart, 45–69).[6] Echoing the title of McNamara's strip, however, all these comics focus on "us boys."

Remembering and recouping the tradition of Funny Girls complicates such viewpoints. While young male protagonists like Buster Brown, Little Jimmy, and Skippy played an instrumental role in popularizing comics in the United States, elementary-aged girls constituted important protagonists as well. As my discussion in the previous chapters demonstrates, characters like

Little Orphan Annie, Little Lulu, and Nancy were among the most successful comics personalities of their day. The popularity of these preadolescent girls, in fact, equaled if not exceeded that of their male counterparts. In so doing, they played a significant role in establishing comics as a leading mode of mass entertainment in the United States while also influencing the genre from a cultural, commercial, and aesthetic standpoint. The impact of Little Lulu, Little Orphan Annie, and Nancy still reverberates through American comics, shaping the plots, characters, and visual appearances of the medium nearly a century later. Mark Newgarden and Paul Karasik, for example, in their classic essay "How to Read Nancy," detail the strategic layout and restrained aesthetic that were the hallmarks of Bushmiller's work: "His gags have the abstract feel of math and *Nancy* was, in fact, a mini-algebraic equation masquerading as a comic strip for close to 50 years" (100). Bushmiller's minimalist style became a signature feature of *Nancy*, and its influence can be seen in a variety of subsequent strips, from Charles Schulz's *Peanuts* (1950–2000) to Jim Davis's *Garfield* (1978–present).

Of course, the young female protagonists showcased in the previous chapters were not the only ones during this era to enjoy commercial success. On the contrary, Little Lulu, Little Orphan Annie, and Nancy were joined by a bevy of additional strips that enjoyed long runs, achieved national notoriety, and starred girl characters. *Little Mary Mixup* (1918–57), *Little Annie Rooney* (1927–66), *The Adventures of Patsy* (1935–55), and *Little Iodine* (1943–83) were tremendously popular. *Little Mary Mixup*, for example, was syndicated soon after its debut in 1917.[7] Although the comic originated as a gag-a-day strip, it soon shifted to an adventure serial. To allow Mary to engage in more dangerous and exciting adventures, her age changed from nine—when the strip began—to the early teens. Over the years, the "spunky auburn-haired heroine [was] mixed up with kidnappings, treasure hunts, and other staples of melodrama" (Goulart, 117–18). During World War II, Mary even got a chance to chase Nazis. As Ron Goulart notes, however, the Sunday strip usually offered a respite from her current adventure by presenting a lighthearted gag (117–18).

Whether Little Mary Mixup was engaging in a silly prank or enmeshed in an intense plot, readers followed her exploits. The comic was hugely popular; it appeared in newspapers around the country for nearly four decades. Additionally, as Don Markstein writes, the strip was "featured in a couple of *Big Little Books*"—which were collections of popular comics published by Whitman Publishing Company—in the early 1930s (Markstein, "Little Mary Mixup," para. 3). In 1940, United Feature Syndicate released a book-length collection of the strips. *Little Mary Mixup* also appeared in the new medium of comic books. In April 1938 the strip was printed in the inaugural volume of *Comics on Parade* (para. 5). In the years to come, it would appear in twenty other issues; in addition, Mary would be featured in forty-one issues of *Tip Top Comics* ("Little Mary Mixup"). Finally, in January 1939, Little Mary Mixup got her own stand-alone comic book series. As the teaser on the cover to the second volume touted, the issue featured "sixty-four pages in full color." While the *Little Mary Mixup* comic book series was short-lived—encompassing just a handful of issues—the newspaper strip ran until 1956, ending only when the cartoonist R. M. Brinkerhoff retired.

Little Annie Rooney was equally popular. Admittedly, when the strip debuted on January 10, 1927, it was a shameless imitation of Harold Gray's *Little Orphan Annie*.[8] Markstein has detailed the numerous areas of overlap between the two. For instance, "Orphan Annie had a constant companion, a dog named Sandy. Annie Rooney's constant companion was a dog named Zero" (Markstein, "Little Annie Rooney," para. 3). Likewise, "Orphan Annie had a characteristic expression, 'Leapin' Lizards!' Annie Rooney's characteristic expression was 'Gloriosky!'" (para. 3). Finally, "Orphan Annie escaped from an orphanage run by the cruel Miss Hannigan [sic]. Annie Rooney's cruel but legal guardian, whom she was constantly on the lam from, was named Miss Meany" (para. 3). Nevertheless, the two characters were not identical. As Richard Beland has noted, "You could tell them apart by their hair: Annie Rooney had a fashionable bob, and Orphan Annie had a tangled mess" (Beland, "Little Annie Rooney," para. 4).[9]

Little Annie Rooney may not have had the most innovative origins, but the strip attained success in its own right. The comic, which was drawn by a handful of different cartoonists over its life span, ran for nearly four decades. Moreover, a variety of strips were reprinted over the years. For example, "*Little Annie Rooney* was the subject of a couple of *Big Little Books*, and publisher David McKay . . . did a slim reprint volume in 1935" (Markstein, "Little Annie Rooney," para. 5). Additionally, the title appeared in several comic books from 1938 to 1948, such as *Feature Book* and *King Comics*, and selected strips were republished by "St. John . . . in its annual (1948–50) *Treasury of Comics*, a 500-page compilation that included *Abbie & Slats*, *Casper the Friendly Ghost* and many others" (para. 5). *Little Annie Rooney* "continued to be syndicated to a respectable number of papers" throughout the 1940s and 1950s (para. 6). The strip finally ceased publication on April 16, 1966, one year short of its fortieth anniversary (para. 6).

Although *The Adventures of Pasty* had a shorter life span, it had an arguably even greater impact on the genre. Created by Mel Graff, the comic "started on March 11, 1935, when young Patsy, an ordinary girl of about 4–6 [years old], was carried away on a kite. Next thing she knew, she was in the magical kingdom of Ods Bodkins, and getting caught up in stories reminiscent of Winsor McCay's *Little Nemo in Slumberland*" (Markstein, "The Adventures of Patsy," para. 3). Patsy did not merely imagine these adventures in the fantasy world of dreams, as did Nemo. On the contrary, she lived them in her waking life. For this reason, *The Adventures of Patsy* is often compared to Milton Caniff's *Dickie Dare*, which debuted the year before and also showcased a juvenile star (para. 3). The sex of the central character, however, was not the only element that differentiated the two comics. As Markstein has written, "Dickie's adventures all took place in books [that Caniff had] read, whereas Mel Graff . . . had no such limits on the things that could happen to Patsy, or the characters she could meet" (para. 3). *The Adventures of Patsy* appeared during a time when both women's gender roles and the cultural construction of girlhood were constricting. As I have written elsewhere on the subject, "Akin to nearly all other periods of national crisis, the Great Depression brought a backlash against iconoclastic gender roles and a return to more conservative mores for women. With the nation experiencing unprecedented levels of unemployment and fears over communist revolution, tradition instead of transgression came to characterize American life" (*Tomboys*, 137). The title character in *The Adventures of Pasty* was presented not simply as a young girl who, with her dark curls, freshly pressed dresses, and ever-present bow in her hair, is cute, but as one who is also courageous. In numerous strips, Patsy solves problems, confronts controversy, and embraces rather than shrinks from thrills.[10]

Finally, but far from insignificantly, is *Little Iodine* (1943–85). Created by Jimmy Hatlo, the character debuted during the 1930s as a secondary figure in his strip *They'll Do It Every Time*. By 1943, however, she had become so popular that she received her own spin-off Sunday comic. "Iodine was the only child of Henry Tremblechin, a Caspar Milquetoast type whom Hatlo used as a recurring victim," Markstein notes ("Little Iodine," para. 2). Akin to all the other young female protagonists profiled in this project, Iodine "was one of those mischievous little girls" (para. 2). In the words of Markstein once again, "Since her dad's main function was to have funny but unpleasant things happen to him . . . her main function was to cause them" (para. 2). Hatlo, in fact, would later characterize Iodine as "the embodiment of all the brats I knew" (quoted in Markstein, "Little Iodine," para. 2). Bratty or not, Iodine was a sensation. Her comic strip appeared in newspapers throughout the country for more than forty years, finally ceasing in 1985.

Although comics such as *Little Iodine, Little Mary Mixup,* and *Little Annie Rooney* were as popular as their counterparts that featured young boys as protagonists, they are not commonly discussed or widely remembered today. Many of the most detailed and authoritative examinations of the origins, history, and evolution of American newspaper comics—such as *The Smithsonian Collection of Newspaper Comics* and *Cartoon America: Comic Art in the Library of Congress*—either wholly omit them or mention them only briefly, suggesting that they are minor strips. However, Little Mary Mixup, Little Annie Rooney, and Little Iodine were all household names for decades, beloved by generations of Americans. These titles enjoyed levels of success on a par with titles like *Skippy, Little Jimmy,* or *Reg'lar Fellers.* In a telling demonstration of the preeminence of Little Annie Rooney, for example, King Features Syndicate issued a promotional card in July 1928 that "bore a number of characters from their cartoon stable. Little Annie Rooney is sitting on the corner of the building at left" (Beland, "Little Annie Rooney," para. 6) (fig. E.1). As Beland goes on to note, the "mischievous waif had only been around for a year and a half, but was already important enough to depict on this card" (para. 6). Moreover, in a powerful indication of Little Annie Rooney's tremendous popularity, she appears in the company of now-classic comics characters such as Felix the Cat, Maggie and Jiggs (from *Bringing Up Father*), Hans and Fritz (from *The Katzenjammer Kids*), and Krazy Kat (para. 6). As this example reveals, placing titles like *Little Annie Rooney* or *Little Mary Mixup* in the company of their newspaper strip peers changes the landscape of comics featuring kids. They demonstrate that this era of "child stars" in classic American comics was not exclusively or even predominantly populated by boys.

Additionally, many of the Funny Girls from these early newspaper strips played a major role in the licensing, branding, and merchandising of comics. Over the course of their careers, characters like Little Orphan Annie, Little Lulu, and Little Annie Rooney lent their likenesses to products so numerous and diverse that they rivaled the merchandizing bonanza associated with Outcault's the Yellow Kid and Buster Brown.[11] As Beland has observed, "An avalanche of merchandise followed" the release of *Little Orphan Annie* ("Merchandise," para. 1). From dolls, toys, jewelry, clothing, baking supplies, and banks to song books, dishes, coloring books, paint sets, handkerchiefs, and board games, Gray's character became the subject of a synergistic product

Epilogue: The Legacy of Classic American Comics Starring Girls   159

Figure E.1. King Features Syndicate promotional card, 1928.

line that has come to typify the licensing of characters in the twenty-first century. At one point there was even a "Little Orphan Annie sweater button to stick on your Little Orphan Annie sweater" (Beland). Moreover, when the sweater needed to be laundered, it could be hung up to dry with a Little Orphan Annie clothespin (Beland).

Little Annie Rooney imitated Gray's strip through its merchandizing campaign as well. During the 1940s and 1950s, Little Annie Rooney was featured on buttons, Christmas cards, paper dolls, jigsaw puzzles, paint books, sheet music, statuettes, transfer decals, lockets, and collectibles (Beland). Indeed, for almost every Little Orphan Annie product, there was a corresponding one featuring Little Annie Rooney.

Little Lulu followed in the commercial footsteps of Little Annie Rooney and Little Orphan Annie. Buell's character adorned seemingly every conceivable item: toys, clothes, games, home decor, dolls, school supplies, paper products, and even household supplies. For this reason, Tom Heintjes has asserted: "In tracing the evolution of marketing consumer products using comics characters, encountering Marge Buell and her moppet creation Little Lulu is inevitable" (para. 1). Astoundingly, however, this condition has not been the case. Ian Gordon's landmark book *Comic Strips and Consumer Culture, 1890–1945*, for example, does not mention Lulu—or Little Annie Rooney. Moreover, he discusses Little Orphan Annie on just one page. Instead, Gordon's examination of the process by which comics came to be so heavily commoditized during the late nineteenth century and the first half of the twentieth focuses on strips such as *Hogan's Alley*, *Buster Brown*, and *Gasoline Alley*.

Adding the tradition of Funny Girls to such discussions provides a more accurate portrait of the commercialization of comics in the United States while it also reveals the significant role that strips starring female characters have played in this phenomenon. Comics that became lucrative licensed properties and launched successful branded characters did not simply feature boys as protagonists but featured girls as well. In this way, the merchandizing of Funny Girls introduces an element of gender diversity to a phenomenon that is commonly framed as being far more monolithic.

Moving the significant presence of young female protagonists from the background to the forefront of discussions about the development of sequential art in the United States likewise complicates standard perceptions about the early decades of comic books. When this new material format debuted in the 1930s, the practice of featuring male central characters simultaneously shifted and stayed the same. While young boys were less likely to be the stars of comic books, adult men emerged to take their place. As historical accounts like Bradford W. Wright's *Comic Book Nation: The Transformation of Youth Culture in America* (2001), David Hajdu's *The Ten-Cent Plague: The Great Comic-Book Scare and How It Changed America* (2008), and Paul Lopes's *Demanding Respect: The Evolution of the American Comic Book* (2009) have all discussed, the appearance of Superman in *Action Comics* in 1938 marked the beginning of what is now commonly known as the Golden Age of comics in the United States. It also marked the moment when the medium became dominated by the superhero genre (Goulart, 118). That said, nearly all these figures were male. In the words of Mike Madrid, "There are a lot of 'men' in comic books: Super*man*, Bat*man*, Spider-*Man*" (*Supergirls*, vi). When female characters did appear during the Golden Age, they were usually secondary figures. As Trina Robbins has observed, "Often they were merely sidekicks of the more important male hero. For the most part, when women appeared in comics they were relegated to the role of girlfriend, and their purpose was to be rescued by the hero" (3).

This situation persisted until the early 1940s with the debut of Wonder Woman. The singularity of Wonder Woman, however, was the exception that proved the rule. In comments that have been echoed by numerous other critics, Sherrie Inness flatly stated: "The first female character to attract a large following challenged the notion that women superheroes in comic books generally had to be subordinate to men; her name was Wonder Woman" (144). Consequently, the history of strong and successful female characters in US comic books is commonly seen as commencing with Wonder Woman. Trina Robbins, in *The Great Women Superheroes* (1996), for example, begins her survey with this character (3–14). As Robbins says about the tremendous popularity and thus historical significance of the comic: "At its peak, the monthly *Wonder Woman* comic book sold around two and a half million copies, and by 1944 she even had her own newspaper comic strip" (5, 7). Likewise, Wonder Woman looms large in Mike Madrid's *The Supergirls: Fashion, Feminism, and the History of Comic Book Heroines* (2009). Madrid identifies a few female characters who precede the famous Amazon—such as Sheena and the Woman in Red—but he still identifies Wonder Woman as a crucial starting point. In fact, the first chapter is titled "The Queen and the Princess." As Madrid explains: "The queen was the first of her kind, but the princess outlived her in life, and in legend. The queen was named Sheena, and the princess was called Wonder Woman. As different as they were from one another, these two sovereigns ruled the early days of comic books as the medium's two popular heroines, and the archetypes that would define the female superhero" (*Supergirls*, 31).

More recently, Madrid has sought to complicate long-standing perceptions about female characters in Golden Age comics. His books *Divas, Dames, and Daredevils: Lost Heroines of Golden Age Comics* (2013) and *Vixens, Vamps, and Vipers: Lost Villainesses of Golden Age Comics* (2014) work to dispel views that comics from this period were populated almost exclusively by male figures. Both texts remind readers about the various "lost heroines" as well as "lost villainesses" of Golden Age comics. To that end, he calls attention to characters ranging from Madame Doom, Skull Lady, and Veda the Cobra Woman to Pat Patriot, Mother Hubbard, and Jill Trent, Science Sleuth. As Madrid explains in the introduction to *Divas, Dames, and Daredevils*, "The heroines in this collection are not among the most famous in comic book history. They are, as the book's title calls them, 'lost' heroines. Some had long careers; some made only one appearance. What they lack in big names they make up with heroic swagger" (17).

While Little Audrey and Li'l Tomboy are not superheroes in the conventional sense of the term, they do have heroic qualities: they are spirited, outspoken, and strong. These characters affirm the existence of powerful female protagonists during the Golden Age of comic books while simultaneously revealing how some of these "supergirls"—to evoke the title of one of Madrid's books—were actual girls, not adult women. In so doing, the tradition of Funny Girls presented in this book reveals that the important work by Robbins and Madrid tells only some of the untold stories about early American comics. In the same way that there is a bevy of lost women superheroes and villainesses, so too is there an equally strong tradition of girl characters who have been historically neglected and critically overlooked. Moreover, unlike the characters that Madrid profiles, these Funny Girls were

Figure E.2. *Little Dot*, vol. 1, no. 56 (May 1960). Harvey Comics.

not secondary characters in a comic book series starring another figure. On the contrary, each had her own multi-issue title.

That said, Little Audrey and Li'l Tomboy were not the only young female protagonists in comic books from this era who merit attention. Little Audrey, for example, had two female friends—Little Dot and Little Lotta—each with her own stand-alone title from Harvey Comics. As Jerry Beck has written, "Little Dot began as a series of one-page 'fillers' in *Sad Sack Comics* (starting with issue #1 in 1949)" (11). Dot was more than merely her name; it was also her passion; this character loved polka dots: she found them, made them, distributed them, and collected them (fig. E.2). In addition, she was always attired in a polka-dotted dress. Even so, this trait was not her only signature quality: she also had a bevy of eccentric aunts and uncles who were always ready to whisk her off for some exciting adventure. "In Dot's universe, each relative has a name to go with his or her profession—so Uncle Gill is fisherman, Aunt Badge a policewoman, and so on. These stories took Dot all over the world, where she played the role of a global peacekeeper and problem-solver" (Beck, 13). For almost half a decade, Dot served largely as a secondary character to Little Audrey. However, when Harvey "began its concerted push toward producing children's comics (and away from adult- and teenage-skewed horror and crime) in 1953, they rewarded a redesigned Dot with her own book" (11). The *Little Dot* comic book was an immediate hit. As Beck has discussed, the title occasionally outsold *Little Audrey* (11–13). The series ran for nearly two decades, ending in 1976 after 164 issues. In addition, it gave rise to a spin-off title, *Little Dot Dotland*, in 1962. The title was aimed at a slightly younger audience and ran for sixty-one issues before ceasing in 1973.

Little Audrey had a second young female friend, a character named Little Lotta (fig. E.3). "Both Little Lotta and Richie Rich debuted as backup features in *Little Dot* #1. Both went on to comics fame in their own rights" (Beck, 13). The *Little Lotta* comic book series began in 1955, and akin to its counterparts, the title character had a distinctive appearance and personality. First and perhaps most noticeably, Lotta was full-figured. Stephen Beck calls Lotta's physique "Rubenesque" (13). The character's signature personality traits were by-products of this feature. Lotta possessed both "Herculean physical strength and an impossibly huge appetite" (13). Indeed, the young girl often seems more like a superhero than an actual person: she single-handedly lifts pianos and consumes entire tables of food.[12] The *Little Lotta* comic book enjoyed a long run, ceasing in 1973. The series was then reprised twice: from 1974 to 1976, and then again from 1992 to 1993.

Collectively, Little Audrey, Little Dot, and Little Lotta became known as the "Harvey Girls." As Sid Jacobson commented, "Dot and Lotta were sort-of designed as companion strips to Audrey. There weren't many little girl books at the time, but they soon became a hot item. Harvey was the only publisher with a group of comics centered around little girls" (quoted in Beck, 11). These three figures were fixtures in the comic book world for decades. Indeed, as Beck rightly notes, "In a world dominated by adolescent millionaires, pint-sized devils, friendly ghosts, and overfed baby ducklings—all males—Harvey Comics had the wisdom and foresight to create and maintain a 'little trio' of female characters, just as mischievous, and just as powerful as the boys" (7). With their distinctive personalities, bold behavior, and powerful sense

Figure E.3. *Little Lotta*, no. 82 (March 1955). Harvey Comics.

of humor, "their comic stories . . . [were] unique, imaginative, and above all, fun" (7).

Harvey Comics was not the only publisher during the postwar period to have its own comic book series starring a spirited young girl; MLJ Magazines did so as well, with Li'l Jinx from the *Archie* series (fig. E.4). Li'l Jinx debuted in the July 1947 issue of the comic. Created by Joe Edwards, "Jinx was so-called because she was (like Edwards's own son) born on Halloween, about a half-dozen or so years ago" (Markstein, "Li'l Jinx," para. 3). The diminutive that preceded her name connected her with comics predecessors such as Little Lulu and Little Iodine—and with good reason. Like these figures, Li'l

Epilogue: The Legacy of Classic American Comics Starring Girls 165

Figure E.4. *Li'l Jinx*, vol. 1, no. 16 (September 1957). Archie Comics Group.

Jinx was as spirited as she was mischievous. Routinely accompanied by a young boy name Charley, who was her best friend, Jinx was involved in one humorous scrape after another: with the other kids in the neighborhood, with her peers at school, and especially with her parents and teachers. In what became a recurring feature of the series, many of the issues had a few rhyming lines at the top of the cover that served as a lead-in to the comic book title—and also summarized the personality of its star. The January 1957 issue, for example, reads: "She's Little Miss Trouble / Everyone thinks / And everyone's right! Meet . . . *Li'l Jinx*." The July 1957 issue took a slightly different approach, but the end result was the same. It promised: "The house

Figure E.5. *Li'l Jinx Giant Laugh-Out*, no. 38 (October 1971). Archie Comics Group.

is all quiet so everyone thinks, / When suddenly, wham, bam, allagazam, here's . . . *Li'l Jinx*."[13]

The *Li'l Jinx* comic book series was comparatively short-lived, running only from 1956 through 1957. That said, the character did not cease to exist when her title did. Instead she continued to appear as filler stories in other *Pep* comics (Markstein, "Li'l Jinx," para. 4). Moreover, Li'l Jinx was revived during the early 1970s. "From 1971–73, she was the star of an extra-thick comic titled *Li'l Jinx Giant Laugh-Out*" (para. 4) (fig. E.5). In many ways,

Epilogue: The Legacy of Classic American Comics Starring Girls

Figure E.6. *Little Iodine*, vol. 1, no. 30 (October–December 1955). Dell Comics.

her reappearance during this era was not surprising, for Li'l Jinx's spirited personality reflected the transformations to female gender roles, national child-rearing practices, and constructions of girlhood that were taking place in the wake of the second-wave feminist movement.

Finally, but far from insignificantly, American comic books during the postwar era were also populated by another female figure: Little Iodine (fig. E.6). This mischievous miscreant with the distinctive swirl of bangs had received her own self-titled newspaper strip in 1943, and she debuted in her own stand-alone comic book in 1950. Released by Dell, the series lasted until 1962, encompassing "56 issues in all" (Markstein, para. 3).[14] Consequently, for nearly a decade and a half, Little Iodine was a fixture both in American daily newspapers and on its comic book racks. This accolade is impressive for any character, but especially for one who was a young girl during a period that is commonly seen as being dominated by the superhero genre, focused almost exclusively on male figures, and—by the mid-1950s—heavily constricted by the Comics Code. Indeed, akin to Li'l Tomboy, Little Iodine was a rascal whose behavior did not conform to the expectations for postwar children in general and young girls in particular, both outside and especially inside of comic books.

Recovering young female protagonists like Little Iodine and L'il Jinx has implications that extend beyond the historical eras in which these characters originally appeared. In the same way that the tradition of Funny Girls changes the way we view American comics during the opening decades of the twentieth century, it likewise alters our perception of developments in the industry during the opening decades of the new millennium. The early twenty-first century is increasingly regarded as a halcyon period for girls and women. Beginning with the tremendous popularity of *Ghost World* during the late 1990s and then accelerating rapidly during the opening decades of the new millennium, the number of female comics characters, fans, and creators increased exponentially. Sherrie Inness, writing in 1999, observed: "Whether they are cartoonists or readers of cartoons, women are invading the formerly predominantly male sanctuary of the comic book, which is perhaps one of the reasons tough women in comic books are appearing with greater frequency than ever before" (141–42). In the years that followed, these sentiments were echoed by numerous other commentators. William Kuskin, in an essay that appeared in 2014, for instance, asserted: "Right now . . . we are in the midst of a revolution of gender in comics. No one need scrape around to find prolific female creators and powerful female characters in mainstream comics. They are front and center" (9). In the following year, Lois E. Huffman and Roslyn P. Moffit wrote an article titled "Girls (of All Ages) Are Wild about Comics and Graphic Novels."

Even a cursory examination of the industry affirms the veracity of these claims. Many of the most popular serialized comic books, such as *Ms. Marvel* (2014–present), *Lumberjanes* (2014–present), and *The Unbeatable Squirrel Girl* (2015–present), feature strong female protagonists. Likewise, a variety of the most commercially successful and critically acclaimed graphic novels—ranging from *Persepolis* (2000), *Fun Home* (2006), and *Smile* (2010) to *Hereville* (2010), *Anya's Ghost* (2011), and *This One Summer* (2014)—showcased a girl as their central character. Finally, in a detail that is just as noteworthy, the majority of these titles were made by female cartoonists. Creators like Raina Telgemeier, Marjane Satrapi, Alison Bechdel, and Mariko Tamaki and Jillian Tamaki represent both the most recognizable and the most celebrated names in the field. Telgemeier, for example, was named Comics Industry Person of the Year in 2014. As one commentator aptly noted, she is "the undisputed Queen of Graphic Novels right now. I don't mean Queen in the patriarchal sense of a woman standing by the side of her king, but in the sense that she is alone at the top of the Comic Book Kingdom (or Queendom, rather)" (Mey, para. 1). Telgemeier's debut graphic novel *Smile* (2010) appeared on the *New York Times* best-seller list for an astounding four consecutive years (Hennum et al.). In 2014, her work occupied the list's top four spots, with her book *Drama* (2012) ranking first, *Smile* second, *Sisters* (2014) third, and *The Baby-Sitters Club* fourth. Given these details, a recent article offering a retrospective look at Telgemeier's work calls her nothing less than "a major force in the comics industry" (Hennum et al.). As discussions by both popular critics and academic scholars assert, one of the factors fueling Telgemeier's success is that her comics "are by a woman, about girls and for girls" (Mey, para. 6).[15]

In the same way that the presence of girls as cartoonists, readers, and fans has expanded in recent decades, so too has the field's depiction of girlhood. Whereas the feisty female figures that populated the classic era of American comics were uniformly white, those who have appeared in the opening decades of the twenty-first century hail from a wider range of racial, ethnic, and cultural backgrounds. Titles like *Moon Girl and Devil Dinosaur* (2015), *Paper Girls* (2015–present), and *Moonshot: The Indigenous Comics Collection* (2015)—along with the aforementioned *Ms. Marvel*, *Lumberjanes*, and *This One Summer*—feature young female protagonists who are black, Asian, Muslim, indigenous, and Latina. In so doing, these works take US comics featuring girls to sociocultural places that titles like *Little Lulu* and *Little Audrey* never ventured. Together with addressing the issue of gender, these titles do so for other equally important vectors of identity. In this way, they disrupt the long-standing construction of girlhood from the standpoint of whiteness while also demonstrating that gender is only one of multiple factors impacting girls. Their identities—akin to their lives—are inherently intersectional.

Although the Funny Girls profiled in previous chapters lamentably do not possess the same level of sociocultural diversity, they change the way that we view the current comics phenomenon. Remembering and recouping these classic American comics starring girls reveals how recent developments in the industry are not something wholly new or radically different; rather, they can be connected with a previous tradition. Little Lulu, Little Audrey, and Li'l Tomboy embody far more than merely the historical predecessors of characters like Callie from *Drama*, Doreen Green from *The Unbeatable Squirrel Girl*, or April from *Lumberjanes*; they can be regarded as their creative, commercial, and cultural foresisters. Nearly a century before April bested the statue of Hercules in an arm-wrestling contest or Callie wowed her classmates with the show-stopping "KA-BOOM!" of the confetti cannon that she had constructed, figures like Little Iodine and Li'l Tomboy were engaging in remarkably similar feats. In so doing, they reveal that it is not simply millennium American comics that feature strong female characters. On the contrary, sequential art in the United States has a long tradition of girl power.

• • •

Moving the cadre of fun, feisty, and formidable female protagonists from the background to the forefront of consideration changes the landscape of American comics, both past and present. Whether in the realm of newspaper strips from the 1920s and 1930s, comic books from the 1940s and 1950s, or graphic novels from the opening decades of the new millennium, the influence of characters like Little Lulu, Little Annie Rooney, and Nancy has been as far-reaching as it has been long lasting. The history of comics in the United States during the early twentieth century has commonly included discussions about the funny papers. If this project has accomplished its purpose, then subsequent accounts will also include a consideration of an equally important element: its Funny Girls.

Notes

INTRODUCTION. "IT'S A BIRD! IT'S A PLANE! IT'S AN ELEMENTARY-AGED GIRL!": REMEMBERING A TIME IN AMERICAN COMICS WHEN YOUNG FEMALE PROTAGONISTS RULED

1. The same observation applies to a segment from Jerry Robinson's *The Comics: An Illustrated History of Comic Strip Art, 1895–2010* (Dark Horse, 2011). Chapter 4 is titled "Girls, Family, and Kids: 1920–1929." By "girls," however, Robinson means adult women and, more specifically, flappers and pink-collar professionals. To be sure, his discussion of the topic of "girls" in comics during the Roaring Twenties concerns the numerous strips that featured young single women who were working at some type of office job. Titles included *Winnie Winkle the Breadwinner*, *Tillie the Toiler*, and *Somebody's Stenog*, among others. Thus, while Robinson refers to the protagonists of these strips as "working girls" or "career girls" (114), they are all adult women.

2. For Meconis's full list of the "top ten criticism mistakes" that both journalists and scholars make when talking about comics, see his full article here: http://www.dylanmeconis.com/how-not-to-write-comics-criticism.

3. For example, Rose O'Neill's *Kewpies* could be added to this list. While these cherub-looking characters are more commonly remembered as dolls and figurines, they first appeared in a comic strip in 1910. As their name implies, the Kewpies were an ensemble cast comprising baby boys and baby girls.

CHAPTER 1. "THEN I COULD HAVE A REAL PAPA AND MAMA LIKE OTHER KIDS": *LITTLE ORPHAN ANNIE*, THE ORPHAN GIRL FORMULA, AND THE NANNY STATE

1. It should be noted that, nearly three decades later, Gray would tell a different story about the origins of *Little Orphan Annie*. In an interview that he gave to *Editor & Publisher* magazine in 1951, he claimed that the title character was inspired by an actual girl whom he met on the streets of Chicago (Heer, "Dream Big," 24). Given that Gray had never mentioned this alternative basis for Annie for nearly thirty years—and did so only after Patterson had died—most agree that "the first version seems far more believable than the second" (Smith, 9). As Bruce Smith speculated, "Perhaps, like many people who are asked

the same question over and over again, Gray decided to amuse himself at *E&P*'s expense by fabricating a new answer" (9).

2. Orphan girls also permeated the burgeoning new arena of commercial film. The actress Mary Pickford, for example, rose to stardom and became one of the most famous celebrities of her day by playing roles of this nature. Indeed, although Pickford would go on to have a long career in Hollywood, she would forever be remembered for what came to be known as her "little girl" roles in movies like *Rebecca of Sunnybrook Farm* (1917), *Daddy-Long-Legs* (1919), and *Pollyanna* (1920).

3. While I specifically mention the work of Mazzenga and Ress here, the same observation applies to many other essays, chapters, and articles. For example, William H. Young's journal article "That Indomitable Redhead: Little Orphan Annie" examines Gray's strip "during two crises: the Depression and World War Two" (309). Likewise, Lyle W. Shannon's essay "The Opinions of Little Orphan Annie and Her Friends" examines strips from 1948 to 1950 (70). Finally, Donald Auster's groundbreaking study "A Content Analysis of *Little Orphan Annie*" spotlights comics from the year 1935 (28).

CHAPTER 2. "I SLANT MY GAGS TO THE LAWRENCE WELK GUM CHEWERS" : NANCY AND THE VAUDEVILLE AESTHETIC

1. The bulk of *Nancy* comics that I discuss in this chapter appear in *The Best of Ernie Bushmiller's "Nancy"*, edited by Brian Walker. My reasons for using this text as my primary source for Bushmiller's material are multifold. Walker's collection is widely available, held by many library collections, and easily purchased at most booksellers. In addition, the volume represents, as the title announces, comics that readers and critics agree embody some of the best *Nancy* strips. Consequently the examples that I cite from this volume are not anomalous. Rather, they represent some of the most publicly popular, critically acclaimed, and commercially successful comics from Bushmiller's series.

2. Of course, racist caricatures, crass ethnic stereotypes, misogynistic portrayals of women, and classist lampoons of the poor were pervasive on the vaudeville stage. As I discuss later, these features even constituted the expected slate of acts and common sources of humor. The presence of these features raises questions about for whom vaudeville was "'clean,' 'wholesome' entertainment, for the whole family." Certainly then, as now, vaudeville depicted while it perpetuated painful prejudice and harmful stereotypes.

CHAPTER 3. FROM BATTLING ADULT AUTHORITY TO BATTLING THE OPPOSITE SEX: LITTLE LULU AS GAG PANEL AND COMIC BOOK

1. Although young children wore white dresses for the first six or so years of their lives, these garments were certainly not uniform. The type and quality of the fabric, along with the style and degree of embellishment on the gowns—in the form of ribbons, lace, trims, pleating, or decorative stitching—varied according to the family's socioeconomic status, the child's cultural and religious background, and the mother's sewing ability. In addition,

the gown's length also changed: the white dresses worn by infants were usually longer to keep their feet and legs warm, while those intended for toddlers and kindergarten-aged children were shorter to allow them a greater range of motion while crawling, walking, and playing. Nonetheless the basic garment was the same for both boys and girls.

2. Admittedly, one comic near the end of the Rand McNally collection does show Little Lulu directing her mischievous energies toward a male peer. In it, Lulu follows behind a chubby boy who is her frequent playmate and suspected boyfriend as he walks on wooden stilts. He is sweating profusely and has an anxious expression on his face as he looks behind him to see that Lulu is carrying a saw and smiling. This panel is the exception, however, not the norm. Of the twenty-nine gag panels contained in the book, in fact, it is the only one that presents Lulu scuffling with a boy. Consequently this plotline represents a departure from the norm.

3. Admittedly, as Craig Shutt notes, this era was a difficult one for many comic book characters and series. "The late 1960s and early 1970s were not a strong period for comics of any kind, with the vaunted Silver Age of superhero comics coming to an end and publishers scrambling to find another high tide to lift all their boats" (40).

CHAPTER 4. IN YOUR DREAMS: *LITTLE AUDREY*, FREUDIAN PSYCHOANALYSIS, AND POSTWAR CHILD PSYCHOLOGY

1. Tennessee Williams was not the only playwright in the 1950s to engage with Freudian themes. One of his main rivals on the American stage during this era was Eugene O'Neill, whose work was also highly psychoanalytic. In 1957, O'Neill posthumously received the Pulitzer Prize for Drama for his portrait of a dysfunctional family in *Long Day's Journey into Night* (1956).

2. Of course, the dream sequences in the cartoon version of *Little Audrey* can also be viewed psychoanalytically. After all, they are dreams and thus, by definition, lend themselves to Freudian analysis. Surely at least some of these story lines can be interpreted as embedding postwar fears, events, and anxieties. As a result, the comic book version of *Little Audrey* exists on a continuum with the animated version. The dream sequences in the print stories echo and even extend a narrative feature from the animated shorts, and in so doing, both versions traffic in the postwar fascination with the somnolent workings of the unconscious mind.

CHAPTER 5. "FROM THE TOP, STUPID!": THE *LI'L TOMBOY* COMIC BOOK SERIES, FEMALE JUVENILE DELINQUENCY, AND THE COMICS CODE

1. This character's precise age is not explicitly stated until the story "Bargain Day," which appears in the March 1957 issue of *Li'l Tomboy*. That said, her physical appearance—height, weight, and so on—and thus her implied age do not change throughout the series. Akin to many other comic book characters, Li'l Tomboy remains frozen in time.

2. In keeping with the cross-promotional practices that were common in the comic book industry at the time, stories featuring Li'l Tomboy also appeared in some of Charlton's other titles. The two-page tale "Li'l Tomboy in Thanks for Disturbing Me," for example, was featured in the November 1957 issue of *Timmy the Timid Ghost*.

3. For more information about the ways in which deviation from white, middle-class women's traditional gender and sexual roles was both socially stigmatized and medically pathologized during the postwar period, see Devlin, "Female Juvenile Delinquency"; and Faderman, *Odd Girls and Twilight Lovers*.

4. For more information on this widespread cultural practice and historical phenomenon, see Rosemarie Garland-Thompson's *Freakery: Cultural Spectacles of the Extraordinary Body* (NYU Press, 1996).

5. Note that the indigenous tribal peoples of Africa are not the only racial or ethnic group through which Li'l Tomboy constructs her identity and uses as a conduit for her mischievous conduct. This character also draws on elements of American Indian culture. The cover image to the September 1957 issue of *Li'l Tomboy*, for example, shows the title character in close-up against a vivid red background. She is dressed in buckskin, wielding a hatchet, and running through the house while yelling "Whooooooooo." The June 1958 issue's cover contains a similar scenario. In what can clearly be seen as a reference to "scalping," it shows Li'l Tomboy wearing a feathered headband, holding a hatchet, and shaving off nearly half of her father's hair with an electric razor while he naps in a chair. Interestingly, no stories in either of these two issues present Li'l Tomboy engaging in any antics of this type. Nonetheless these cover images are clearly being used to attract juvenile consumers, catch their attention, and get them to pick up—and hopefully purchase—the comic. Moreover, the kinship between the "wild" and "uncivilized" acts of the indigenous peoples of North America and Li'l Tomboy's own "wild" and "uncivilized" conduct is clear. So even though postwar juvenile delinquents did not draw on American Indian culture to authorize their rebellion from middle-class suburban whiteness, it is worth calling attention to these elements because they help in the construction, as well as the expression, of Li'l Tomboy's "wild" behavior. Incidentally, Li'l Tomboy was not the only publication to forge a connection between white tomboyism and American Indian tribalism. On the contrary, it was a well-established trope in American culture in general and especially in its books for young readers by the 1950s. For more on this issue, see Abate, "Becoming a 'Red-Blooded' American."

6. For both an accounting of these titles and a detailed discussion of their content, see Nyberg, *Seal of Approval*, chap. 2.

7. The CMAA was not the first time that comic book publishers had formed a professional organization in an attempt to regulate themselves. Back in 1948—amid similar public criticisms about the harmful nature of comics, many of which were levied by Fredric Wertham—the industry created the Association of Comics Magazine Publishers (ACMP). This trade association likewise created its own code of standards that was "similar to that of the film industry" (Nyberg, 104). That said, the ACMP never possessed the power or achieved the prominence of the CMAA. Many publishers refused to join the association, and those who did routinely broke ranks and refused to abide by the standards. While the

ACMP was never officially dissolved or disbanded, it was an organization that existed in name only. By 1954, in fact, when the CMAA was created, "there were only three publishers left in the organization and the prepublication review process had been abandoned" (Nyberg, 35). For more on the origins, history, and decline of the ACMP, see Nyberg, *Seal of Approval*.

8. Note that the restrictions imposed by the Comics Code were not the only reason for this decline; other cultural issues, economic factors, and social forces were at play. As Jean-Paul Gabilliet has commented, comic book sales actually began dipping in 1953, a year before the Senate hearings and the creation of the CMAA. As he explains, "The supply of comic books had skyrocketed in 1951–1952 and probably reached the upper limit of what the demand could absorb—or, precisely, could not absorb" (47). Together with simple market saturation, comic books were facing increased competition from other forms of leisure-time entertainment, namely, the rise of television. "In cultural terms," Gabilliet argues, "an important factor was the spectacular rise of television: 23.5 percent of American households owned a television set in 1951 compared to 34.2 percent the following year" (47). These figures would only increase: "From the start of the 1950s onward, the most determinant factor for the purchase of a television set was not the household's revenue or social class but the presence of children, who had so far been the largest segment of comic book readers" (Gabilliet, 47).

EPILOGUE. FROM LI'L TO BIG: THE LEGACY OF CLASSIC AMERICAN COMICS STARRING GIRLS

1. Of course, given the success of *The Katzenjammer Kids*, the strip inspired numerous imitators: Gene Carr's *Stepbrothers* and H. H. Knerr's *Die Fineheimer Twins* are perhaps the two most notable among them. For more both on the original comic by Rudolph Dirks and on these two knockoff strips, see Goulart, *The Funnies*.

2. The popularity of McCay's *Little Nemo* inspired a bevy of other fantasy-themed comics starring young boys, including W. O. Wilson's *The Wish Twins and Aladdin's Lamp* (1904–8), Gustave Verbeek's *The Terrors of the Tiny Tads* (1905–14), and Frank King's *Bobby Make-Believe* (1915–19). Indeed, in language that reveals the kinship that *Bobby Make-Believe* had with *Little Nemo*, Ron Goulart observed: "Another daydreamer, Bobby escaped the perils and perplexities of boyhood by imagining himself in adventurous settings" (45). As even this brief discussion indicates, "Dreamland became a popular kid hangout during the first decade of the century," in large part due to the work of Winsor McCay (Goulart, 18).

3. *Buster Brown* was preceded by another, less-successful, strip by Outcault that also showcased a young protagonist: *Pore Li'l Mose* (1900–1902). As Jerry Robinson has noted, *Pore Li'l Mose* was "the first strip with a principal character who was black" (27). That said, from the visual representation of the title character to the plots featured in the strips, the comic was steeped in racist stereotypes about African Americans. For more on *Pore Li'l Mose*, see Bernard A. Drew's *Black Stereotypes in Popular Series Fiction, 1851–1955: Jim Crow Era Authors and Their Characters* (McFarland, 2015).

4. During the course of its run, *S'matter Pop?* was also titled *Say, Pop!* and *Nippy's Pop* (Robinson, 109).

5. This observation holds true for *Just Kids*, though the comic technically features an ensemble cast that includes two girl characters. The strip routinely spotlights Mush Stebbins and his pals Fatso Dolan and Pat Finnegan, not Mush's younger sister, Stelle, or his love interest, Marjory Jones.

6. Goulart does not include the publication dates for these comics. Instead I have taken them from Allan Holtz's *American Newspaper Comics: An Encyclopedic Reference* (University of Michigan Press, 2012). I want to thank Susan Liberator at the Billy Ireland Cartoon Library and Museum for her help in verifying the publication dates for these comics, along with many of the others mentioned throughout this project.

7. *Little Mary Mixup* was not the first American newspaper strip to star a spunky little girl. On the contrary, several additional, albeit less successful, titles preceded it. As Goulart reports, "*The Angel Child*, begun in April 1902 by Kate Carew, was about a sweet-seeming blond little girl who was continually plotting and carrying out mischievous schemes" (16). Along the same lines, "A similar page was *Mama's Angel Child*, which came along a few years later" (16). The strip was drawn by Penny Ross and was rendered in a beautiful art nouveau style. The title "Mama's Little Angel" was ironic, for the comic "featured a misbehaving little blond girl named Esther. It was a depressing page, since everybody knew what a brat little Esther was. Her peers shunned her. Most parents didn't want anything to do with her, and even her mother wasn't that fond of her" (16). Not all the young female characters in early newspaper comics were so insufferable, however. In the words of Goulart, "There were also a number of little girls who truly were angelic, and numbingly cute on top of that" (17). Most of these figures were created by Grace Drayton. "Best remembered today for inventing the Campbell Soup Kids, Drayton drew children who were always about five years old, dimpled, encased in baby fat, and given to lisping and baby talk" (17). As Goulart explains, "Among her early comic section entries were *Naughty Toodles*, *Dottie Dimple*, *Dimples*, and *The Turr'ble Tales of Kaptain Kidd*" (17). Finally, but far from insignificantly, the fantasy craze that appeared in the wake of Winsor McCay's *Little Nemo* included a few strips that starred young girls, such as Peter Newell's *The Naps of Polly Sleepyhead* (1906–7) and W. O. Wilson's *Madge the Magician's Daughter* (1906–7). Thus, though I begin my discussion of girls in newspaper comics with *Little Mary Mixup* in 1917, the tradition can be traced back more than a decade earlier.

8. Of course, Gray's strip was not the only cultural entity with which *Little Annie Rooney* possessed a kinship. The comic also shared its name with a well-known Irish folk song and with a 1925 film starring Mary Pickford.

9. *Little Annie Rooney* was not the only strip that appeared in the wake of *Little Orphan Annie*, mimicked its basic premise, and attempted to capitalize on its massive popularity. Al Zere's *Two Orphans* also functioned in this way. As Ron Goulart has said about this comic, Zere "covered all his bases and peoples [in] his new strip with one little girl orphan and one little boy orphan plus a dog. True to the Harold Gray tradition, both little Tess and little Bub had no pupils in their eyes. The dog didn't either. Despite all this, *Two Orphans* did not last long" (83). The comic was canceled a few months after it debuted.

10. *The Adventures of Patsy* is significant not simply for the portrayal of its young title character. As Markstein has written, "Depending on how you define the term, Patsy's recurring rescuer, the Phantom Magician, may have been the first superhero in comics" (para. 2). Making his first appearance on April 15, 1935—less than two months after the strip debuted—this figure was "a tall, handsome man in swashbuckling clothes [who] appeared in a puff of smoke" and had the ability to conjure items out of thin air (para. 2). An immediate hit with audiences, the Phantom Magician made regular appearances in the strip thereafter.

11. *Little Mary Mixup* and *Little Iodine* also became licensed properties, though not on the same scale. In 1922, Mary and her friend Peggy were sold as paper dolls, and Little Iodine "starred in a live-action feature film, released by United Artists on October 20, 1946" (Markstein, para. 4).

12. Of course, the latter behavior may have been impressive, but it was not seen as commendable. Instead, Lotta's appetite was presented as the reason for her physical appearance. Phrased more bluntly, it was an act of body-shaming the character for failing to conform to conventions about women's physique.

13. Some of these lead-ins to the title of *Li'l Jinx* sexualized the elementary-aged character. For example, the one that appeared at the top of the November 1956 issue announced, "She's always in mischief, / This cute little minx / And that's why they call her . . . *Li'l Jinx*."

14. Six more issues, titled *Jimmy Hatlo's Little Iodine*, were released by Page Comics.

15. Telgemeier's success is not all cause for celebration. As Debbie Reese, Laura M. Jiménez, and I have all written, Telgemeier's graphic novels contain many problematic portrays of US history, racial and ethnicity diversity, and indigeneity that greatly undercut such praise. Telgemeier's *Drama* (2012), for example, traffics in myths about the plantation South and romanticized views of antebellum life. *Ghosts* (2016) not only appropriates the Day of the Dead but also omits the genocide of indigenous peoples and the erasure of Mexican people, history, and culture in California. As even these brief examples attest, assessments of Telgemeier's work that are unequivocally laudatory are only possible when her novels are viewed from a perspective that is culturally, racially, and historically limited—and even exclusionary. For more on this issue, see Debbie Reese's review of *Ghosts* on her website American Indians in Children's Literature; Laura M. Jiménez's post "*Ghosts*: A Swing and a Hard Miss," on her blog *Booktoss*; and my article "'Springtime in the South Is like a Song in My Heart': Raina Telgemeier's *Drama*, the Romanticization of the Plantation South, and the Romance Plot," in *Children's Literature in Education*.

Works Cited

Entries are organized chapter by chapter.

INTRODUCTION. "IT'S A BIRD! IT'S A PLANE! IT'S AN ELEMENTARY-AGED GIRL!": REMEMBERING A TIME IN AMERICAN COMICS WHEN YOUNG FEMALE PROTAGONISTS RULED

Bechdel, Alison. *Fun Home: A Family Tragicomic*. New York: Mariner, 2006.
Berlatsky, Noah. "The Female Thor and the Female Comic-Book Reader." *Atlantic*, July 21, 2014. http://www.theatlantic.com/entertainment/archive/2014/07/just-how-many-women-read-comic-books/374736.
Bernstein, Robin. *Racial Innocence: Performing American Childhood and Race from Slavery to Civil Rights*. New York: NYU Press, 2011.
Brainard, Joe. *The Nancy Book*. New York: Siglio, 2008.
Brosgol, Vera. *Anya's Ghost*. New York: Square Fish, 2011.
Danziger-Russell, Jacqueline. *Girls and Their Comics: Finding a Female Voice in Comic Book Narrative*. Lanham, MD: Scarecrow, 2013.
Deutsch, Barry. *Hereville: How Mirka Got Her Sword*. New York: Amulet, 2010.
Hamrah, A. S. "The Beckett/Bushmiller Letters." *American Reader*, 2013. http://theamericanreader.com/the-beckettbushmiller-letters.
Horn, Maurice. *Women in the Comics*. 3rd ed. New York: Chelsea House, 2001.
Larrick, Nancy. "The All-White World of Children's Literature." *Saturday Review*, September 11, 1965, 63–65, 84–85.
Madrid, Mike. *Divas, Dames, and Daredevils: Lost Heroines of Golden Age Comics*. Minneapolis, MN: Exterminating Angel Press, 2013.
Madrid, Mike. *The Supergirls: Fashion, Feminism, Fantasy, and the History of Comic Book Heroines*. Minneapolis, MN: Exterminating Angel Press, 2009.
Madrid, Mike. *Vixens, Vamps, and Vipers: Lost Villainesses of Golden Age Comics*. Minneapolis, MN: Exterminating Angel Press, 2014.
Maxwell, Erin. "Women Quietly Become a Force in the Comic Book World." *Variety*, October 6, 2015. http://variety.com/2015/biz/news/women-comic-books-gotham-academy-1201610869.

Mazzenga, Maria. "The Home Front's Cartoony Face: World War Two through Orphan Annie's Eyes." *Prospects* 28 (October 2004): 429–63.

McCloud, Scott. "Girls Are Taking the Comic Book World by Storm." *Time*, May 1, 2015. http://time.com/3841761/scott-mccloud-free-comic-book-day.

Meconis, Dylan. "How Not to Write Comics Criticism." September 2012. http://www.dylan meconis.com/how-not-to-write-comics-criticism.

Mey. "Drawn to Comics: Raina Telgemeier's NYT Bestselling Graphic Novels Are Perfect for Middle School Girls." Autostraddle, August 11, 2015. http://www.autostraddle.com/tag/drawn-to-comics.

Mullaney, Dean, and Bruce Canwell. "Editors' Note." In *The Complete Little Orphan Annie*, vol. 1, *Will Tomorrow Ever Come? Daily Comic Strips, 1924–1927*, ed. Dean Mullaney and Bruce Canwell, 5. San Diego, CA: IDW, 2008.

Newgarden, Mark, and Paul Karasik. "How to Read Nancy." In *The Best of Ernie Bushmiller's "Nancy"*, ed. Brian Walker, 98–105. New York: Henry Holt, 1988.

Ress, Stella. "Bridging the Generation Gap: Little Orphan Annie in the Great Depression." *Journal of Popular Culture* 43, no. 4 (August 2010): 782–800.

Robbins, Trina. *From Girls to Grrrlz: A History of Female Comics from Teens to Zines*. San Francisco: Chronicle Books, 1999.

Robbins, Trina. *The Great Women Superheroes*. Northampton, MA: Kitchen Sink Press, 1996.

Robinson, Jerry. *The Comics: An Illustrated History of Comic Strip Art, 1895–2010*. Milwaukie, OR: Dark Horse, 2011.

Satrapi, Marjane. *Persepolis*. New York: Pantheon, 2000.

Stevenson, Noelle, Grace Ellis, Shannon Watters, and Brooke A. Allen. *Lumberjanes*. Vol. 1, *Beware the Kitten Holy*. Los Angeles: BOOM!, 2014.

Tamaki, Mariko, and Jillian Tamaki. *This One Summer*. New York: First Second, 2014.

Telgemeier, Raina. *Smile*. New York: Scholastic, 2010.

Weales, Gerald. "Arf! The Life and Hard Times of Little Orphan Annie, 1935–1945, by Harold Gray." *North American Review* 256, no. 1 (Spring 1971): 80.

CHAPTER 1. "THEN I COULD HAVE A REAL PAPA AND MAMA LIKE OTHER KIDS":
LITTLE ORPHAN ANNIE, THE ORPHAN GIRL FORMULA, AND THE NANNY STATE

Alcott, Louisa May. *Eight Cousins*. 1875. New York: Dell, 1988.

Alger, Horatio. *Ragged Dick*. 1868. New York: Signet Classics, 2014.

Allen, Frederick Lewis. *Only Yesterday: An Informal History of the 1920s*. New York: Harper and Row, 1931.

Auster, Donald. "A Content Analysis of *Little Orphan Annie*." *Social Problems* 2, no. 1 (July 1954): 26–33.

Burnett, Frances Hodgson. *A Little Princess*. 1905. London: Collector's Library, 2007.

Burnett, Frances Hodgson. *The Secret Garden*. 1911. New York: Barnes and Noble, 2005.

Burroughs, Edgar Rice. *Tarzan of the Apes*. 1918. New York: Penguin, 1990.

Cohen, Sharon. "'Annie' Comic Ends, but the Redhead's Fate Uncertain." *USA Today*, June 13, 2010.

Cummins, Susanna Maria. *The Lamplighter*. 1854. New Brunswick, NJ: Rutgers University Press, 1988.

Doherty, Brian. "Yesterday Is Tomorrow: Revisiting Annie as the New Deal Dawns." *Reason* 41, no. 1 (May 2009).

"Fascism in the Funnies." *New Republic*, September 18, 1935, 147.

Gatewood, Worth. Foreword to *The History of Little Orphan Annie*, by Bruce Smith, vii–ix. New York: Ballantine, 1982.

Gray, Harold. *The Complete Little Orphan Annie*. Vol. 1, *Will Tomorrow Ever Come? Daily Comic Strips, 1924–1927*, ed. Dean Mullaney and Bruce Canwell. San Diego, CA: IDW, 2008.

Gubar, Marah. "The Teflon Kid: How Annie Enables Apathy about Inequality." *Public Books*, January 5, 2014.

Harvey, R. C. "The Orphan's Epic." *Comics Journal*, May 20, 2013.

Heer, Jeet. "CR Holiday Interview #2: Jeet Heer on Little Orphan Annie." *Comics Reporter*, December 23, 2008. http://www.comicsreporter.com/index.php/cr_holiday_interview_2_jeet_heer_on_little_orphan_annie.

Heer, Jeet. "Dream Big and Work Hard." In *The Complete Little Orphan Annie*, by Harold Gray, vol. 1, 11–27. San Diego, CA: IDW, 2008.

Heer, Jeet. "Harold Gray and the Limits of Conservative Anti-Racism." *Comics Journal*, July 7, 2014.

Mazzenga, Maria. "The Home Front's Cartoony Face: World War Two through Orphan Annie's Eyes." *Prospects* 28 (October 2004): 429–63.

Mills, Claudia. "Children in Search of a Family: Orphan Novels through the Century." *Children's Literature in Education* 18, no. 4 (1987): 227–39.

Montgomery, L. M. *Anne of Green Gables*. 1908. London: Collector's Library, 2014.

Montgomery, L. M. *Emily of New Moon*. New York: A. L. Burt, 1923.

Mullaney, Dean, and Bruce Canwell. "Editors' Note." In *The Complete Little Orphan Annie*, vol. 1, *Will Tomorrow Ever Come? Daily Comic Strips, 1924–1927*, ed. Dean Mullaney and Bruce Canwell, 5. San Diego, CA: IDW, 2008.

Negra, Diane. *Off-White Hollywood: American Culture and Ethnic Female Stardom*. London: Routledge, 2001.

Nelson, Claudia. *Little Strangers: Portrayals of Adoption and Foster Care in America, 1850–1929*. Bloomington: Indiana University Press, 2003.

Nodelman, Perry. "Progressive Utopia; or, How to Grow Up without Growing Up." *Children's Literature Association Quarterly* (1979): 146–54.

"Orphan Stories." *Children's Literature Review*. Farmington Hills, MI: Gale, 2009. http://www.encyclopedia.com/children/academic-and-educational-journals/orphan-stories.

Pazicky, Diana Loercher. *Cultural Orphans in America*. Jackson: University Press of Mississippi, 1998.

Porter, Eleanor H. *Pollyanna*. 1911. Charlottesville: University of Virginia Library, 1996.

Ress, Stella. "Bridging the Generation Gap: *Little Orphan Annie* in the Great Depression." *Journal of Popular Culture* 43, no. 4 (2010): 782–800.
Riley, James Whitcomb. "Little Orphant Annie." In *Completed Works*. Indianapolis: Bobbs-Merrill, 1916.
Sanders, Joe Sutliff. *Disciplining Girls: Understanding the Origins of the Classic Orphan Girl Story*. Baltimore, MD: Johns Hopkins University Press, 2011.
Shannon, Lyle W. "The Opinions of Little Orphan Annie and Her Friends." *Public Opinion Quarterly* 18, no. 2 (Summer 1954): 169–79.
Singley, Carol. *Adopting America: Childhood, Kinship, and National Identity in Literature*. New York: Oxford University Press, 2011.
Smith, Bruce. *The History of Little Orphan Annie*. New York: Ballantine, 1982.
Southworth, E. D. E. N. *The Hidden Hand*. 1859. New Brunswick, NJ: Rutgers University Press, 1988.
St. Germain, Amos. "The Flowering of Mass Society: A Historical Overview of the 1920s." In *Dancing Fools and Weary Blues: The Great Escape of the Twenties*, ed. Lawrence R. Broer and John D. Walther, 13–44. Bowling Green, OH: Bowling Green State University Popular Press, 1990.
Twain, Mark. *The Adventures of Huckleberry Finn*. 1884. New York: Dover, 2009.
Warner, Susan. *The Wide, Wide World*. 1850. New York: Feminist Press, 1987.
Weales, Gerald. "Arf! The Life and Hard Times of Little Orphan Annie, 1935–1945, by Harold Gray." *North American Review* 256, no. 1 (Spring 1971): 80.
Webster, Jean. *Daddy-Long-Legs*. 1912. New York: Grosset and Dunlap, 1940.
Wiggin, Kate Douglas. *Rebecca of Sunnybrook Farm*. 1903. New York: Penguin, 2005.
Wojcik, Pamela Robertson. "Little Orphan Annie as Streetwalker." In *Picturing Childhood: Youth in Transnational Comics*, ed. Mark Heimermann and Brittany Tullis, 13–29. Austin: University of Texas Press, 2017.
Young, William H. "That Indomitable Redhead: Little Orphan Annie." *Journal of Popular Culture* 8, no. 2 (Fall 1974): 309–16.
Zelizer, Viviana A. Rotman. *Pricing the Priceless Child: The Changing Social Value of Children*. Princeton, NJ: Princeton University Press, 1994.

CHAPTER 2. "I SLANT MY GAGS TO THE LAWRENCE WELK GUM CHEWERS":
NANCY AND THE VAUDEVILLE AESTHETIC

Bushmiller, Ernie. *The Best of Ernie Bushmiller's "Nancy."* Ed. Brian Walker. New York: Henry Holt, 1988.
Clowes, Daniel. Foreword to *Nancy Is Happy: Complete Dailies, 1943–1945*, by Ernie Bushmiller, 4–5. Seattle, WA: Fantagraphics, 2012.
DiMeglio, John E. *Vaudeville U.S.A.* Bowling Green, OH: Bowling Green State University Popular Press, 1973.
Editors. Introduction to *Nancy Is Happy: Complete Dailies, 1943–1945*, by Ernie Bushmiller, 6–7. Seattle, WA: Fantagraphics, 2012.

Erdman, Andrew K. *Blue Vaudeville: Sex, Morals, and the Mass Marketing of Amusement, 1895–1915*. Jefferson, NC: McFarland, 2004.

Gabler, Neal. "Neal Gabler." In *Television's Changing Image of American Jews*, ed. Neal Gabler, Frank Rich, and Joyce Antler, 3–12. Los Angeles: Norman Lear Center, 2000.

Garofalo, Reebee. *Rockin' Out: Popular Music in the USA*. Upper Saddle River, NJ: Pearson, 2011.

Gilchrist, Guy. "About Nancy." Nancy and Sluggo. http://nancyandsluggo.com.

Glenn, Susan A. "A Hero! Is Dot a Business?": Vaudeville Comedy and American Popular Entertainment." *Reviews in American History* 23, no. 4 (1995): 650–57.

Hamrah, A. S. "The Beckett/Bushmiller Letters." *American Reader*, 2013. http://theamericanreader.com/the-beckettbushmiller-letters.

Harvey, R. C. "The Lawrence Welk of Cartoonists: Ernie, Nancy, and the Bushmiller Society." *Comics Journal*, April 10, 2012. http://www.tcj.com/the-lawrence-welk-of-cartoonists-ernie-nancy-and-the-bushmiller-society.

Hodin, Mark. "Class, Consumption, and Ethnic Performance in Vaudeville." *Prospects* 22 (August 1997): 193–210.

Jenkins, Henry. *What Made Pistachio Nuts? Early Sound Comedy and the Vaudeville Aesthetic*. New York: Columbia University Press, 1992.

Jones, Gavin. *Strange Talk: The Politics of Dialect Literature in Gilded Age America*. Berkeley: University of California Press, 1999.

Keightley, Keir. "Hogan's *Tin Pan Alley*: R. F. Outcault and Popular Sheet Music." *Musical Quarterly* 98 (2015): 29–56.

Kimball, Robert, and Linda Emmet, eds. *The Complete Lyrics of Irving Berlin*. Winona, MN: Hal Leonard, 2000.

Levine, Lawrence. *Highbrow/Lowbrow: The Emergence of Cultural Hierarchy in America*. 1988. Cambridge, MA: Harvard University Press, 1999.

Markstein, Don. "Nancy." Toonopedia.com. http://www.toonopedia.com/nancy.htm.

McCloud, Scott. "Five Card Nancy." http://www.scottmccloud.com/4-inventions/nancy/index.html.

McLean, Albert F., Jr. *American Vaudeville as Ritual*. Louisville: University of Kentucky Press, 1965.

Nasaw, David. *Going Out: The Rise and Fall of Public Amusements*. New York: Basic Books, 1993.

Newgarden, Mark, and Paul Karasik. "How to Read Nancy." In *The Best of Ernie Bushmiller's "Nancy"*, ed. Brian Walker, 98–105. New York: Henry Holt, 1988.

Sammond, Nicholas. *The Birth of an Industry: Blackface Minstrelsy and the Rise of American Animation*. Durham, NC: Duke University Press, 2015.

Slide, Anthony. *The Encyclopedia of Vaudeville*. Jackson: University Press of Mississippi, 2012.

Slide, Anthony. *The Vaudevillians: A Dictionary of Vaudeville Performers*. Westport, CT: Arlington House, 1981.

Sobel, Bernard. *A Pictorial History of Vaudeville*. New York: Citadel Press, 1961.

Staples, Shirley. *Male-Female Comedy Teams in American Vaudeville, 1865–1932.* 1981. Ann Arbor, MI: UMI Research, 1984.
Steiner, Wendy. "The Clearest Eye." *New York Times*, April 5, 1992.
Taubman, Howard. *The Making of American Theatre.* New York: Putnam, 1967.
Walker, Brian, ed. *The Best of Ernie Bushmiller's "Nancy."* New York: Henry Holt, 1988.
Young, Hershini Bhana. *Haunting Capital: Memory, Text and the Black Diasporic Body.* Lebanon, NH: University Press of New England, 2006.

CHAPTER 3. FROM BATTLING ADULT AUTHORITY TO BATTLING THE OPPOSITE SEX: *LITTLE LULU* AS GAG PANEL AND COMIC BOOK

Brink, Carol Ryrie. *Caddie Woodlawn.* 1935. New York: Macmillan, 2006.
Cogan, Francis B. *All-American Girl: The Ideal of Real Womanhood in Mid-Nineteenth Century America.* Athens: University of Georgia Press, 1989.
Gorman, Michele. "Graphic Novels: For Tween Girls." *Teacher Librarian* 33, no. 3 (Fall 2006): 22.
Heintjes, Tom. "Marge and Lulu: The Art of the Deal." *Hogan's Alley*, May 22, 2012.
Hughes, L. Patrick. "When All the Experts Got It Wrong: Harry Truman's Upset Presidential Victory, 1948." Faculty Research and Resource Pages. History Department. Austin Community College. http://www2.austincc.edu/lpatrick/his1302/WhenAllTheExperts1.html 2000.
"Little Lulu." Dark Horse Comics. http://www.darkhorse.com/Books/13-390/Little-Lulu-Vol-9-Lucky-Lulu-TPB.
Maccoby, Eleanor Emmons. *The Two Sexes: Growing Up Apart, Coming Together.* Cambridge, MA: Harvard University Press, 1998.
Maglaty, Jeanne. "When Did Girls Start Wearing Pink? *Smithsonian*, April 7, 2011. http://www.smithsonianmag.com/arts-culture/when-did-girls-start-wearing-pink-1370097/?no-ist.
Marge. *Little Lulu.* Chicago: Rand McNally, 1936.
Marge. *Oh, Little Lulu!* David McKay, 1943.
Marlo Thomas and Friends. *Free to Be You and Me.* Bell Records/Arista Records, 1972. CD.
Meyerowitz, Joanne. Introduction to *Not June Cleaver: Women in Postwar America, 1945–1960*, 1–16. Philadelphia: Temple University Press, 1994.
Morris, Gary. "Film Sissies." *GLBTQ: An Encyclopedia of Gay, Lesbian, Bisexual, Transgender and Queer Culture.* http://www.glbtq.com/arts/film_sissies.html.
Murray, Janet Horowitz. "Feminist Fables: The Little Lulu Library." *Women's Review of Books* 7, no. 3 (December 1989): 13.
Paoletti, Jo B. *Pink and Blue: Telling the Boys from the Girls in America.* Bloomington: Indiana University Press, 2012.
Raiteri, Steve. "Graphic Novels [Book Reviews]." *Library Journal*, May 15, 2005, 98–103.
Rhoades, Shirrel. *Comic Books: How the Industry Works.* Peter Lang, 2008.

Sanders, Joe Sutliff. "Good and Funny, Old and New." *Teacher Librarian* 38, no. 1 (October 2010): 69.

Shutt, Craig. "Little Lulu, Big Media Star." *Hogan's Alley* 15 (2007): 32–43.

Spiegelman, Art, and Françoise Mouly. "Out of the Trash and into a Treasury." In *The Toon Treasury of Classic Children's Comics*, ed. Art Spiegelman and Françoise Mouly, 8–14. New York: Abrams, 2009.

Stanley, John, Irving Tripp, and Marge. *Giant Size Little Lulu*. Vol. 1. Milwaukie, OR: Dark Horse, 2010.

Walker, Mort. *The Lexicon of Comicana*. 1980. iUniverse, 2000.

CHAPTER 4. IN YOUR DREAMS: *LITTLE AUDREY*, FREUDIAN PSYCHOANALYSIS, AND POSTWAR CHILD PSYCHOLOGY

Beaty, Bart. *Fredric Wertham and the Critique of Mass Culture*. Jackson: University Press of Mississippi, 2005.

Beck, Jerry. Introduction to *Harvey Comics Classics*, vol. 5, *The Harvey Girls: The Harvey Girls: Little Audrey, Little Dot, and Little Lotta*, ed. Leslie Cabarga, 7–15. Milwaukie, OR: Dark Horse, 2009.

Booker, Ken. *The Post-utopian Imagination: American Culture in the Long 1950s*. Westport, CT: Greenwood, 2002.

Botkin, Benjamin A. *A Treasury of American Folklore*. 1944. New York: Crown, 1965.

Buhle, Mari Jo. "Feminism, Freud, and Popular Culture." *Chronicle of Higher Education* 45, no. 22 (February 5, 1999).

"Business Girl." In *Harvey Comics Classics*, vol. 5, *The Harvey Girls: Little Audrey, Little Dot, and Little Lotta*, ed. Leslie Cabarga, 81–85. Milwaukie, OR: Dark Horse, 2009.

Cabarga, Leslie. "Production Notes from the Editor." In *Harvey Comics Classics*, vol. 5, *The Harvey Girls: Little Audrey, Little Dot, and Little Lotta*, ed. Leslie Cabarga, 15. Milwaukie, OR: Dark Horse, 2009.

Carosso, Andrea. *Cold War Narratives: American Culture in the 1950s*. Bern, Switzerland: Peter Lang, 2012.

"Carpet Bagger." In *Harvey Comics Classics*, vol. 5, *The Harvey Girls: Little Audrey, Little Dot, and Little Lotta*, ed. Leslie Cabarga, 60–64. Milwaukie, OR: Dark Horse, 2009.

"The Culture of the 1950s." United States History, October 4, 2014. http://countrystudies.us/united-states/history-117.htm.

David, Robert. "Freud, Lacan, and the Subject of Cultural Studies." *College Literature* 18, no. 2 (June 1991): 22–37.

"Domino Theory." History.com. 2009. http://www.history.com/topics/cold-war/domino-theory.

Dunar, Andrew J. *America in the Fifties*. Syracuse, NY: Syracuse University Press, 2006.

Freud, Sigmund. *The Interpretation of Dreams*. 1899, 1915. New York: Barnes and Noble Classics, 2005.

Freud, Sigmund. *On Dreams*. Trans. M. D. Eder. 1911. Digireads, 2009.
"Freud in Oz." Publisher's summary. https://www.upress.umn.edu/book-division/books/freud-in-oz.
Frost, Jennifer. "Movie Star Suicide, Hollywood Gossip, and Popular Psychology in the 1950s and 1960s." *Journal of American Culture* 34, no. 2 (2011): 113–23.
Hale, Nathan G. *The Rise and Crisis of Psychoanalysis in the United States: Freud and the Americans, 1917–1985*. New York: Oxford University Press, 1995.
Halliwell, Martin. *American Culture in the 1950s*. Edinburgh University Press, 2007.
Harvey Comics. "Little Audrey." Harvey Comics Database Wiki. http://harveycomicsdatabase.wikia.com/wiki/Little_Audrey.
Kidd, Kenneth B. *Freud in Oz: At the Intersections of Psychoanalysis and Children's Literature*. Minneapolis: University of Minnesota Press, 2011.
Kramer, Yale. "Freud and the Culture Wars." *National Affairs* 124 (Summer 1996): 37–51.
LaPierre, Patrick. "Sigmund Freud and American Democratic Realism, 1915–1963." Paper presented at the Annual Meeting of the Midwest Political Science Association. Chicago, IL. April 3–6, 2008.
"Little Audrey (Comic Book Character)." Comic Book Realm. http://comicbookrealm.com/report/character/3308/little+audrey.
MacKenzie, W. Leslie. Introduction to *On Dreams*, by Sigmund Freud, trans. M. D. Eder, v–xxxii. 1914. Digireads, 2009.
Maurer, Maurer, ed. *Combat Squadrons of the Air Force: World War II*. Alan F. Simpson Historical Research Center and Office of Air Force History, Headquarters USAF, 1982.
"Midsummer Day's Dream." In *Harvey Comics Classics*, vol. 5, *The Harvey Girls: Little Audrey, Little Dot, and Little Lotta*, ed. Leslie Cabarga, 96–100. Milwaukie, OR: Dark Horse, 2009.
Nyberg, Amy Kiste. *Seal of Approval: The History of the Comics Code*. Jackson: University Press of Mississippi, 1998.
Pressman, Jack D. "American Analyzed." *Reviews in American History* 24, no. 3 (1996): 476–81.
Samuel, Lawrence. *Freud on Madison Avenue: Motivational Research and Subliminal Advertising in America*. Philadelphia: University of Pennsylvania Press, 2010.
Shumway, David R. "Watching Elvis: The Male Rock Star as Object of the Gaze." In *The Other Fifties: Interrogating Midcentury American Icons*, ed. Joel Foreman, 124–43. Urbana: University of Illinois Press, 1997.
Thwaites, Tony. *Reading Freud: Psychoanalysis as Cultural Theory*. Los Angeles: Sage, 2007.
United States Air Force Historical Division. Department of the Air Force. *Combat Squadrons of the Air Force: World War II*. Washington, DC, 1969.
Walden, Daniel, and Helena Poch. "Psychoanalysis of Dreams: Dream Theory and Its Relationship to Literature and Popular Culture: Freud, Billy Joel, Appelfeld, and Abe." *Journal of Popular Culture* 32, no. 1 (Summer 1998): 113–20.
"Who Killed Cock Robin." In *Harvey Comics Classics*, vol. 5, *The Harvey Girls: Little Audrey, Little Dot, and Little Lotta*, ed. Leslie Cabarga, 126–31. Milwaukie, OR: Dark Horse, 2009.
Wright, Bradford W. *Comic Book Nation: The Transformation of Youth Culture in America*. Baltimore, MD: Johns Hopkins University Press, 2003.

CHAPTER 5. "FROM THE TOP, STUPID!": THE *LI'L TOMBOY* COMIC BOOK SERIES, FEMALE JUVENILE DELINQUENCY, AND THE COMICS CODE

Abate, Michelle Ann. "Becoming a 'Red-Blooded' American: White Tomboyism and American Indian Tribalism in *Caddie Woodlawn*." *Mosaic: A Journal for the Interdisciplinary Study of Literature* 41, no. 4 (2008): 143–59.

Abate, Michelle Ann. *Tomboys: A Literary and Cultural History*. Philadelphia: Temple University Press, 2008.

Beaty, Bart. *Fredric Wertham and the Critique of Mass Culture*. Jackson: University Press of Mississippi, 2005.

Breines, Wini. "The 'Other' Fifties: Beats and Bad Girls." In *Not June Cleaver: Women and Gender in Postwar America, 1945–1960*, ed. Joanne Meyerowitz, 382–408. Philadelphia: Temple University Press, 1994.

Breines, Wini. "Postwar White Girls' Dark Others." In *The Other Fifties: Interrogating Midcentury American Icons*, ed. Joel Foreman, 53–77. Urbana: University of Illinois Press, 1997.

Breines, Wini. *Young, White, and Miserable: Growing Up Female in the Fifties*. Chicago: University of Chicago Press, 2001.

Caponegro, Ramona. "Where the 'Bad' Girls Are (Contained): Representations of the 1950s Female Juvenile Delinquent in Children's Literature and the *Ladies' Home Journal*." *Children's Literature Association Quarterly* 34, no. 4 (Winter 2009): 312–29.

Cavan, Ruth Shonle. *Juvenile Delinquency*. Philadelphia: J. B. Lippincott, 1964.

"The Comics Code." Code of the Comic Magazine Association of American, Inc. As Adopted in 1954. http://www.comicartville.com/comicscode.htm.

Cooke, Jon B., and Christopher Irving. "The Charlton Empire: A Brief History of the Derby, Connecticut, Publisher." *Comic Book Artist*, no. 9 (August 2000). TwoMorrows Publishing.

Cross, Gary. *The Cute and the Cool: Wondrous Innocence and Modern American Children's Culture*. New York: Oxford University Press, 2004.

Danziger-Russell, Jacqueline. *Girls and Their Comics: Finding the Female Voice in Comic Book Narrative*. Lanham, MD: Scarecrow, 2013.

Devlin, Rachel. "Female Juvenile Delinquency and the Problem of Sexual Authority in America, 1945–1965." In *Delinquents and Debutantes: Twentieth-Century American Girls' Cultures*, ed. Sherrie A. Inness, 83–106. New York: NYU Press, 1998.

Doherty, Thomas. *Teenagers and Teenpics: The Juvenilization of American Movies in the 1950s*. Philadelphia: Temple University Press, 2002.

Duncan, Randy. "Charlton Comics." *Encyclopedia of Comics and Graphic Novels*. Vol. 1. Ed. M. Keith Booker. Santa Barbara, CA: Greenwood/ABC-CLIO.

Faderman, Lillian. *Odd Girls and Twilight Lovers: A History of Lesbian Life in Twentieth Century America*. New York: Penguin, 1991.

Fine, Benjamin. *1,000,000 Delinquents*. New York: Signet, 1957.

Foreman, Joel. Introduction to *The Other Fifties: Interrogating Midcentury American Icons*, 1–23. Urbana: University of Illinois Press, 1997.

Fyvel, T. R. *Troublemakers: Rebellious Youth in an Affluent Society*. 1961. New York: Schocken, 1966.

Gabilliet, Jean-Paul. *Of Comics and Men: A Cultural History of American Comic Books*. Trans. Bart Beaty and Nick Nguyen. Jackson: University Press of Mississippi, 2010.
Hajdu, David. *The Ten-Cent Plague: The Great Comic-Book Scare and How It Changed America*. New York: Farrar, Straus and Giroux, 2008.
[Johnson, Frank (artist).] "All Bankers Beware." *Li'l Tomboy* 14, no. 97 (January 1958): n.p.
[Johnson, Frank (a).] "Are You for Real?" *Li'l Rascal Twins* 1, no. 8 (January 1958): n.p.
[Johnson, Frank (a).] "At the Zoo." *Li'l Tomboy* 14, no. 96 (November 1957): n.p.
[Johnson, Frank (a).] "At the Zoo." *Li'l Rascal Twins* 1, no. 6 (September 1957): n.p.
[Johnson, Frank (a).] "Baby Sitter First Class." *Li'l Tomboy* 14, no. 98 (March 1958): n.p.
[Johnson, Frank (a).] "Bargain Day." *Li'l Tomboy* 14, no. 93 (March 1957): n.p.
[Johnson, Frank (a).] "Can't Tell a Book by Its Cover." *Li'l Tomboy* 14, no. 95 (September 1957): n.p.
[Johnson, Frank (a).] "Driving Lesson." *Li'l Tomboy* 14, no. 95 (September 1957): n.p.
[Johnson, Frank (a).] "First Movie." *Li'l Tomboy* 14, no. 93 (March 1957): n.p.
[Johnson, Frank (a).] "Ghost in the House." *Li'l Tomboy* 14, no. 106 (October 1959): n.p.
[Johnson, Frank (a).] "A Girl on the Team." *Li'l Tomboy* 14, no. 92 (October 1956): n.p.
[Johnson, Frank (a).] "Goes Shopping." *Li'l Tomboy* 14, no. 95 (September 1957): n.p.
[Johnson, Frank (a).] "The Hair-Raiser." *Li'l Tomboy* 14, no. 94 (January 1957): n.p.
[Johnson, Frank (a).] "Let Us into the Ballgame." *Li'l Rascal Twins* 1, no. 7 (November 1957): n.p.
[Johnson, Frank (a).] "Li'l Genius and Li'l Tomboy." *Li'l Genius* 1, no. 11 (October 1956): n.p.
[Johnson, Frank (a).] "Lost and Found." *Li'l Rascal Twins* 1, no. 7 (November 1957): n.p.
[Johnson, Frank (a).] "Making like a Lady." *Li'l Tomboy* 14, no. 106 (October 1959): n.p.
[Johnson, Frank (a).] "Monkey Business." *Li'l Rascal Twins* 1, no. 10 (June 1958): n.p.
[Johnson, Frank (a).] "Office Pest." *Li'l Tomboy* 14, no. 98 (March 1958): n.p.
[Johnson, Frank (a).] "Reel Robbery." *Li'l Rascal Twins* 1, no. 12 (November 1958): n.p.
[Johnson, Frank (a).] "Sign Happy." *Li'l Tomboy* 14, no. 105 (August 1959): n.p.
[Johnson, Frank (a).] "That's Show Business." *Li'l Rascal Twins* 1, no. 16 (August 1959): n.p.
[Johnson, Frank (a).] "Vacation Bound." *Li'l Tomboy* 14, no. 103 (March 1959): n.p.
[Johnson, Frank (a).] "A Visit with Aunt Penelope." *Li'l Tomboy* 14, no. 103 (March 1959): n.p.
[Johnson, Frank (a).] "We Love Her Just as She Is." *Li'l Tomboy* 14, no. 92 (October 1956): n.p.
Ketcham, Hank. *Hank Ketcham's Complete Dennis the Menace, 1953–1954*. Seattle, WA: Fantagraphics Books, 2006.
Lindner, Robert. "The Mutiny of the Young." In *Must You Conform?* by Robert Lindner, 3–28. New York: Rinehart, 1956.
Lindner, Robert. "Raise Your Child to Be a Rebel." *McCall's*, February 1956, 31, 100–104.
Lynn, Susan. "Gender and Progressive Politics: A Bridge to Social Activism of the 1960s." In *Not June Cleaver: Women and Gender in Postwar America, 1945–1960*, ed. Joanne Meyerowitz, 103–27. Philadelphia: Temple University Press, 1994.
Medovoi, Leerom. *Rebels: Youth and the Cold War Origins of Identity*. Durham, NC: Duke University Press, 2005.
Meyerowitz, Joanne. Introduction to *Not June Cleaver: Women and Gender in Postwar America, 1945–1960*, ed. Joanne Meyerowitz, 1–16. Philadelphia: Temple University Press, 1994.

Nyberg, Amy Kiste. *Seal of Approval: The History of the Comics Code*. Jackson: University Press of Mississippi, 1998.

Palladino, Grace. *Teenagers: An American History*. New York: Basic Books, 1997.

Robbins, Trina. *From Girls to Grrrlz: A History of Female Comics from Teens to Zines*. San Francisco: Chronicle Books, 1999.

Wertham, Fredric. *Seduction of the Innocent*. 1954. Laurel, NY: Main Road Books, 2004.

Wright, Bradford W. *Comic Book Nation: The Transformation of Youth Culture in America*. Baltimore, MD: Johns Hopkins University Press, 2001.

York, Rafiel. "Rebellion in Riverdale." In *Comic Books and the Cold War, 1946–1962: Essays on the Graphic Treatment of Communism, the Code and Social Concerns*, ed. Chris York and Rafiel York, 103–14. Jefferson, NC: McFarland, 2012.

EPILOGUE. FROM LI'L TO BIG: THE LEGACY OF CLASSIC AMERICAN COMICS STARRING GIRLS

Abate, Michelle Ann. "'Springtime in the South Is like a Song in My Heart': Raina Telgemeier's *Drama*, the Romanticization of the Plantation South, and the Romance Plot." *Children's Literature in Education*. Forthcoming.

Abate, Michelle Ann. *Tomboys: A Literary and Cultural History*. Philadelphia: Temple University Press, 2008.

Beck, Jerry. Introduction to *Harvey Comics Classics*, vol. 5, *The Harvey Girls: Little Audrey, Little Dot, and Little Lotta*, ed. Leslie Cabarga, 7–15. Milwaukie, OR: Dark Horse, 2009.

Becker, Stephen D. *Comic Art in America: A Social History of the Funnies, the Political Cartoons, Magazine Humor, Sporting Cartoons, and Animated Cartoons*. New York: Simon and Schuster, 1959.

Beland, Richard. "Little Annie Rooney." *Jungle Frolics*, July 2013. http://junglefrolics.blogspot.com/2013/07/little-annie-rooney.html.

Beland, Richard. "Little Orphan Annie: Merchandise." *Jungle Frolics*, January 12, 2012. http://junglefrolics.blogspot.com/2012/01/little-orphan-annie-merchandise.html.

Blackbeard, Bill, and Martin Williams, eds. *The Smithsonian Collection of Newspaper Comics*. New York: Harry N. Abrams, 1977.

Gordon, Ian. *Comic Strips and Consumer Culture, 1890–1945*. Washington, DC: Smithsonian Institution Press, 1998.

Goulart, Ron. *The Funnies: 100 Years of American Comic Strips*. Holbrook, MA: Adams, 1995.

Hajdu, David. *The Ten-Cent Plague: The Great Comic-Book Scare and How It Changed America*. New York: Farrar, Straus and Giroux, 2008.

Heintjes, Tom. "Marge and Lulu: The Art of the Deal." *Hogan's Alley*, May 22, 2012.

Hennum, Shea, J. A. Micheline, Caitlin Rosberg, and Oliver Sava. "Raina Telgemeier's *Smile* Signaled a Sea Change in Comics Still Felt Today." *AV Club*, June 29, 2016. http://www.avclub.com/article/raina-telgemeiers-smile-signaled-sea-change-comics-238414.

Horn, Maurice. "100 Years of Comics: An Introduction." In *100 Years of American Newspaper Comics: An Illustrated Encyclopedia*, ed. Maurice Horn, 11–19. New York: Gramercy, 1996.

Huffman, Lois E., and Roslyn P. Moffit. "Girls (of All Ages) Are Wild about Comics and Graphic Novels." NCRA: North Carolina Reading Association, June 1, 2015. http://www.ncreading.org/girls-of-all-ages-are-wild-about-comics-and-graphic-novels.

Inge, M. Thomas. *Comics as Culture*. Jackson: University Press of Mississippi, 1990.

Inness, Sherrie A. *Tough Girls: Women Warriors and Wonder Women in Popular Culture*. Philadelphia: University of Pennsylvania Press, 1999.

Jiménez, Laura M. "Ghosts: A Swing and a Hard Miss." *Booktoss*, September 18, 2016. https://booktoss.blog/2016/09/18/ghosts-swing-and-a-hard-miss.

Katz, Harry, ed. *Cartoon America: Comic Art in the Library of Congress*. New York: Harry N. Abrams, 2006.

Kuskin, William. "V Is for Villainess." Foreword to *Vixens, Vamps, and Vipers: Lost Villainesses of Golden Age Comics*, by Mike Madrid, 6–9. Minneapolis, MN: Exterminating Angel Press, 2014.

"Little Mary Mixup." Comic Vine. http://comicvine.gamespot.com/little-mary-mixup/4005-33171.

Lopes, Paul. *Demanding Respect: The Evolution of the American Comic Book*. Philadelphia: Temple University Press, 2009.

Madrid, Mike. *Divas, Dames, and Daredevils: Lost Heroines of Golden Age Comics*. Minneapolis, MN: Exterminating Angel Press, 2013.

Madrid, Mike. *The Supergirls: Fashion, Feminism, Fantasy, and the History of Comic Book Heroines*. Minneapolis, MN: Exterminating Angel Press, 2009.

Madrid, Mike. *Vixens, Vamps, and Vipers: Lost Villainesses of Golden Age Comics*. Minneapolis, MN: Exterminating Angel Press, 2014.

Markstein, Don. "The Adventures of Patsy." Toonopedia.com. 2005. http://www.toonopedia.com/phanmagi.htm.

Markstein, Don. "Li'l Jinx." Toonopedia.com. http://www.toonopedia.com/liljinx.htm.

Markstein, Don. "Little Annie Rooney." Toonopedia.com. 2008. http://www.toonopedia.com/annieroo.htm.

Markstein, Don. "Little Iodine." Toonopedia.com. 2010. http://www.toonopedia.com/iodine.htm.

Markstein, Don. "Little Mary Mixup." Toonopedia.com. 2005. http://www.toonopedia.com/mixup.htm.

Mey. "Drawn to Comics: Raina Telgemeier's NYT Bestselling Graphic Novels Are Perfect for Middle School Girls." Autostraddle, August 11, 2015. http://www.autostraddle.com/tag/drawn-to-comics.

Montclare, Brandon, Amy Reeder, and Natacha Bustos. *Moon Girl and Devil Dinosaur*. Vol. 1, *BFF*. New York: Marvel, 2016.

Newgarden, Mark, and Paul Karasik. "How to Read Nancy." In *The Best of Ernie Bushmiller's "Nancy"*, ed. Brian Walker, 98–105. New York: Henry Holt, 1988.

Nicholson, Hope. *Moonshot: The Indigenous Comics Collection*. Cupertino, CA: Alternative Comics, 2015.

Reese, Debbie. "Not Recommended: *Ghosts* by Raina Telgemeier." *American Indians in Children's Literature*, September 17, 2016. https://americanindiansinchildrensliterature.blogspot.com/2016/09/not-recommended-ghosts-by-raina.html.

Robbins, Trina. *The Great Women Superheroes*. Northampton, MA: Kitchen Sink, 1996.

Robinson, Jerry. *The Comics: An Illustrated History of Comic Strip Art, 1895–2010*. Milwaukie, OR: Dark Horse, 2011.

Vaughan, Brian K., and Cliff Chiang. *Paper Girls*. Vol. 1. Berkeley, CA: Image Comics, 2016.

Walker, Brian. *Children of the Yellow Kid: The Evolution of the American Comic Strip*. Seattle: University of Washington Press, 1998.

Walker, Brian. *The Comics: The Complete Collection*. New York: Abrams, 2011.

Wallace, Derek. "The Yellow Kid." *Virtue* 1, no. 14 (July 2005). www.virtuemag.com/articles/the-yellow-kid.

Wood, Mary. Introduction to *The Yellow Kid on the Paper Stage*. February 2, 2004. University of Virginia Law School. http://xroads.virginia.edu/~ma04/wood/ykid/intro.htm.

Wright, Bradford W. *Comic Book Nation: The Transformation of Youth Culture in America*. Baltimore, MD: Johns Hopkins University Press, 2001.

Index

Page numbers in **bold** indicate illustrations.

Abbie & Slats, 156
ACMP (Association of Comics Magazine Publishers), 174n7
Action Comics, 160
adoption, as American literary trope, 39
Adventure Time with Orphan Annie (radio broadcast), 15
Adventures of Patsy, The, 13, 155, 157, 177n10
African Americans. *See* racial dynamics
Albee, Edward Franklin, 49
Alcott, Louisa May: *Eight Cousins* (1875), 18; *Little Women* (1868), 68
Alger, Horatio, *Ragged Dick* (1868), 17
All About Eve (film, 1950), 96
Allen, Frederick Lewis, 31
Allen, Gracie, 44, 52, 53–54, 55
American character, orphan character and/as, 32–40
American Indian culture. *See* Native American culture
American society, transformation of (in 1920s), 31
Angel Child, The, 176n7
Anya's Ghost (graphic novel, 2011), 12, 168
Archie, 6, 13, 115, 147
Association of Comics Magazine Publishers (ACMP), 174n7
Astaire, Fred, 44
Aunt Jemima, 56
Auster, Donald, 172n3
Autograph Company, 80

Autostraddle, 3
Ayers, Dick, 134
Baby-Sitters Club, The, books, 169
Barrie, J. M., *Peter Pan* (1904), 113
Barrymore, Ethel, 44
Barrymore, Lionel, 44
Batgirl, 3
Baum, Frank L., *The Wizard of Oz* (1900), 113
Beat Generation, 117, 129
Beaty, Bart, 92, 94
Bechdel, Alison, 169
Beck, Jerry, 90, 162, 163
Beck, Stephen, 163
Becker, Stephen, 153, 154
behavioral and social codes, 7–8; American society of 1920s questioning, 31–32; *Little Iodine* defying, 168; *Little Lulu*, prewar-era conflict between adults and children in, **64**, 65, 71–77, **73**, 75–79; *Little Orphan Annie*, defying "good" orphan girl stereotype, 25–32, **26–30**; *Nancy*, wholesome and family-friendly code of vaudeville and, 49–50, 172n2. *See also* Comics Code; juvenile delinquency
Beland, Richard, 156, 158
Bell, Cece, 3
Berlatsky, Noah, 4
Berle, Milton, 44, 45

Bernstein, Robin, 13
Big Little Books, 155, 156
Bishop, Walter, 154
Blackboard Jungle (film, 1955), 125
Blosser, Merrill, 154
blue and pink, gendered/nongendered use of, 66, 67, 69
Bobby Bumps (animated shorts, 1915–1925), 153
Bobby Make-Believe, 175n2
Botkin, Benjamin A., 91
Brainard, Joe, 5
branding, licensing, and merchandising, 8, 158–60; of *Buster Brown*, 153–54, 158; Freudian theory in postwar advertising, 96–97; of *Kewpies*, 171n3; of *Little Annie Rooney*, 159; of *Little Audrey*, 91, 98; of *Little Iodine*, 177n11; of *Little Lulu*, 8, 63–64, 80–81, 91, 159; of *Little Mary Mixup*, 177n11; of *Little Orphan Annie*, 158–59; of the Yellow Kid, 152, 158
Brando, Marlon, 96
Breiner, Wini, 128–29
Brice, Fanny, 44
Bringing Up Bill, 154
Bringing Up Father, 158
Brink, Carol Ryrie, *Caddie Woodlawn* (1935), 68
Brosgol, Vera, 12
Buell, Marjorie Henderson (Marge), 4, 9, 63, 71, 80–82, 90–91, 159. See also *Little Lulu*
Bugs Bunny, 61–62
Buhle, Mary Jo, 94
Bulwer-Lytton, Edward, 72–73, **73**
Burnett, Frances Hodgson: *A Little Princess* (1905), 18; *The Secret Garden* (1911), 18
Burns, George, 44, 48, 52, 53–54, 55
Burroughs, Edgar Rice, *Tarzan of the Apes* (1912), 17–18
Bushmiller, Ernest, Sr., 47
Bushmiller, Ernie, 4, 5, 9, 41, 42, 45–47, 48, 50, 51, 55, 56, 155. See also *Nancy*
Buster Brown, 153–54, 158, 159

Buster Brown Shoe Co., 153–54
Butler, Judith, 124
Buttons and Fatty, 154
Byrnes, Gene, 154

Cabarga, Leslie, 98
Campbell Soup Kids, 176n7
Caniff, Milton, 157
Cantor, Eddie, 44, 48, 52, 54
Canwell, Bruce, 5, 16
Caponegro, Ramona, 125, 127
Carew, Kate, 176n7
Carosso, Andrea, 96–97
Carr, Gene, 154, 175n1
Carroll, Lewis, *Alice's Adventures in Wonderland* (1865), 113
Carter, Ad, 154
Cartoon America: Comic Art in the Library of Congress (2006), 158
Casper the Friendly Ghost, 91, 149, 156
Cat on a Hot Tin Roof (film, 1958), 96
Cavan, Ruth Shonle, 127–28
CENSORED box used in *Li'l Tomboy*, 138–39, **139**
Chaplin, Charlie, 44, 48
Charlton Publications, 6, 11, 114, 115, 116, 138, 147, 149–51
Chicago Tribune, 16
childhood and youth, changing perceptions of: age and gender of main character in *Li'l Tomboy* used to elude Comics Code censorship, 146–47; in *Little Orphan Annie*, 20–22; sexual segregation of American childhood, development of, 66–71. See also juvenile delinquency
Chub's Big Brother, 154
Clowes, Daniel, 42
CMAA (Comics Magazine Association of America), 132–34, 137, 139, 146, 148, 150, 174n7
Cogan, Francis B., 68
Cold War anxieties, in *Little Audrey*, 104–6, **105, 106**

Index

comic book sales, decline in (early 1950s), 148, 175n8
Comics Code: age and gender of *Li'l Tomboy* main character used to elude censorship by, 146–47; Charlton Publications' response to, 149–51; creation and functioning of, 132–37; effects on comic book industry, 137, 148–50; Freudian theory and, 112; juvenile delinquency and comics reading linked, 130–32; *Li'l Tomboy* and, 11, 116, 130, 136–47, **139, 141, 143–45**; *Little Iodine* and, 168; Marvel Comics' 1971 defiance of, 137; seal of approval, 138; women as censors, 135
Comics Code Authority, 11, 116, 133, 135, 136, 137, 138, 149
Comics Magazine Association of America (CMAA), 132–34, 137, 139, 146, 148, 150, 174n7
Comics on Parade, 156
comics with young female protagonists. *See* young female protagonists in classic American comics
commercialization. *See* branding, licensing, and merchandising
communist/McCarthy anxieties, in *Little Audrey*, 110–11
Cooke, Jon B., 150
Crestwood/Mainline Comics, 149
crime and criminals, in *Li'l Tomboy*, 141–43, **143**, 150
Crosby, Bing, 56
Crosby, Percy, 154
Cross, Gary, 147
cross-promotional appearances of characters in other comics, 174n2
Cul de Sac, vii
Cummins, Susanna Maria, *The Lamplighter* (1854), 18

Danziger-Russell, Jane, 3; *Girls and Their Comics: Finding a Female Voice in Comic Book Narrative* (2013), 14

Davis, Jim, 155
delinquents. *See* juvenile delinquency
Dell Publications, 81, 148, 167
Dennis the Menace, 70, 114, 115, 147
Depression. *See* Great Depression
Devlin, Rachel, 125, 127
Dickens, Charles, 24
Dickie Dare, 157
DiMeglio, John E., 43, 44, 45, 46, 47, 48, 49, 62
Dimples, 176n7
Dirks, Rudolph, 46, 153, 175n1
Doherty, Thomas, 125
domino theory anxieties, in *Little Audrey*, 107
Dottie Dimple, 176n7
Drake, Arnold, 86
Drama (graphic novel, 2012), 169, 170, 177n15
Drayton, Grace, 176n7
dream analysis. *See* Freud, Sigmund, and Freudian psychoanalysis; *Little Audrey*
Dunar, Andrew J., 98
Duncan, Randy, 149

EC Comics, 148
Edwards, Joe, 164
Eisenhower, Dwight D., 125
Erdman, Andrew K., 43, 49
Erikson, Erik, 95

Famous Studios, 90
Fanon, Frantz, 59
Farr, Jack, 154
Fawcett Publications, 149, 150
Feature Book, 156
Feininger, Lyonel, 153
Felix the Cat, 61–62, 158
feminism, 7, 13, 36, 82, 83, 84, 86, 117, 130, 167
Fera, A. C., 154
Fields, Lew, 52, 53
Fields, W. C., 44
Fine, Benjamin, *1,000,000 Delinquents* (1955), 125

Fineheimer Twins, Die, 175n1
firearms, depiction of, in *Li'l Tomboy*, 140–41, **141**
Foote, Cone & Belding (advertising company), 80
Foreman, Joel, 117, 128–29
Freckles and His Friends, 154
Freud, Sigmund, and Freudian psychoanalysis: *Civilization and Its Discontents*, 95; Clark University lectures (1909), 94; comics, therapeutic and pernicious views of, 112–13; *The Interpretation of Dreams* (1899), 92, 98–99; *Little Audrey* critiquing, 92–93, 101, 111–12, 113; *On Dreams* (1901/1952/1963), 98–100, 103, 109; postwar ascendancy of Freudian theory, 91–92, 93–97, 111, 173n1
Fritzi Ritz, 4–5, 41, 48
Fromm, Erich, 95
Fun Home (2006), 3, 168
Funny Animals and funny animal comics, 150–51

Gabilliet, Jean-Paul, 132–33, 175n8
Garfield, 155
Gasoline Alley, 159
Gatewood, Worth, 15, 37
gender roles, 7–8; American society of 1920s questioning, 31–32; Comics Code censors, women as, 135; in Great Depression era, 157; juvenile delinquency as defiance of, 127–28; *Li'l Tomboy* challenging, 115–16, 117–24, **118**; *Li'l Tomboy* main character's age and gender used to elude Comics Code, 146–47; *Little Lotta*, body-shaming in, 177n12; *Little Lulu*, as proxy for gender war between women and men, 87–88; *Little Lulu*, postwar conflict between boys and girls in, 65–66, 81–87, **84**, **85**, 89; *Little Lulu*, reasons for loss of popularity of, 86–87; *Little Orphan Annie*, defying "good" orphan girl stereotype, 25–32, **26–30**; "the other 1950s," nonconformist women in, 116, 117–19; redomestication campaign of 1950s, 88, 117; sexual segregation of American childhood, development of, 66–71; Wertham's condemnation of comics and, 131–32

Ghost World, 168
Ghosts (graphic novel, 2016), 177n15
Gilchrist, Guy, 42–43
Girl Power movement, 7
girls as comics characters. *See* young female protagonists in classic American comics
Glenn, Susan A., 51, 54
Golding, William, *The Lord of the Flies* (1954), 95
Goldmark, Daniel, 62
Gone with the Wind (film, 1939), **56**
Gordon, Ian, 154; *Comic Strips and Consumer Culture, 1890–1945* (1998), 159
Gorman, Michele, 89
Goulart, Ron, 155, 175n2, 176n7, 176n9; *The Funnies: 100 Years of American Comic Strips* (1995), 154
Graff, Mel, 157
Gray, Harold, 5, 15–16, 17, 19, 29, 37–38, 156, 171n1, 176n9. *See also Little Orphan Annie*
Great Depression: gender roles affected by, 157; *Little Lulu* and, 65, 71; *Little Orphan Annie* and, 5, 17, 32, 34, 38, 172n3; sexual segregation of American childhood, development of, 69–70

Hajdu, David, 130, 134, 148; *The Ten-Cent Plague: The Great Comic-Book Scare and How It Changed America* (2008), 160
Hale, Nathan C., 92
Hallmark greeting cards, 80
Hamrah, A. S., 5
Harvey, Alfred, 91
Harvey, R. C., 37, 42, 54, 55, 56
Harvey Publications/Harvey Comics, 91, 98, 149, 163–64
Hatlo, Jimmy, 157–58

Hays Code, 133
Heath, Russ, 134
Heer, Jeet, 24, 37
Heintjes, Tom, 65, 82, 86, 159
Held, Virginia, 125
Hemingway, Ernest, 66
Hereville (graphic novel, 2010), 3, 168
Hitchcock, Alfred, 96
Hodin, Mark, 43, 44
Hogan's Alley, 46, 152–53, 159
Hope, Bob, 44, 45, 56
Horn, Maurice: *Women in the Comics* (1971/1981/2001), 6; *World Encyclopedia of Comics* (1976), 55
Horney, Karen, 95
Hot Stuff, 149
Houdini, Harry, 46
Huffman, Lois E., 168

Inness, Sherrie, 160, 168
Irving, Christopher, 150

Jenkins, Henry, 48, 50, 54, 55
Jessel, George, 52
Jim Crow, **59**
Jiménez, Laura M., 177n15
Johnson, Frank, 147
Jolson, Al, 44, 56, 57, **58**
Jones, Gavin, 43, 52, 55
Just Boy (later *Elmer*), 154
Just Kids, 154, 174n5
juvenile delinquency: as 1950s problem, 116, 125–26, 127–29; comics reading linked to, 130–32; co-opting elements of black culture, 128–29; gender roles, as defiance of, 127–28; *Li'l Tomboy*, as juvenile delinquent, 115–16, 125–30, **128**, **129**; *Li'l Tomboy* main character's age and gender used to elude accusations of, 146–47

Karasik, Paul, 5, 50, 51, 55, 155
Katzenjammer Kids, The, 46, 88, 153, 158, 175n1
Keaton, Buster, 44

Keightley, Keir, 46
Keith, B. F., 49
Kennedy, John F., 97
Kewpies, 171n3
Kidd, Kenneth B., *Freud in Oz: At the Intersections of Freud and Psychoanalysis* (2011), 113
Kin-der-Kids, The, 153
King, Frank, 175n2
King Comics, 156
King Features Syndicate, 158, **159**
Kirby, Jack, 149
Kleenex ads, *Little Lulu* in (1944–1960), 63, 80
Knerr, H. H., 175n1
Kramer, Yale, 94–95, 111
Kuskin, William, 168

Ladies' Home Journal, 67, 132
Lady in the Dark (play/film, 1944), 96
language: CENSORED box used in *Li'l Tomboy*, 138–39, **139**; dialect, use of, in *Nancy*, 9, 42, 49, 52–53; slang, use of, in *Li'l Tomboy*, 145–46
LaPierre, Patrick, 95
Lawrence Welk Show, The (TV show), 42, 45
Lee, Gypsy Rose, 44
Leigh, Vivian, **56**, 96
licensing. *See* branding, licensing, and merchandising
Li'l Genius and Li'l Genius character, 11, 113, 115, 116, 126, 130, 136, 137, 141–42, 146, 147, 151
Li'l Jinx, 13, 164–67, **165**, **166**, 168, 177n13
Li'l Jinx Giant Laugh-Out, **166**
Li'l Rascal Twins, 115, 126, 130, 136–43, **143**
Li'l Tomboy, 11, 114–51; age and gender of main character used to elude Comics Code censorship, 146–47; CENSORED box used in, 138–39, **139**; Charlton Publications' response to Comics Code and, 149–51; Comics Code and, 11, 116, 130, 136–47, **139**, **141**, 143–45; crime and criminals in, 141–43, **143**, 150; dynamite stick replacing *i* in title, 139–40, 150;

firearms, depiction of, 140–41, **141**; *Funny Animals* and funny animal comics, 150–51; gender stereotypes challenged by, 115–16, 117–24, **118**; heroic qualities of, 161; importance in comic book history, 170; as juvenile delinquent, 115–16, 125–30, **128, 129**; *Li'l Genius*, debut in (1956), 114, 136, 137, 151; *Li'l Rascal Twins* as spin-off from, 115, 126, 130, 136–43, **143**; *Little Iodine* compared, 168; police, treatment of, 143–45, **144, 145**, 150; popularity of, 115; racial dynamics in, 13, 128–30, 174n5; scholarly attention, lack of, 115; slang, use of, 145–46; unchanging age and appearance of, 173n1

Li'l Tomboy characters: Aunt Penelope, 122; grandmother, 122; Li'l Genius (cousin Ollie), 126, 130, 136, 141–42, 146, 147, 151; neighborhood boys, 122–24

Lindner, Robert, 121, 140

Little Annie Rooney, 13, 155, 156, 158, **159**, 170, 176nn8–9

Little Audrey, 6, 10–11, 90–113; animated shorts (from 1947), 90–91, 173n2; branding, licensing, and merchandising, 91, 98; "Carpet Bagger" (1953), 101–7, **102–6**; Cold War anxieties in, 104–6, **105, 106**; comic book series (1948–1976), 91, 172n3; comic strip (1951), 91, 98; communist/McCarthy anxieties in, 110–11; as critique of Freudian theory, 92–93, 101, 111–12, 113; domino theory anxieties in, 107; dream sequences in, 91, 100–112, **102–6, 109, 110**, 173n2; Freud's *Interpretation of Dreams* and *On Dreams*, 92, 98–100, 102–3; Harvey Girls, as one of, 163–64; heroic qualities of, 161; importance in comic book history, 170; jokes based on, 91; *Little Lulu*, as imitation of, 90–91; long decade of 1950s as heyday of, 97–98; "Midsummer Day's Dream" (1953), 107–8; phobic behavior in, 107; popularity of, 90, 91; postwar ascendancy of Freudian theory and, 91–92, 93–97, 111, 173n1; sexual anxiety in, 109–10, **110**; "Who Killed Cock Robin" (1953), 109–11, **109, 110**

Little Audrey characters: Little Dot and Little Lotta, 13, 96, 162, 163; Melvin, 107–8; Mr. Turtle and Mr. Ostrich, **109**, 110–11; Tiny, 101, 106, 107

Little Dot, 13, 96, 149, 162–64, **162**

Little Dot Dotland, 163

little girls as comics characters. *See* young female protagonists in classic American comics

Little Iodine, 13, 155, 157–58, 164, 167–68, **167**, 170, 177n11, 177n14

Little Jimmy, 154, 158

Little Lotta, 13, 96, 162, 163–64, **164**, 177n12

Little Lulu, 4, 9–10, 63–89; adults and children, prewar-era conflict between, **64**, 65, 71–77, **73**, **75–79**; as animated character (1940s–1990s), 63, 79, 90; boys and girls, postwar conflict between, 65–66, 81–87, **84, 85**, 89; branding, licensing, and merchandising of, 8, 63–64, 80–81, 91, 159; as comic book series (*Marge's Little Lulu*, 1948–1984), 64–65, 81–86, **84, 85**, 87; as comic strip (1945–1969), 63, 86; as gag panel (1935–1944), 63, **64**, 65, 71–77, **73, 75–79**, 80; importance in comic book history, 170; in Kleenex ads (1944–1960), 63, 80; *Li'l Jinx* and, 164; *Little Audrey* as imitation of, 90–91; loss of popularity from 1970s, 86–87; modern popularity of, 5; *Oh, Little Lulu!* collection (1943), 74–77; Orphan Annie compared, 5; as proxy for gender war between women and men, 87–88; Rand McNally collection (1936), 72–74, 173n2; sexual segregation of American childhood, development of, 66–71, 86–87; transition from gag panel written by woman to comic book written by two men, 65–66, 81–82

Little Lulu characters: Alvin Jones, 82, 83; Annie Inch, 82, 83; in comic book series, 82; in gag panels, 74, 76–77, **76**, **79**, 173n2; Tubby Tomkins, 74, 76–77, **76**, **79**, 82, 83, 84–86, **84**
Little Mary Mixup, 13, 155–56, 158, 177n11
Little Nemo in Slumberland, 88, 153, 157, 175n2, 176n7
Little Orphan Annie, vii, 5, 9, 15–40; adoption, as American literary trope, 39; American character, orphan character and/as, 32–40; branding, licensing, and merchandising, 158–59; childhood and youth, changing perceptions of, 20–22; continuing popularity of, 5, 15–16, 39–40; development of (debut 1924), 15–16, 171–72n1; engagement with orphan girl tradition, 16–24, **21**; familial boundaries, moving beyond, 32–36; Great Depression and, 5, 17, 32, 34, 38, 172n3; influences on, 24; *Little Annie Rooney* imitating, 156, 159; Little Lulu compared, 5; reorphaning of, 32, 34; sassiness and scrappiness defying "good" orphan girl behavioral code, 25–32, **26–30**; scholarly work on, 6, 38–39; sociopolitical commentary in, 17, 33–34, 35–38; sympathetic and sentimental aspects of, 18–20, 22–24, 38
Little Orphan Annie characters: Daddy Warbucks, 16, 17, 23–24, 29–30, 33, 34, 35, 36, 37, 40; Miss, 20, **21**, 22, **26**, 27, 34; Miss Hannigan, 156; Mr. Willis, 34, 35; Mrs. Bottle, 22; Mrs. Warbucks, 22, 23, 34; Sandy (dog), 16, 28, **30**, 34, 37, 156; Silo family, 34–36
Little Orphan Annie musical/films, 5, 15
Little Orphan Annie radio broadcasts, 5, 15
Lloyd, Harold, 46
Lopez, Paul, *Demanding Respect: The Evolution of the American Comic Book* (2009), 160
Lott, Eric, 56

Lulu. See *Little Lulu*
Lumberjanes, 3, 168, 169, 170

Maccoby, Eleanor Emmons, 66, 70–71
MacKenzie, W. Leslie, 103, 109
Mad, 148
Madge the Magician's Daughter, 176n7
Madrid, Mike, 160; *Divas, Dames, and Daredevils: Lost Heroines of Golden Age Comics* (2012), 6, 161; *The Supergirls: Fashion, Feminism, Fantasy, and the History of Comic Book Heroines* (2009), 6, 161; *Vixens, Vamps, and Vipers: Lost Villainesses of Golden Age Comics* (2014), 6, 161
Maeder, Jay, 37
Maglaty, Jeanne, 66, 69
Mama's Angel Child, 176n7
Mammy characters, **56**
Markstein, Don, vii, 155, 156, 157, 176n10
Marshall, Richard, 153
Marvel Comics, 137
Marx, Groucho, 46
Maxwell, Erin, 4
Mazzenga, Maria, 6, 15, 38
McCall's magazine, 121
McCarthy, Joseph, 111
McCay, Winsor, 153, 157, 175n2, 176n7
McClintock, Anne, 59
McCloud, Scott, 3, 50–51; *Understanding Comics* (1993), viii
McKay, David, 156
McLean, Albert F., 44
McNamara, Tom, 154
Meconis, Dylan, 8–9
Medovoi, Leerom, 116
Mellin's baby food, 67–68
merchandising. See branding, licensing, and merchandising
Metalious, Grace, *Peyton Place* (1956), 95
Meyerowitz, Joanne, 117
Mickey Mouse, 61–62
Mike and Meyer (Joe Weber and Lew Fields), 52, 53

Mills, Claudia, 17, 19, 25
Milne, A. A., *Winnie the Pooh* (1926), 113
MLJ Magazines, 164
Moffit, Roslyn P., 168
Montgomery, L. M., 24; *Anne of Green Gables* (1908), 18; *Emily of New Moon* (1923), 18
Moon Girl and Devil Dinosaur, 169
Moonshot: The Indigenous Comics Collection (2015), 169
Morrison, Toni, *Playing in the Dark*, 62
Motion Picture Association of America (MPAA), 132–33
Motley, Willard, *Knock on Any Door* (1950), 125
Mouly, Françoise, 88
MPAA (Motion Picture Association of America), 132–33
Ms. Marvel, 3, 168, 169
Muggs and Skeeter, 154
Mullaney, Dean, 5, 16
Murphy, Charles F., 133–37
Murray, Janet Horowitz, 81, 82–83

Nabokov, Vladimir, *Lolita* (1955/1958), 95–96
Nancy, 4–5, 9; blackface minstrelsy and racial stereotypes in, 13, 56–62, **57–61**; Bushmiller and vaudeville, 45–47; comedic delivery in, 54–55, 155; comedy team, Nancy and Sluggo as, 9, 49, 51–54; critical reception of, 41–42; dialect, use of, 9, 42, 49, 52–53; *Fritzi Ritz* (comic), debuting in (1933), 4–5, 41, 48; importance in comic book history, 170; *The Lawrence Welk Show* compared, 42, 45; performer, Nancy as, 48–49, 51–52; physical appearance of, 57–59; popularity of, 5, 41; scholarly work on, 6; simplicity of humor, 55–56; simplicity of style, 50–51, 155; slapstick and satire, use of, 51–52; variety programs and vaudeville, 42, 43–44; vaudeville aesthetic of, 42–43, 48–56, 62; vaudeville as popular entertainment, development of, 43–45; wholesome and family-friendly code of, 49–50, 172n2
Nancy (Warhol painting, 1961), 5
Nancy characters: Aunt Fritzi (Fritzi Ritz), 48, 52, 57, 59, 62; Marigold, **59**; Sluggo, 5, 9, 42, 49, 52–54, **59**, 62; Trixie, 54
Nancy Book, The (Brainard, 2008), 5
Nancy Is Happy: Complete Dailies, 1943–1945, 61
Naps of Polly Sleepyhead, The, 176n7
Nasaw, David, 43
Native American culture: modern comics with indigenous protagonists, 169; white tomboyism associated with, 174n5
Naughty Toodles, 176n7
Nelson, Claudia, 16, 21
New Deal, 17, 34, 37–38
New Republic, 37
New York Daily News, 5, 15, 18
New York World, 46, 152
Newell, Peter, 176n7
Newgarden, Mark, 5, 50, 51, 55, 155
Newman, Paul, 96
Nodelman, Perry, 23
North by Northwest (film, 1959), 96
Nyberg, Amy Kiste, 132, 134, 135, 137, 145, 174n7

O'Neill, Eugene, *Long Day's Journey into Night* (1956), 173n1
O'Neill, Rose, 171
orphan girl formula. See *Little Orphan Annie*
Outcault, Richard F., 46, 152–53, 158, 175n3

Packard, Vance, *The Hidden Persuaders* (1957), 97
Palladino, Grace, 127
Paoletti, Jo B., 66, 67–68, 70, 86–87
Paper Girls, 169
Paramount Pictures, 79, 90
Patterson, Joseph Medill, 16, 18
Payne, C. M., 154

Pazicky, Diana Loercher, 19
Peanuts, vii, 155
Pep comics, 166
Persepolis (graphic novel, 2000), 3, 168
Phantom Magician, in *The Adventures of Patsy*, 177n10
phobic behavior, in *Little Audrey*, 107
Pickford, Mary, 172n2, 176n8
pink and blue, gendered/nongendered use of, 66, 67, 69
police, treatment of, in *Li'l Tomboy*, 143–45, **144, 145**, 150
Pollock, Jackson, 96
Pore Li'l Mose, 175n3
Porter, Eleanor, 24; *Pollyanna* (1911), 18
Pressman, Jack D., 93, 94
Progressive era, 20, 68
Publishers Weekly, 114

racial dynamics: dirt, racial blackness associated with, 59–60, **60**; in early twentieth-century comics generally, 13; effects of Harlem Renaissance and African American culture in 1920s, 31; juvenile delinquency and co-opting elements of black culture, 128–29; in *Li'l Tomboy*, 13, 128–30, 174n5; in modern graphic novels and comics, 169; Nancy, blackface minstrelsy and racial stereotypes in, 13, 56–62, **57–61**; *Pore Li'l Mose*, 175n3; in Telgemeier's graphic novels, 177n15; tomboys and wild or uncivilized behavior, racial/ethnic reading of, 129–30, 174n5; vaudeville, minstrelsy and racial stereotyping in, 56, 172n2. *See also* Native American culture
Raiteri, Steve, 64, 83
Rawhide Kid, The, 134
Reader's Digest, 132
Rear Window (film, 1954), 96
Rebel without a Cause (film, 1955), 116
Reese, Debbie, 177n15
Reg'lar Fellers, 154, 158
Ress, Stella, 6, 38

Rice, T., **59**
Richie Rich, 91, 147, 149, 163
Riley, James Whitcomb, "Little Orphant Annie" (poem, 1885), 18, 21–22
Robbins, Trina: *From Girls to Grrrlz: A History of Women's Comics from Teens to Zines* (1999), 6; *The Great Women Superheroes* (1996), 6, 160–61
Robinson, Edward G., 46
Robinson, Jerry, 152, 154; *The Comics: An Illustrated History of Comic Strip Art, 1895–2010* (2011), 171n1
Rogers, Will, 44
Rogoff, Herb, 135
Roosevelt, Franklin Delano, 17, 34, 37, 66
Rosediger, David, 56
Ross, Penny, 176n7
Roth, Michael S., 97
Rothko, Mark, 96
Rourke, Constance, 50
Royle, Edwin, 44

Sad Sack Comics, 162
Salinger, J. D., *The Catcher in the Rye* (1951), 95, 113
Sammond, Nicholas, 61–62
Sanders, Joe Sutliff, 16, 18, 25, 32–33, 89
Santa's Surprise (animated film, 1947), 90
Satrapi, Marjane, 169
Saturday Evening Post, 4, 9, 63, 65, 71, 74, 79, 80, 82
Schulz, Charles, vii, 155
second-wave feminism, 7, 86, 167
Sendak, Maurice, *Where the Wild Things Are* (1963), 113
sexual anxiety in *Little Audrey* dream sequence, 109–10, **110**
sexualization of *Li'l Jinx*, 177n13
Shannon, Lyle W., 39–40, 172n3
Shutt, Craig, 63–64, 71, 72, 79, 81, 82, 86, 173n3
Simon, Joe, 149
Singley, Carol, 16, 18, 25, 32, 39
Sisters (graphic novel, 2014), 169

Skippy, 154, 158
Slampyak, Ted, 30–31
Slide, Anthony, 53; *The Vaudevillians: A Dictionary of Vaudeville Performers* (1981), 46
S'matter Pop? (aka *Say, Pop!* and *Nippy's Pop*), 154, 176n4
Smile (graphic novel, 2010), 3, 12, 168, 169
Smith, Bruce, 16; *The History of Little Orphan Annie* (1982), 38–39
Smithsonian Collection of Newspaper Comics, The (1977), 158
social codes. *See* behavioral and social codes
Somebody's Stenog, 171n1
Southworth, E. D. E. N., *The Hidden Hand* (1859), 18
Spiegelman, Art, 51, 88
Spock, Benjamin, *The Common Sense Book of Baby and Child Care* (1946), 96
St. Germain, Amos, 31
St. John (publishing company), 92, 156
Stanley, John, 64, 65, 81–82, 87. *See also Little Lulu*
Staples, Shirley, 55
Steiner, Wendy, 52
Stepbrothers, 175n1
Streetcar Named Desire, A (film, 1951), 96
superhero genre, 4, 160–61, 168, 177n10
Superior Comics, 149
Superman, 160
Swinnerton, James, 154

Tamaki, Mariko and Jillian, 3, 12, 169
Taubman, Howard, 45
Taylor, Elizabeth, 96
Telgemeier, Raina, 3, 12, 169, 177n15
Terrors of the Tiny Tads, The, 175n2
Texaco Star Theater (TV show), 45
They'll Do It Every Time, 157
This One Summer (graphic novel, 2014), 12, 168, 169
Thompson, Richard, vii
Thwaites, Tony, 98

Tillie the Toiler, 171n1
Timmy the Timid Ghost, 174n2
Tin Pan Alley, 46
Tip Top Comics, 156
Toll, Robert, 56
Treasury of Comics, 156
Tripp, Irving, 64, 65, 81, 87. *See also Little Lulu*
Trulock, Mrs. Guy Percy, 137
Truman, Harry S., 88
Tucker, Sophie, 44
Turr'ble Tales of Kaptain Kidd, The, 176n7
Twain, Mark, *The Adventures of Huckleberry Finn* (1884), 17
Two Orphans, 176n9

Unbeatable Squirrel Girl, The, 3, 168, 170
United Feature Syndicate, 155–56
US Air Force, 521st Air Defense Group, 104–5, **105**
Us Boys, 154

variety programs and vaudeville, 42, 43–44
vaudeville. *See Nancy*
Verbeek, Gustave, 175n2
Vertigo (film, 1958), 96

W. W. Norton, 99
Walker, Brian, 41, 42, 46, 50–51, 52, 56, 154; *The Best of Ernie Bushmiller's "Nancy"* (1988), 47, 172n1
Warhol, Andy, *Nancy* (1961), 5
Warner, Susan, 24; *The Wide, Wide World* (1850), 18, 36
Waters, Ethel, 44
Weber, Joe, 52, 53
Webster, Jean, *Daddy-Long-Legs* (1912), 18
Wertham, Fredric, 7, 112, 113, 130–32, 133, 135, 140, 148; *Seduction of the Innocent* (1954), 131, 132
West, Mae, 44
Western Publishing Company, 80–81
Wheeler, Shannon, 41

white dresses, girls and boys both clothed in, 66–67, 172n1
Whitman Publishing Company, 155
Whittington, Larry, 48
Wiggin, Kate Douglas, 24; *Rebecca of Sunnybrook Farm* (1903), 18
Williams, Bert, 44, 56
Williams, Tennessee, 96, 173n1; *Cat on a Hot Tin Roof* (1955), 96; *The Glass Menagerie* (1944), 96; *A Streetcar Named Desire* (1947), 96
Wilson, W. O., 175n2, 176n7
Winnie Winkle, 153
Winnie Winkle the Breadwinner, 171n1
Wish Twins and Aladdin's Lamp, The, 175n2
Wojcik, Pamela Robertson, 32
Wonder Woman, 115, 131–32, 160–61
Wood, Mary, 152
Wright, Bradford W., 112, 114, 131, 132, 133, 135–36, 137, 148–50; *Comic Book Nation: The Transformation of Youth Culture in America* (2001), 160

Yellow Kid, The, and the Yellow Kid character, 46, 88, 152–53, 158
York, Rafiel, 127
Young, Hershini Bhana, 59–60
Young, William H., 38, 40, 172n3

young female protagonists in classic American comics, 3–14, 152–70; artistic medium versus material format, 12; branding, licensing, and merchandising of, 8, 158–60 (*see also* branding, licensing, and merchandising); historical background to comics with child protagonists, 152–54; importance of, 4–5, 154–58, 161–62, 169–70; legacy of, 11–12; methodological approach, 8–9, 12–13; mixed-gender audience for comics, in first half of twentieth century, 4, 114; questioning of gender roles, societal status, and behavioral codes in, 7–8 (*see also* behavioral and social codes; gender roles); racial dynamic of, 13; rise of female fans and female cartoonists in millennial American society and, 3, 14, 168–70; scholarly study of, 5–8, 13, 158; superhero genre and, 4, 160–61, 168, 177n10. *See also* specific comics by title
youth. *See* childhood and youth, changing perceptions of; juvenile delinquency

Zelizer, Viviana, 20–21
Zere, Al, 154, 176n9
Ziff-Davis Publications, 135